Religious symbols and their functions

Religious symbols and their functions

Based on Papers read at the Symposium on Religious Symbols and their Functions held at Åbo on the 28th–30th of August 1978

Edited by
HARALDS BIEZAIS

Distributed by

Almqvist & Wiksell International
Stockholm/Sweden

ISBN 91-22-00199-9

Printed in Sweden by
Almqvist & Wiksell, Uppsala 1979

Contents

Die Hauptprobleme der religiösen Symbolik

Von HARALDS BIEZAIS

1. Im Leben des Einzelnen als auch religiöser Gruppen ist das religiöse Symbol von zentraler Bedeutung. Damit ist auch das gesteigerte Interesse für Probleme, die mit ihm verbunden sind, zu erklären[1]. Ich kann hier nur auf einige dieser Probleme hinweisen, die so bedeutsam sind, daß man an ihnen nicht vorbeikommt, ohne danach seinen Standpunkt zu präzisieren. Dagegen glaube ich nicht, daß man versuchen müßte, eine mehr oder weniger vollständige systematische oder historische Übersicht über diese Probleme zu geben[2], denn eine solche würde für die Erörterung der Probleme nichts Neues bringen.

1.1. Das besondere Interesse unserer Zeit am Symbol steht in engem Zusammenhang mit der Weiterbildung und Entwicklung von Ansichten, wie sie die Theoretiker der Psychoanalyse Freud und Jung geäußert haben.

Ihre Grundthese lautet, daß die Aktivitäten der menschlichen Psyche sich von Zeit zu Zeit in Symbolen äußern, welche vom Unterbewußtsein bestimmt werden[3]. Die symbolischen Bilder würden in Wirklichkeit durch erblicherweise übernommene Inhalte des kollektiven Unterbewußtseins bestimmt. Nur die Formen, welche diese Inhalte annehmen und durch welche sie sich äußern, würden durch die jeweiligen Erfahrungen und Erlebnisse mitbestimmt[4]. So wird also verständlich, daß die symbolischen Formen im Verhältnis zum Inhalt von sekundärer Bedeutung sind. Der Einfluß dieser Theorie hat sich, ungeachtet der wesentlichen biologischen Einschränkung und Einseitigkeit des Symbolbegriffs[5], auch tiefgreifend auf die Forschungen über die religiöse Symbolik ausgewirkt.

---

[1] Einen weiten Überblick über diese Forschungen bieten die entsprechenden Bibliographien und besonderen Sammlungen. *Bibliographie* 1968 ff.; *Symbolon* 1960 ff. Cf. auch Giedion, 78, mit seinen Aussagen.

[2] Ein Beispiel dafür, daß es nicht möglich ist, Symbole zu systematisieren und zu gruppieren, oder, richtiger, daß dies nur nach rein subjektiv ausgewählten Grundsätzen erfolgen kann, bietet Assagioli 34 ff.

[3] Cf. Moody 12 f.

[4] Ib.

[5] Gegen Jungs Theorie hat sich Jaspers, 1946, 277, gewandt: „In der verstehenden Psychologie ist besonders zu unterscheiden das Symbol als *Träger persönlich gültiger Bedeutungen* aus der eigenen Lebensgeschichte, als Ersatzbildung usw. von dem Symbol als *umgreifenden Bedeutungsträger immanenter Transzendenz*. Jenes läßt Jung sich gründen im persönlichen Unbewußten, dieses im kollektiven Unbewußten." Er lehnt die Psychoanalyse und ähnliche Theorien grundsätzlich ab 1947, 1040: „Die psychoanalytischen Deutungen werden im Ganzen zur Grimasse eines Lesens der Chifferschrift, wie sie einem glaubenslosen Zeitalter gemäß war. Statt auf die Wirklichkeit transzendenten Seins hin wird auf das seelisch-unbewußte Geschehen hin gedeutet. Statt Erhellung und Glaube wird scheinerklärung und Aberglaube vollzogen." Cf. auch Bertalanffy 47 ff.; besonders Wisse 134 f.

1.2. Großen Einfluß auf das Verständnis des Symbolbegriffs überhaupt und damit auch auf das religiöse Symbol hat Cassirer ausgeübt[6]. Ausgehend von der deutschen idealistischen Philosophie, hat er seine Philosophie der symbolischen Formen entwickelt. Er hat sich hauptsächlich sprachpsychologischer und ethnologischer Materialien bedient. Er hält sich auch konsequent an die zu seiner Zeit herrschende Vorstellung einer Entwicklungsgeschichte. Praktisch wirkt sich das so aus, daß er mit Hilfe umfangreichen Materials zu beweisen sucht, daß auf dem Gebiet der symbolischen Formen eine Entwicklung von einer ,,sinnlich aufgefaßte[n] Wirklichkeit" über eine mythische Weltauffassung zur Religion zu beobachten sei. Die letzte Entwicklungsstufe sei die Religionsphilosophie. Seine Absicht war es, den Dualismus zu überwinden, der zwischen der empirischen und der außerempirischen Welt besteht: ,,Immer wieder sind wir im Laufe unserer Untersuchung zu der Ensicht geführt worden, daß der echte und wahrhafte Begriff des 'Symbolischen' sich den herkömmlichen metaphysischen Einteilungen und Dualismen nicht fügt, sondern daß er ihren Rahmen sprengt. Das Symbolische gehört niemals dem 'Diesseits' oder 'Jenseits', dem Gebiet der 'Immanenz' oder 'Transzendenz' an: sondern sein Wert besteht eben darin, daß es diese Gegensätze, die einer metaphysischen Zweiweltentheorie entstammen, überwindet. Es ist nicht das Eine oder das Andere, sondern es stellt das 'Eine im anderen' und das 'Andere im Einen' dar. So konstituiert die Sprache, der Mythos, die Kunst je ein selbständiges und charakteristisches Gefüge, das seinen Wert nicht dadurch erhält, daß in ihm ein äußeres und jenseitiges Dasein irgendwie 'abgespiegelt' erscheint. Ihr Gehalt wird ihnen vielmehr dadurch zuteil, daß sie, je nach einem eigenen ihnen innewohnenden Bildungsgesetz, eine eigentümliche und selbständige, in sich geschlossene Welt des Sinnes aufbauen."[7]

Mit seinen Vorstellungen schließt sich Cassirer der ,,Erkenntnislehre" der Neukantianer an[8]. Der tiefe Eindruck, den die erstgenannte Schule hinterlassen hat, ist bei der sogenannten Eranos-Gruppe (Eliade, Kerény u.a.) zu erkennen, während die letztgenannte viele theologisch orientierte Denker (Bultmann, Wach, Tillich u. a.) beeinflußt hat.

---

[6] Sein dreibändiges Werk, ,,Die Philosophie der symbolischen Formen", erschien bereits 1923–1929. Auf den Einfluß von Cassirers Gedanken auf andere Forscher (Plachte, Urban) hat Looff, 44, hingewiesen, der auch vom Standpunkt der protestantischen Theologie Kritik geäußert hat (96ff.).

[7] Cassirer 3,404f. Goodman, 228, hat erkannt, daß auch die heutige positivistische Philosophie die symbolischen Ausdrucksformen auf eine frühere Entwicklungsstufe verweist: ,,[...] these were ages of myth, when people living in a fearful and uncontrollable environment could not distinguish magic and science, nor saga and history, nor dream and empirical experience; the poets were the prophets, historians, philosophers, and scientists. In the course of time, poetry was replaced by philosophy and history; and these in turn have given way to special physical sciences and positivist sociology. In our time, literature can be merely decoration or entertainment or exercise in emotional noises."

[8] Cf. Bertalanffy 43.

2. Bedeutungsvoller und fruchtbarer ist es jedoch, sich mit jenen Standpunkten und Begriffsdefinitionen bekannt zu machen, welche immer noch die heutigen Diskussionen über das Wesen des religiösen Symbols, seine Struktur und seine Funktionen bestimmen. Verständlicherweise herrschen gerade in der Frage der Definition des Symbols größte Unklarheiten und Widersprüche[9]. Es ist nicht meine Aufgabe, diese hier im einzelnen darzustellen. Damit aber die im folgenden vorgetragenen Gedanken besser verständlich sind, müssen hier dennoch ein paar früher geäußerte Definitionen des Symbols erwähnt werden.

2.1. Bis in die letzte Zeit dominieren in Diskussionen über das religiöse Symbol die von Tillich geäußerten Gedanken, mit denen er bereits 1928 hervorgetreten ist[10]. Seine Ansicht ist auch deshalb bedeutsam, weil sie die kirchliche Theologie stark beeinflußt hat. Diese Theorie ist aus einem gewissen Gegensatz zu Cassirers kritischem Idealismus erwachsen. Tillich charakterisiert die Struktur des Symbols durch vier Merkmale: ,,Das erste und grundlegende Merkmal des Symbols ist die *Uneigentlichkeit*. Sie besagt, daß der innere Akt, der sich auf das Symbol richtet, nicht das Symbol meint, sondern das in ihm Symbolisierte. [...]

Das zweite Merkmal des Symbols ist die *Anschaulichkeit*. Sie besagt, daß ein wesensmäßig Unanschauliches, Ideelles oder Transzendentes im Symbol zur Anschauung und damit zur Gegenständlichkeit gebracht wird. Die Anschaulichkeit braucht keine sinnliche zu sein. Sie kann ebensogut eine vorgestellte sein. [...]

Das dritte Merkmal des Symbols ist die *Selbstmächtigkeit*. Sie besagt, daß das Symbol eine ihm selbst innewohnende Macht hat, die es von dem bloßen in sich ohnmächtigen Zeichen unterscheidet. Dieses Merkmal ist maßgebend für die Trennung von Zeichen und Symbol. Das Zeichen ist willkürlich austauschbar. Es hat keine Notwendigkeit, weil es keine innere Macht hat. Das Symbol hat Notwendigkeit. Es kann nicht ausgetauscht werden. Es kann nur verschwinden durch Verlust seiner inneren Mächtigkeit, durch Symbolzerfall. Und es kann nicht erfunden, sondern nur geschaffen werden. [...]

Das vierte Merkmal des Symbols ist die *Anerkanntheit*. Sie besagt, daß das Symbol sozial eingebettet und getragen ist. Es ist also nicht so, daß eine Sache erst Symbol ist und dann Anerkennung findet, sondern Symbolwerdung und Anerkennung gehören zusammen. Der symbolschaffende Akt ist ein Sozialakt, auch wenn er in einem Einzelnen zuerst durchbricht. Der Einzelne kann sich Zeichen machen für seine privaten Bedürfnisse;

---

[9] Skorupski 117ff.; Wisse 3, 21f.; Urban 580ff.; dazu Firth 50ff.

[10] Hier und im folgenden habe ich die Ausgabe seiner Gesammelten Werke (von 1964) benutzt, in der in unveränderter Form sein Aufsatz ,,Das religiöse Symbol" abgedruckt ist, der zum ersten Male in: ,,Blätter für deutsche Philosophie" 1 (1928), 277ff., erschien. Er wurde wiederholt in deutscher und englischer Sprache in verschiedenen Ausgaben veröffentlicht.

Symbole kann er nicht machen; wird ihm etwas zum Symbol, so immer im Hinblick auf die Gemeinschaft, die sich darin wiedererkennen kann. [...]

Diese allgemeinen Merkmale des Symbols gelten – wie die Einzelbeispiele zeigten – auch für die religiösen Symbole. Die religiösen Symbole sind vor den übrigen dadurch ausgezeichnet, daß sie Veranschaulichung dessen sind, was die Sphäre der Anschauung unbedingt übersteigt, des im religiösen Akt Letztgemeinten, des Unbedingt-Transzendenten. [...]

Die religiösen Symbole sind weder gegenständlich, noch geistig-sinnhaft fundiert, sie sind unfundiert, religiös gesprochen, sie sind Gegenstand des Glaubens. Sie haben kein anderes Recht als das der *Vertretung* des Unanschaubar-Transzendenten, das ihrer nicht bedarf, um zur Existenz zu kommen. Auf dieser Tatsache beruht die eigentümliche Zweischichtigkeit der religiösen Symbole."[11]

Kurz gesagt, Tillich behauptet, daß das Symbolbewußtsein nicht im Symbol selbst verwirklicht sei, sondern in dem, was damit symbolisiert werde. Durch das Symbol werde das Unsichtbare sichtbar gemacht. Ferner besitzte das Symbol selbst eine bestimmte Kraft, die aber den symbolischen Zeichen fehle. Wie bereits gesagt, hat Tillichs Symbolbegriff das Symbolverständnis der Theologie stark beeinflußt. Dagegen wurden jedoch Einwendungen erhoben, sowohl von der empirisch ausgerichteten Religionswissenschaft als auch besonders von seiten der orthodoxen Theologie[12].

2.2. In unserer Darstellung des Symbols wollen wir uns nun auch den Definitionen des Symbols durch Mensching zuwenden. Wie mir scheint, erweitern diese den Begriff Symbol bedeutend und helfen, den von Tillich dogmatisch eingeschränkten Begriff „gläubiger Realismus" zu überwinden. Mensching hat sich wie folgt geäußert: „Symbol ist alles, was zu einer von sich selbst verschiedenen *Wirklichkeit* in einem *sachlich notwendigen* Verhältnis der Repräsentation steht, wobei das Repräsentierte je nach Art des Symbols in eine *verschiedene Nähe zum Symbol* tritt."

Zu dieser Definition hat er folgende Erklärungen geliefert:

„a) 'Symbol ist *alles* ...': mit diesem Satze ist bereits a priori gesagt, daß der Symbolcharakter einer Sache nicht auf bestimmte konkrete Dinge beschränkt ist, sondern daß prinzipiell *alles* zum Symbol werden kann, sofern es den in der weiteren Formel angegebenen Bedingungen genügt. Der Symbolcharakter also liegt nicht in irgendeiner Sache an sich, sondern in gewissen zu untersuchenden *Beziehungen* dieser Sache zu etwas Anderem. [...]

b) 'was zu einer *von sich selbst verschiedenen Wirklichkeit* ...': das ist die zum Symbolcharakter einer Seinsform notwendige andere Größe. Diese

---

[11] Tillich 1964, 196ff. Manchmal spricht er von 5 Merkmalen (cf. 1973, 5). Royce, 20, hat bei Tillich 6 solcher Merkmale festgestellt.

[12] Dagegen werden Einwände, auch von seiten der Psychologen, erhoben, z. B. Royce 19ff.

andere Größe nennen wir die vom Symbol gemeinte ,,Wirklichkeit". Dabei ist natürlich festzustellen, daß unter ,,Wirklichkeit" die verschiedenen Möglichkeiten der Realität und nicht etwa nur die gewöhnlich als Wirklichkeit bezeichnete konkrete Welt sinnlicher Erfahrung zu verstehen ist.

c) 'in einem *sachlich notwendigen* Verhältnis der *Repräsentation* steht ...': Die Beziehung zu jener anderen Wirklichkeit ist nach zwei Seiten hin zu charakterisieren. Einerseits muß das Verhältnis sachlich notwendig sein. Auf dieses Moment der Notwendigkeit, und zwar einer aus der Sache heraus und nicht durch Zufall gestifteten Notwendigkeit ist das größte Gewicht zu legen. [...] Und das zweite charakterisierende Moment ist die Bezeichnung des Verhältnisses von Symbol und gemeinter Wirklichkeit als Repräsentation.

d) 'wobei das Repräsentierte je nach Art des Symbols in eine verschiedene *Nähe* zum Symbol tritt.' Die Repräsentation der gemeinten Wirklichkeit durch das Symbol ist in den verschiedenen Arten möglicher Symbolbegriffe nicht von gleicher Art. Es wird sich zeigen, daß eine wesentliche Differenzierung der Symbolarten gerade darin besteht, daß die gemeinte Wirklichkeit mehr oder weniger nahe an das Symbol heranrückt, ja gelegentlich selbst in das konkrete Symbol eintritt."[13]

Menschings Gedanken sind kurz gefaßt folgende: Symbol kann jede Erscheinung sein, die notwendig eine andere von dieser unterschiedliche Erscheinung vertritt. Mit diesen wenigen Beispielen aus der gegenwärtigen Diskussion über das Symbol sind wir bei der Wesensfrage angelangt[14].

3. Diskussionen darüber, warum der Mensch Symbole benutzt, sind überflüssig, insbesondere deshalb, weil man auf diese Frage nicht genetisch antworten kann. Man kann zwar vermuten, weshalb der Mensch des Neolithikums die elementarsten geometrischen Zeichen – Punkte und Striche – oder auch komplizierte geometrische Muster in die Wände seiner Höhlen eingraviert hat, man kann aber nicht einmal mit gewisser Sicherheit sagen, ob er das aus spielerischer Freude getan hat oder ob damit auch irgendwelche religiöse Erlebnisse und Ideen verbunden waren. Die Genese des Gebrauchs von Symbolen ist nicht aufzuklären[15]. Um sagen zu können, ob diese Zeichen einen Sinn haben, müßte man wissen, zu welchem Zweck

[13] Mensching 1930, 1070. Er ist später noch einmal auf den Begriff und die Struktur des Symbols zurückgekommen: ,,Symbol ist alles, was für ein Subjekt zu einer von sich selbst verschiedenen im Symbol gemeinten Sinnwirklichkeit in ein Verhältnis der Repräsentation gesetzt wird" (1955, 362).

[14] Zum Vergleich können wir hier auf verschiedene andere Definitionen hinweisen: in der Philosophie auf Seiffert 25f.; Friedmann 29; in der Soziologie auf Parsons 416; Thass-Thienemann 17ff.; in der Psychologie auf Jaspers 1947, 1032; 1956, 150.

[15] Das wird mehrfach vermerkt. So Langer, Susanne 41: ,,This basic need, which certainly is obvious only in man, is the *need of symbolization*. The symbol-making function is one of man's primary activities, like eating, looking, or moving about. It is the fundamental process of his mind, and goes on all the time. Sometimes we are aware of it, sometimes we merely find its results, and realize that certain experiences have passed through our brains and have been digested there." Ähnlich auch Mensching 1955, 362; Giedion 87.

sie angebracht wurden. Dies wird deutlicher bei der Betrachtung der Funktionen von Sprachzeichen. Es ist wahr, daß z.B. im geschriebenen Wort „Berg" vier verschiedene Zeichen zu sehen sind, in der Aussprache dieses Wortes dagegen hören wir vier Laute verschiedenen Klanges. Weder die geschriebenen Zeichen noch die hörbaren Laute haben alle zusammen oder einzeln irgendeine symbolische Bedeutung. Sie können als Sinnwirklichkeit von Menschen verschiedener ethnischer Gruppen und Kulturen erkannt und gehört werden, ohne daß sich deshalb mit dieser Sinnwirklichkeit die Vorstellung von einem Berg assoziieren würde, d.h. eine andere Sinnwirklichkeit, die diese Zeichen und Laute symbolisieren. Aber nur für die Menschen und die Gemeinschaft, welche einer besonderen Kultureinheit angehören, die die deutsche Sprache versteht, werden diese Zeichen und Laute symbolisch, d.h. sie erhalten einen Sinninhalt[16]. Dieses einfache Beispiel bestätigt das vorhin Gesagte, daß ein Zeichen für sich allein kein Symbol bedeutet, und es zeigt auch, daß die genetische Frage als solche für die Problematik des Gebrauchs von Symbolen nicht wichtig ist. Wichtiger ist es, das Symbol in seiner Struktur und seinen Funktionen zu erkennen.

3.1. Wenn wir uns zunächst der Frage der Symbolstruktur zuwenden, so sollten wir uns daran erinnern, daß die bisherige Forschung besonders den dualistischen – ich möchte lieber sagen: den bipolaren – Charakter des Symbolbegriffs betont hat, wie mir scheint, mit Recht. Das Symbol umfaßt immer sowohl die zu symbolisierende Wirklichkeit als auch die Wirklichkeit des Symbolisierenden. Doch verwirrt sich diese grundlegende, an sich klare Selbstverständlichkeit in dem Moment, wenn man versucht, die Beziehungen dieser beiden Strukturelemente zu klären. Es handelt sich um ein Problem, das viele heftige Diskussionen hervorgerufen hat.

Wiederholt wurde behauptet, daß alles zum Symbol für alles werden könne. Formal ist diese Behauptung richtig, soweit sie rein theoretisch bleibt. Doch zeigt die empirische Erfahrung, daß die Möglichkeiten prak-

---

[16] Cf. bei Segerstedt das Kapitel „Der Laut wird zum Symbol" (26ff., besonders 38 und 43). Die Sinngebung des Wortes faßt er in folgender Weise auf: „Wir fassen das Ergebnis dahin zusammen, daß ein Wort keinen *Sinn* bekommen kann, insofern es nicht in eine allgemeine Situation eingesetzt wird. Hingegen wird das Wort zum Symbol, weil es auf ein System gesellschaftlicher Normen hinweist, die das Wort teils mit der allgemeinen Situation verbinden, *teils* aus dieser allgemeinen Situation herausgreifen. Wörter, die als Teile des Ganzen zu Repräsentanten des Ganzen werden, sind Symbole des Ganzen. Wenn wir sagen, die Wörter seien Symbole, so ist es dieses Ganze, dessen Symbole sie sind. Wir sagten also *nicht,* die Wörter ständen als Symbole des Gedankens an das Objekt und auch nicht als Symbole des Objekts. Wir sagten nicht, ein Mensch sähe zuerst einen Gegenstand, zum Beispiel einen Stuhl, darauf denke er Stuhl und suche nun ein Symbol für seinen *Gedanken* Stuhl, das er endlich im *Worte Stuhl* findet. Das Wort ist nach unserer Auffassung Symbol für eine Reihe von Verhalten, die zu einer allgemeinen Situation vereinigt sind. Daß gerade ein bestimmtes Wort verwendet wird, beruht auf einem System gesellschaftlicher Normen, so wie auch unser Verhalten im übrigen auf einem System von Normen beruht" (57).

tisch sehr eingeschränkt sind[17]. Schon allein die Tatsache, daß erfahrungsgemäß niemals alles zur Symbolisierung von allem verwendet wurde, läßt uns aufmerken. Es ist nur die Frage, was dafür bestimmend ist, daß die Zahl der benutzten Symbole sehr klein ist. Das umfangreiche religionsgeschichtliche Material zeigt unmißverständlich, daß die Auswahl von Symbolen festgelegt und historisch gebunden ist. Darüber braucht man sich nicht zu streiten. Es ist nur die Frage, wodurch diese Auswahl bestimmt wird. Die Antworten können sehr verschieden sein. Die einen behaupten, daß die freie Wahl des Subjekts und dessen Ziel, das mit der Symbolisierung erreicht werden soll, bestimmend seien. Die anderen behaupten, die soziale Struktur, der das Individuum angehört, sei maßgebend für die Auswahl. Die Funktionalisten meinen, daß alle psychischen Aktivitäten von dem Wunsch nach Sicherung der Stabilität der sozialen Struktur motiviert seien[18]. Ohne sich in diese breite Diskussion einzulassen, kann man sagen, daß man es im einen wie im anderen Fall mit einer Auswahl zu tun hat. Zum Verständnis des Wesens des Symbols trägt die Behauptung wenig bei, daß alles zum Symbol für alles werden könne. Das Symbol ist das Ergebnis einer Auswahl. Daher ist zum richtigen Verständnis seiner Struktur die Frage der Auswahl wichtig.

Auch Mensching hat die Wichtigkeit dieser Frage erkannt. Er hat versucht, darauf mit dem Hinweis zu antworten, wie wir bereits gelesen haben, daß zwischen dem zu Symbolisierenden und dem Symbolisierenden „ein sachlich notwendiges Verhältnis" bestehe. Diese Antwort ist formal richtig, denn es ist nicht anzunehmen, daß die Auswahl des Symbols nur auf Zufall oder rationaler Willkür beruht, ohne die Fähigkeit, Wesentliches auszusagen, d. h. die zu symbolisierende Wirklichkeit zu repräsentieren. Aber das genügt nicht, denn die folgende Frage lautet: Wer bestimmt, was „sachlich notwendig" ist? Mit anderen Worten: von wem hängt es ab, daß ein besonderes Symbol mit etwas Bestimmtem, was symbolisiert werden soll, verbunden wird? Daß diese Frage angebracht ist, ist aus den Fällen zu erkennen, in denen ein und dieselbe zu symbolisierende Erscheinung in verschiedenen Religionen unterschiedliche Symbole erhält. Im germanischen Fruchtbarkeitskult symbolisieren der Eber bzw. die Sau die Fruchtbarkeit, in verschiedenen Gegenden Kleinasiens ist es die Frau mit vielen Brüsten (Artemis von Ephesus), im Hinduismus Schiwa mit vielen Armen. Warum so viele verschiedene Symbole zur Darstellung ein und desselben religiösen Phänomens – der Fruchtbarkeit – geschaffen wurden, ist schwer mit „sachlicher Notwendigkeit" zu erklären, wenn man nicht weitere Gründe aufzeigt, die dafür maßgebend sind. Das erwähnte Beispiel läßt vermuten,

[17] Dazu hat sich bereits Saussure, 103, bekannt: „Le symbole a pour caractère de n'être jamais tout à fait arbitraire; il n'est pas vide, il y a un rudiment de lieu naturel entre le signifiant et le signifié. Le symbole de la justice, la balance, ne pourait pas être remplacé par n'importe quoi, un char, par exemple."

[18] Ausführlicher habe ich mich dazu, 1976, 19ff., geäußert.

daß die Auswahl des Symbols von dem zu symbolisierenden Gegenstand unabhängig ist. Hier mag noch an einige symbolische Darstellungsweisen der hl. Maria erinnert werden: den Stern, die Rose, die Hirtin u. v. a. Es gibt nur ein Wesen Maria, aber es wird verschieden symbolisiert. Vielleicht möchte man hier ergänzen, es sei damit zu erklären, daß Maria in verschiedenen Funktionen auftrete, die später die Auswahl der Symbole bestimmt hätten. Dann könne man sagen, daß abhängig davon, in welchen Funktionen sie erscheint, die entsprechenden Symbole in „sachlicher Notwendigkeit" ausgewählt worden seien. Doch diese Ergänzung bestätigt gerade das, was ich sagen wollte: Nicht das zu symbolisierende Objekt – die hl. Maria – ist diejenige, die sich in verschiedenen funktionellen Situationen befindet, sondern das Subjekt. In Übereinstimmung damit wählt es das entsprechende Symbol, das ihm in dieser Situation „sachlich notwendig" erscheint. Man könnte noch weitergehen und die funktionelle Situation analysieren und damit deren Struktur bestimmen. Dadurch könnten die Motive des Subjekts für die Auswahl von Symbolen noch klarer werden. Hier wollen wir uns auf die Feststellung beschränken, daß die Auswahl des Symbols von der funktionellen Situation des Individuums abhängig ist. Mit anderen Worten, die Auswahl des Symbols ist stets durch seine Subjektbezogenheit bestimmt.

Aus dieser Erkenntnis ergibt sich, daß die These, alles könne für alles zum Symbol werden, auf die konkret gegebene Subjektbezogenheit einzuschränken ist. Wenn man die Möglichkeiten zur Auswahl von Symbolen in der Weise erweitern würde, daß diese Auswahl durch das zu symbolisierende Objekt bestimmt oder zumindest mitbestimmt wird, dann wäre die These von der prinzipiellen Möglichkeit, alles könne durch alles symbolisiert werden, nicht aufrecht zu erhalten. Der Vorgang der Symbolisierung ist einseitig. In verschiedenen Religionen kennt man eine Sonnensymbolik – vom einfachen geometrischen Kreis bis zu so ausdrucksvollen Gestalten wie einer schönen Frau und einem bärtigen König. Dadurch wird ein übriges Mal bestätigt, daß es nicht das Objekt des religiösen Erlebnisses ist[19], sondern dessen Träger, das Subjekt, das die Auswahl des Symbols trifft.

3.2. Aus dem Gesagten wird deutlich, daß damit die anfangs angesprochene Frage des bipolaren Charakters des Symbols aktualisiert wird. Es handelt sich um die Frage nach der empirischen Ausdrucksform des Symbols und dessen transzendentem Inhalt. Die Behauptung, daß das empirisch gegebene religiöse Symbol immer eine nichtempirische Wirklichkeit darstelle, ist schon fast zum Axiom geworden. Erinnern wir uns hier nur an die im vorangegangenen Zitat wiedergegebenen Gedanken von Tillich: „Die religiösen Symbole sind vor den übrigen dadurch ausgezeichnet, daß sie Veranschaulichung dessen sind, was die Sphäre der Anschauung unbedingt übersteigt, des im religiösen Akt Letztgemeinten, des Unbedingt-Trans-

---

[19] Cf. Fawcett 33.

zendenten."[20] Das Unbedingt-Transzendente ist verstanden als Gott. Mit besonderem Pathos hat Leese das betont: „Religiöse Symbole sind nicht willkürliche Zeichen, die man nach Belieben erfinden und deren Bedeutung man auf dem Wege der Verabredung festsetzen könnte (Allegorie), religiöse Symbole sind nicht abstrakte Schemata, die in keinem inneren Verhältnis zu dem stehen, worauf sie hinweisen, religiöse Symbole sind dem menschlichen Zugriff weitgehend entzogene Wesenheiten (essentiae), die mit einer das Gefühl tief erregenden Seinsmächtigkeit geladen sind, die dem Ungeheuren rufen, weil dieses sich in ihnen offenbart. [...] Für ein religiöses Symbol sind zwei Voraussetzungen konstitutiv: eine erlebende Seele und ein zu erlebendes Göttliches. Das religiöse Symbol selbst stellt mit seiner Dialektik von Eigentlichkeit und Uneigentlichkeit, von Anschaulichkeit und Unanschaulichkeit, von Sinnlichkeit und Unsinnlichkeit, von Immanenz und Transzendenz die Mittlerschaft, den Kontakt zwischen beiden her."[21]

Leeses Worte enthüllen, daß er von einer sachlichen Darstellung des Wesens des Symbols zu einem Bekenntnis seiner religiösen Überzeugung übergewechselt ist. Das Symbol ist für ihn zu einer Aussage über die göttliche Offenbarung geworden. Wenn wir diesen Teil seiner Äußerungen beiseite lassen, wird jedoch deutlich, daß er das Problem der Bipolarität ganz richtig erkannt hat. Diese ist das Grundmerkmal der Struktur des religiösen Symbols. Es will immer mit „irgend etwas" „irgend etwas" anderes aussagen. Damit ist das Problem jedoch nicht erschöpft.

Ist diese Bipolarität ontologisch oder psychologisch bestimmt? Daß das „Unbedingt-Transzendente" (Tillich) und „entzogene Wesenheiten (essentiae)" (Leese) ontologisch zu verstehen sind, ist außer Zweifel. Es ist die transzendente Wirklichkeit, die durch den Akt der religiösen Symbolisierung in die Sinnwirklichkeit übertragen wird. Diese ontologische Bipolarität bestimmt das Verständnis des theologischen Symbols. Es ist nur die Frage, ob sie aufrecht erhalten werden kann. Daß es mit dem ontologischen Verständnis seine Schwierigkeiten hat, wurde, wie es scheint, bereits von Mensching zugegeben, wie seine Überlegungen über die Beziehungen der symbolisierenden Wirklichkeit zum Symbol zeigten. In diesem Zusammenhang spricht er von „verschiedener Nähe zum Symbol" und „daß die gemeinte Wirklichkeit mehr oder weniger nahe an das Symbol herantritt". Schon dieser Gedanke der verschiedenen Entfernung beider Sphären ist bezeichnend. Sein Gedankengang mündet konsequenterweise in der Behauptung, daß die zu symbolisierende Wirklichkeit „gelegentlich selbst in das konkrete Symbol eintritt". Diese Aussage zeigt, daß die Bipolarität zwischen dem zu Symbolisierenden und dem Symbolisierenden in

---

[20] Tillich 1964, 197. Ebenso erwähnt auch Leese, 1934, 8, in diesem Zusammenhang das „Letzt-Wirkliche".

[21] Leese 1934, 10.

einer gewissen Situation verschwunden ist. An ihre Stelle ist zweifellos die Identität getreten. In diesem Fall handelt es sich um ein Erlebnis von anderer Qualität, nämlich um ein direktes, undifferenziertes religiöses Erlebnis. Das ist dann kein Symbolisierungsakt mehr[22]. Das hat auch Kahler erkannt: ,,Religious and artistic imagery arose in common. Earliest images, prehistoric cave paintings, are not symbols as yet, they are virtual acts of seizure; they do not signify or represent, they actually *are* the creatures represented. They do not point to prototypes, they are pointed at with the points of arrows. Similarly, the original totemistic idol, as long as the deity is believed to be actually present in the image, is not a likeness of the worshipped being, it is the being itself. Only when a difference is felt between the visually present idol and a remote, or temporarily absent, deity, when the image turns into a mere residue or residence of the deity, only then does the image become a symbol.“[23]

Dieses Hineingleiten in die Identität, wobei der Symbolisierende völlig mit dem zu Symbolisierenden übereinstimmt, zeigt, daß diese Möglichkeit der Struktur des Symbols widerspricht. Die Bipolarität ist daher als wesentliches Kennzeichen der Struktur des Symbols anzusehen[24].

Einerseits haben wir bereits vorhin auf die Schwierigkeiten bezüglich der ontologischen Bipolarität hingewiesen, da sie im faktischen Symbolisierungsakt empirisch nicht zu begründen ist. Andererseits aber sagten wir soeben, daß die Bipolarität wesensmäßig zur Symbolstruktur gehöre. Dieser scheinbare Widerspruch läßt die Bipolarität des Symbols unter einem anderen Aspekt betrachten. Der wahre Grund, weshalb die These von der ontologischen Bipolarität nicht aufrecht erhalten werden kann, liegt im Ge-

---

22 Hier kann man auf eine Diskussion hinweisen, die manchmal recht scharfe Formen angenommen hat, nämlich darüber, ob der Himmel mit Gott identisch ist oder ob der Himmel nur eine Ausdrucksform für Gott (ein Symbol) ist. Darüber habe ich mich, 1961, 20ff., ausführlicher geäußert. Mir scheint, daß Giedion, 87, den Zusammenhang zwischen Symbol und Realität beim prähistorischen Menschen und die spätere Entwicklung richtig erkannt hat: ,,The essential nature of the symbol has always consisted in this urge to express the inherently inexpressible, but in primitive times the crystallization of a concept in the form of a symbol portrayed reality before that reality came to pass. *The symbol itself was reality* [kursiv von H. B.], for it was believed to possess the power of working magic, and thus of directly affecting the course of events: the wish, the prayer, or the spell to be fulfilled. Herein lies the contrast between the function of the symbol in prehistory and in later periods. In Greece the symbol was not only a means of recognition. It also developed a spiritual content and became an abstract concept. It was not an independent agent.“ Es dürfte darüber kein Zweifel bestehen, daß mit Dyaus, Jupiter u. a. anfangs der Himmelsgott selbst bezeichnet wurde, aber ebenso zweifellos ist der Himmel erst auf einer späteren Stufe der Abstraktion, und nicht nur in der christlichen Theologie, sondern auch in anderen religiösen Systemen (Brahmaismus, Buddhismus), zum Aufenthalt Gottes oder zu dessen Erscheinungsform geworden, also zu einem Symbol.

23 Kahler 61.

24 Sehr bestimmt wird dieser Gedanke auch von Seiffert, 27, gestützt: ,,Die Dualität, die bezeichnend ist für das Sinnbild, kann auf keine Weise eliminiert werden.“ Ein andermal spricht er von ,,Zwiegesichtigkeit“ (9). Ungeachtet seines Bestrebens, die Bipolarität zu überwinden, ist Jaspers gezwungen, von ,,Zweideutigkeit“ zu sprechen (1946, 277).

brauch des Begriffs „Wirklichkeit". Im einen Fall ist die Rede von der Sinnwirklichkeit (vom Symbolisierenden bzw. vom Symbol), im anderen Fall handelt es sich um das „Letzt-Wirkliche" (das Religiöse, Gott). Solch eine attributive Bestimmung des Wirklichkeitsbegriffs kann jedoch keine größere Klarheit bringen, da es bei der Frage hier nicht um die Wirklichkeit als solche geht. In beiden Fällen ist die Rede von einer *subjektbezogenen Wirklichkeit*. Es ist das Subjekt, das in seiner psychischen Aktivität im Falle der religiösen Symbolisierung in seinem religiösen Leben den Inhalt seines Erlebnisses durch etwas Anderes indirekt ausdrückt. Wenn man unbedingt den Begriff der Bipolarität gebrauchen möchte, dann muß man ihm in diesem Fall im Gegensatz zur ontologischen Bipolarität einen anderen Inhalt geben. Dann müßte man von einer psychologischen Bipolarität sprechen. Hier ist zu bemerken, daß die Übertragung des Symbolinhalts von der ontologischen auf die psychologische Ebene nichts an der formalen Struktur des Symbolbegriffs ändert, d. h. deren Bipolarität weder einschränkt noch aufhebt.

3.3. Obgleich ich mich zum bipolaren Charakter der Symbolstruktur bekannt habe, meine ich doch, daß man die Ansichten nicht unbeachtet lassen kann, die seinerzeit versucht haben, diesen bipolaren Charakter zu überwinden, wenn auch mit anderer Begründung. So spricht bereits Cassirer vom „Begriff des mit sich selbst identischen Symbolischen". In letzter Konsequenz möchte er, wie er sagt, den Dualismus überwinden. „Wir können 'Bedeutung' nicht anders als durch Rückbeziehung auf die 'Anschauung" erfassen – wie uns Anschauliches nie anders als im 'Hinblick' auf Bedeutung 'gegeben' sein kann. Halten wir hieran fest, so entgehen wir damit der Gefahr, daß das Symbolische unserer Erkenntnis sich in sich selber spaltet, daß es gewissermaßen in einen 'immanenten' und einen 'transzendenten' Bestandteil auseinanderbricht. Das Symbolische ist vielmehr Immanenz und Transzendenz in Einem: Sofern in ihm ein prinzipiell überanschaulicher Gehalt in anschaulicher Form sich äußert."[25]

Cassirer begründet seine Ansicht mit der Entwicklung der Menschheit. Diese komme von mythischen Vorstellungen, die mit Hilfe von Symbolen ausgedrückt werden, zu immer höherer Entwicklung. Dabei wähle sie, um ihren Vorstellungen Ausdruck zu verleihen, begriffliche Formulierungen. Mit anderen Worten: die Entwicklung gehe vom Konkreten zum Abstrakten. Nur die sinnliche Auffassung der Welt verwende die mythischen und religiösen Symbole. Auf einer höheren Entwicklungsstufe verlören diese religiösen Symbole ihren Ursinn, ihren Zusammenhang mit dem Mythischen und Religiösen. An ihre Stelle würden Begriffsbildungen treten[26]. Diese These, die offensichtlich unter dem seinerzeitigen Einfluß

[25] Cassirer 3, 447.

[26] Das hat Looff, 41, richtig erkannt: „Mit dieser Symboldeutung wäre das religiöse Symbol, das seiner Eigenart gemäß doch nie auf einen Hinweis auf etwas außer ihm bzw. über ihm verzichten kann, weil es von der

der evolutionistischen Ideologie entstanden ist, ist jedoch nicht zu halten. Auch ist es nicht nachprüfbar, daß die mythische Weltanschauung durch ein begriffsmäßiges Denken überwunden wird.

3.4. Der zweite Versuch, die ontologische Bipolarität zu überwinden, ist mit dem Namen Jaspers verbunden. Er ist nach einer anderen philosophischen Konzeption unter starkem Einfluß des Existentialismus, insbesondere nach dem Verständnis von Heidegger, angelegt. Jaspers bekennt sich im Prinzip zur Transzendenz: ,,Sein ist für uns, sofern es im Dasein zur Sprache wird. Ein bloßes Jenseits ist leer und so gut, als ob es nicht wäre. Daher fordert die Möglichkeit der Erfahrung eigentlichen Seins *immanente Transzendenz.*

Diese Immanenz aber hat einen offenbar paradoxen Charakter. *Immanent* ist grade in *Unterscheidung vom Transzendenten* im Bewußtsein überhaupt das für jedermann übereinstimmend Erfahrbare, die Welt. Immanent ist dann die *existentielle Gewißheit des Selbstseins,* welches zwar keinem Bewußtsein überhaupt mehr zugänglich, aber sich selbst gegenwärtig ist im *Unterschied vom Sein der Transzendenz,* das für Existenz als das ist, worauf als eigentliches Sein sie sich bezieht. Wird aber das Sein der Transzendenz der Existenz gegenwärtig, so nicht als es selbst – denn es besteht keine Identität von Existenz und Transzendenz –, sondern als *Chiffre* und auch so nicht als Gegenstand, der dieser Gegenstand ist, sondern gleichsam *quer zu aller Gegenständlichkeit.* Die immanente Transzendenz ist *Immanenz,* die sogleich wieder *verschwand;* sie ist *Transzendenz,* die im Dasein *Sprache als Chiffre* wurde. Wie im Bewußtsein überhaupt das Experiment der Mittler zwischen Subjekt und Objekt ist, so die Chiffre zwischen Existenz und Transzendenz.“[27]

In diesen Sätzen treffen wir auf zwei Begriffe, die eine Erklärung verlangen: ,,Chiffre“ und ,,immanente Transzendenz“. Die Chiffre ist eine besondere Erscheinungsform der Transzendenz. Das ist als Paradoxon zu verstehen, denn in der Chiffre wird die Transzendenz weder zum Objekt, noch wird das objektiv Seiende zum Subjekt[28]. Solch eine Chiffre ist demnach ein Symbol. Was will Jaspers mit dem ebenso paradoxen Begriff

---

dialektischen Entgegensetzung von Immanenz und Transzendenz lebt, als einer durch den fortschreitenden Erkenntnisprozeß überwundenen Begriffsform zugehörig erkannt. In der Tat sicht Cassirer die religiöse Entwicklung in der prophetisch-monotheistischen Religion im Sinne einer wachsenden Ablösung von allem Dinglichen.“ Die gleichen Gedanken werden auch bei Bevan, 295 ff., wiedergegeben: ,,So far as the intellectual concept stands for a Reality which differs from it, it is a symbol only. So far as it corresponds with the Reality, it is not a symbol, but the actual truth. All our effort to think true thoughts about God is an effort to get rid of the symbolical character of our conceptions, to change them from symbols into precise apprehensions. And if there has been any progress in thought about God between the primitive level and that of a twentieth-century philosopher, progress has consisted in freeing conceptions from symbolical imagery.“ Cf. auch Kahler 55, 64 f.

[27] Jaspers 1956, 136 f.

[28] Der Begriff Chiffre steht in Jaspers‘ Erkenntnistheorie im Mittelpunkt, und er kommt wiederholt darauf zurück. Cf. auch 1947, 33 ff.

,,immanente Transzendenz" ausdrücken? In Wirklichkeit will er damit zwei Dinge ablehnen. Erstens, daß man mit Hilfe des Symbols das Transzendente als seiendes Objekt anerkennen könne. Zweitens, daß das Subjekt die Fähigkeit ,,der Wahrnehmung und des Hervorbringens metaphysischer Erfahrung" habe. ,,In beiden Fällen würde die unergründliche Dialektik des Chiffreseins aufgehoben. Es bliebe ein Jenseits als Transzendenz und ein Diesseits als empirisches Erleben. [. . .] Nachdem Transzendenz und Immanenz als das einander schlechthin Andere gedacht sind, müssen sie vielmehr in der Chiffre als *immanente Transzendenz* ihre gegenwärtige Dialektik für uns werden, wenn nicht Transzendenz versinken soll."[29] Wie diese Worte deutlich machen, will Jaspers eine Möglichkeit finden, um in seinem System der existentiellen Philosophie auch der Transzendenz einen Platz einzuräumen. Und hier wird nicht nur klar, daß er mit dem Begriff der ,,immanenten Transzendenz" den bipolaren Charakter des Symbols zu überwinden trachtet, sondern auch der Widerspruch dieser Konstruktion zur Grundkonzeption deutlich, dem Subjekt als letztem Deuter des Symbolinhalts, denn diesem ist die Transzendenz in seiner existentiellen Situation nicht zugänglich. ,,Das Sein der Transzendenz an sich ist unabhängig von mir, als solches aber nicht zugänglich. Diese Weise der Zugänglichkeit eignet nur Dingen in der Welt. Von der Transzendenz aber vernehme ich nur soviel, als ich selbst werde; erlahme ich, so trübt sie sich in ihrer an sich steten Gegenwärtigkeit; erlösche ich bis zum Dasein eines bloßen Bewußtseins überhaupt, ist sie verschwunden; erfasse ich sie, so ist sie für mich das Sein, das allein ist und ohne mich bleibt, was es ist."[30]

Indem Jaspers seine Stellungnahme in dieser Weise präzisiert, ist er gezwungen, seinen erkenntnistheoretischen Subjektivismus zuzugeben. Davon, ob eine Behauptung der Wahrheit entspreche, überzeuge er sich als Subjekt selbst: ,,*Ich überzeuge mich durch das, was ich selbst bin und will, nicht durch Verstand und empirische Beobachtung*. Der Maßstab ist nicht mehr der einer wissenschaftlichen methodischen Untersuchung mit einem Endergebnis, sondern die Frage ist die nach existentiell wahrer und existentiell ruinöser Chiffresprache."[31]

Sein Versuch, die ontologische Bipolarität mit Hilfe des Begriffs der immanenten Transzendenz zu überwinden, ist lediglich von tendenzieller Bedeutung. Auf diese Weise kann man sie aus erkenntnistheoretischen Gründen nicht überwinden.

Wenn man an der vorhin dargelegten Struktur des Symbols festhält, ist es möglich, den Gedanken der Identität noch weiter zu vertiefen. Die Behauptung von zwei völlig getrennten Elementen – dem Symbolisierenden und dem zu Symbolisierenden – in der Struktur des Symbols zeigt einen nur scheinbaren Widerspruch. Das wird deutlich, wenn man nach dem

---

[29] Jaspers 1956, 137.
[30] Ib.
[31] Ib. 148.

Wesen der zu symbolisierenden Wirklichkeit fragt. Die Theoretiker der religiösen Symbolik, mit Tillich an der Spitze, betonen besonders die transzendente Wirklichkeit, die mit Hilfe eines Symbols ausgedrückt werde. Das gleiche mit anderen Worten: Es ist die besondere Funktion des religiösen Symbols, dem Menschlichen das Göttliche verständlich zu machen, den Kontakt zwischen Gott und dem Menschen zu festigen[32].

Zu diesen Ansichten ist zu bemerken, daß die transzendente Wirklichkeit in religiösem Zusammenhang immer erlebte Wirklichkeit ist. Die Welt des Heiligen hat sich stets im Bewußtsein des Individuums gebildet. Sowohl die zu symbolisierende als die symbolisierende Wirklichkeit sind Strukturelemente ein und desselben religiösen Erlebens. Mit anderen Worten, der Akt der Symbolisierung ist ein synthetischer Vorgang, in dem die ontologische Bipolarität in Form des Erlebnisses überwunden ist[33]. Es genügt, hier darauf hinzuweisen, daß man bei ähnlichen Erlebnissen auf dem Gebiet der Musik, der bildenden Kunst und der Literatur auch nicht von ontologisch bipolaren oder dualistischen Erscheinungen zu sprechen pflegt. Das bedeutet jedoch nicht, wie schon vorhin bemerkt, daß man im Symbolerlebnis nicht einige Strukturelemente aufzeigen könnte, die eine Bipolarität in psychologischer Hinsicht nicht ausschließen.

4. Von den Problemen der religiösen Symbolik steht neben dem Wirklichkeitsproblem auch das Wahrheitsproblem im Mittelpunkt. Das religiöse Symbol hat wie alle Symbole kommunikative Bedeutung. Mit seiner Hilfe wird eine Wahrheit bekanntgemacht. Um seine Funktion zu erfüllen, muß es in Zusammenhang mit der Kultur stehen, in deren Rahmen die Kom-

---

[32] Ich meine, daß das Fußen auf der ontologischen Wirklichkeit in seiner Konsequenz den eigentlichen Symbolisierungsakt unmöglich macht. Das spiegelt sich auch in den bezeichnenden Worten von Tillich, 1964, 212, wider: „Aber gegen diesen Gedanken, der namentlich in der Gegenwart eine ungeheure Entlastung des religiösen Bewußtseins bedeuten würde, eine Befreiung von der Last fragwürdiger Symbolik, erhebt sich ein schwerwiegender Einwand: Voraussetzung eines unmythischen Redens vom Unbedingt-Transzendenten ist die religiöse Möglichkeit, gleichsam durch die Wirklichkeit hindurchzureden. Diese Möglichkeit aber setzt eine in Gott stehende Wirklichkeit voraus, d.h. diese Wirklichkeit ist eschatologisch und nicht gegenwärtig. Für die Gegenwart gilt, daß bestimmte Wirklichkeiten mit Symbolkraft über die anderen gestellt werden müssen und in diesem Darüberstehen Ausdruck dafür sind, daß die Wirklichkeit an sich nicht im Unbedingten steht. Nur sofern das *eschaton* im Gegenwärtigen als lebendige Macht wirkt, könnte diese Macht zu Worten führen, in denen die Wirklichkeit nicht überschritten ist, sondern in der Wirklichkeit durch die Wirklichkeit hindurchgesprochen wird." Aus diesen unklaren, in paradoxer form ausgedrückten Sätzen wird dennoch eines klar – Tillichs Flucht in die Eschatologie. Damit hat er die Grenzen der kritischen Forschung überschritten und ist in unkontrollierbare Spekulationen hineingeraten. Doch war er dazu gezwungen, um an dem unmöglichen Dualismus von empirischem Symbol und transzendenter Wirklichkeit festzuhalten.

[33] Meinen eigenen Gedanken sehr nahe kommt in diesem Fall Leese 1948, 439: „Insofern also trägt die Gottesanschauung der Religion des protestantischen Menschen *synthetischen* Charakter. In ihr wirkt sich letztlich die Dialektik von 'Grund' und 'Abgrund', der 'Analogia Entis' und des 'Ganz Anderen' aus, aber diese Dialektik nicht statisch, sondern dynamisch verstanden."

munikation stattfindet. Einfacher ausgedrückt, darin besteht der soziale Charakter des Symbols. Wir können hier nicht weiter darauf eingehen, obwohl auch diese Frage von zentraler Bedeutung ist, denn von ihr hängt die Kraft des Symbols ab[34]. In den Diskussionen über den Wahrheitsgehalt des Symbols herrscht verhältnismäßig große Einmütigkeit, nämlich insofern, daß die mit Hilfe eines Symbols ausgedrückte Wahrheit sich nicht in rationale Kategorien einreihen läßt. Damit erhebt sich die Frage nach den verschiedenen Begriffen der Wahrheit. Meiner Meinung nach ist dieser Widerspruch wegen seiner prinzipiellen Natur nicht aufzulösen[35]. Man kann nur den verschiedenen Inhalt dieses Begriffs präzisieren. Das hilft, müßige Diskussionen und Gegensätzlichkeiten bezüglich des rational bestimmten und des praktisch verwendeten symbolischen Wahrheitsbegriffs in der Religion zu vermeiden. Ferner hilft es auch, Einblick in die Funktionen des religiösen Symbols zu gewinnen.

Wenn man über die Kraft der Wahrheitsaussage von Symbolen spricht, wird unter anderem behauptet, daß man diese in zwei Typen einteilen könne: in diskursive und nicht-diskursive Symbole. Zu letzteren gehörten die religiösen Symbole[36]. Zur ersten Gruppe würden demnach Symbole gehören, die dazu dienen, die rationale Wahrheit auszudrücken. Diese Einteilung berührt verständlicherweise sehr stark die Religionswissenschaft. Wenn diese darauf Anspruch erheben will, eine Wissenschaft zu sein, kann sie auf den Gebrauch solcher Symbole, wie sie dem diskursiven Denken

---

[34] Tillich spricht in diesem Zusammenhang von ,,Selbstmächtigkeit" des Symbols (1964, 196), Giedion von ,,potent symbol" (37); von ,,Macht des Wortes" im weiteren Sinne spricht Segerstedt (57).

[35] Dieser unausgeglichene Gegensatz der Ansichten wird eindrucksvoll durch folgende einander widersprechende Behauptungen charakterisiert: ,,Das Kriterium der Wahrheit eines Symbols kann natürlich nicht der Vergleich mit der Wirklichkeit sein, auf die es hinweist, wenn diese Wirklichkeit gerade das schlechthin Unfaßbare ist. Die Wahrheit eines Symbols ruht in seiner inneren Notwendigkeit für das symbolschaffende Bewußtsein. Zweifel an seiner Wahrheit zeigen eine Änderung des Bewußtseins, eine neue Stellung zum Unbedingt-Transzendenten an. Das einzige Kriterium, das überhaupt in Frage kommt, ist dieses, daß das Unbedingte in seiner Unbedingtheit rein erfaßt wird. *Ein Symbol, das dieser Anforderung nicht genügt, das ein Bedingtes zur Würde des Unbedingten erhebt, ist zwar nicht unrichtig, aber dämonisch.*" (Tillich 1964, 208.)

Den entgegengesetzten Standpunkt vertritt Leese 1948, 404: ,,Allein, der Grad der Ausdruckskraft für das Unbedingt-Transzendente, so wichtig er ist, kann unmöglich das alleinige Kriterium für die Wahrheit eines religiösen Symbols sein. Es läge in ihm noch nicht die mindeste Begründung dafür, etwa die christliche Symbolwelt der islamischen oder buddhistischen, der spätjüdischen oder neuplatonistischen mit ihrer starken Betonung der göttlichen Transzendenz vorzuziehen."

Indem er sich zum ontologischen Charakter des Symbols bekennt, erklärt Wisse seine ausgesprochen theologische Position und begründet sie in der Offenbarung (180f.). Das hat den Wert einer objektiven Erkenntnis (229ff.). Natürlich bringt diese Einstellung nichts Wesentliches in die Diskussion über das Symbol, sondern stellt lediglich Wisses gläubiges Bekenntnis dar.

[36] Cf. Bertalanffy 361ff. Auch Langer, Susanne 97. Sie benutzt anstelle des Terminus ,,nicht-diskursiv" den Ausdruck ,,presentational symbolism", doch mit der gleichen Absicht, die Unterscheidung verschiedener Kategorien von Symbolen zu ermöglichen. Cf. auch Fingesten 150.

bekannt sind, nicht verzichten. Das wird auch von der Theologie bestätigt, die, wenn sie auch von gewissen Annahmen ausgeht, dennoch das System ihrer Erkenntnisse im Einklang mit den Prinzipien des diskursiven Denkens bildet. In dieser Hinsicht unterscheidet sie sich nicht von der Mathematik. Daß es sich so verhält, zeigen sehr anschaulich die Versuche der Religionsphilosophie, unter dem Einfluß der analytischen Philosophie die Funktionen Gottes mit Hilfe mathematischer Formeln auszudrücken. Gleichzeitig aber zeigen diese Versuche die tiefe Kluft zwischen den durch mathematische Formeln ausgedrückten Funktionen Gottes und dem im praktischen religiösen Leben empfundenen Gott. Das weist ein weiteres Mal auf die Notwendigkeit hin, von verschiedenen Symboltypen zu sprechen, wenn auch nur von den vorhin erwähnten diskursiven und nicht-diskursiven Symbolen. Das bedeutet, daß die im diskursiven Denken und damit auch von der Theologie benutzten Symbole sich ihrem Wesen nach von den Symbolen unterscheiden, wie sie in der Religion, der Kunst, der Literatur usw. anzutreffen sind. Um diesen Unterschied zu betonen, pflegt man in letzter Zeit die im diskursiven Denken verwendeten Symbole Zeichen zu nennen[37].

4.1. Die Ausdrücke ,,Zeichen" und ,,Symbol" verhelfen zu größerer Klarheit im Gebrauch des Symbolbegriffs; aus diesem Grunde betrachten wir sie hier näher. Vielfach wurde bereits darauf hingewiesen, daß auch in der Forschung nicht selten Ausdrücke der Umgangssprache benutzt werden, die vieldeutig sind. So ist es besonders in der Praxis mit diesen beiden Begriffen geschehen. Das hat auch die sachliche Darstellung des religiösen Symbolbegriffs sehr erschwert. ,,Das Wort Symbol hat im *Sprachgebrauch* einen vielfachen Sinn. Es wird im weitesten Sinn gebraucht für bloße Zeichen, für Gleichnisse und Vergleiche in der Welt, für Schemata und Abkürzungen der Anschauung, für alles Bedeutungshafte. Es ist jeweils zu fragen: Symbol wofür? Ist eine Antwort durch einen Gegenstand in der Welt möglich, so handelt es sich um kein eigentliches Symbol. Das 'wofür' ist hier nur im Symbol selber da und außerdem kein Gegenstand, es sei denn in transzendierenden philosophischen Begriffen."[38]

Hier wird auf die bedeutungsvollste Eigenschaft des Ausdrucks ,,Zeichen" eingegangen, die auch beim Gebrauch dieses Begriffs zu beachten ist. Von ,,Zeichen" kann man in den Fällen sprechen, wenn damit ein Gegenstand (empirisch oder ideell gegeben) bezeichnet werden soll[39]. In Wirklich-

---

[37] Die im diskursiven Denken verwendeten Symbole sind in Wirklichkeit frei gewählte Zeichen, die nach Belieben austauschbar sind. Ähnlich ist es in der Theologie, deren Symbole Zeichen bzw. Hilfsmittel sind, um den Inhalt der Religion in Formen des diskursiven Denkens auszudrücken. Die Probleme, die mit dem Gebrauch von ,,Zeichen" und ,,Symbolen" verbunden sind, haben seit Saussure, 103, die Gedanken der Wissenschaftler, insbesondere auf dem Gebiet der strukturellen Linguistik und der analytischen Philosophie, stark beschäftigt. Unter deren Einfluß, insbesondere dank Levy-Strauss, ist daher auch ein Widerhall in der Religionswissenschaft festzustellen. Cf. Schiwy 61 ff.

[38] Jaspers 1946, 277.

[39] Münzhuber 64: ,,Zeichen, die in sich keinen verstehbaren Gehalt bergen, sind von Menschen gemacht, um etwas ideal oder real

keit ist es das Kennzeichen des Gegenstandes. Eine andere Eigenschaft besteht darin, daß man das Zeichen als solches von Fall zu Fall frei wählen und nach Belieben auch frei wechseln kann. Häufig gebraucht man in der Umgangssprache zur Bezeichnung der Staatsfahne oder des Staatswappens und ähnlichen ein symbolisches Wort. In Wirklichkeit sind dies Zeichen, die die oberste administrative Macht des Staates nach Belieben wechseln kann (zur Zeit wird in Schweden erwogen, das Staatswappen zu ändern). Zusammenfassend kann man mit Fawcett sagen: ,,The associations of the sign are with objective, empirical thinking, whereas the symbol (again, as we shall see) is associated with the emotional and existential levels of human operation."[40]

Wiederholt ist zu betonen, daß ,,symbol is not created arbitrarily in the way that a sign can be. The symbol does, however, share with the sign the capacity to stand for something other than itself, but in a way which opens up possibilities which are closed to the sign. We have already noted that signs become really powerful, at least in a religious context, only when they are associated with a symbol. [...]

Symbols are not created, but born out of life. They do not come into being like signs as a result of the creative faculty of man's imagination."[41]

Einfacher gesagt, das Zeichen ist ein Hilfsmittel, ein Arbeitsrequisit, sowohl im täglichen Leben als auch in der wissenschaftlichen Arbeit, um die Orientierung und die Kommunikation innerhalb einer Gruppe zu erleichtern. Diese Kommunikation ist, dank der Konvention, rational, bestimmt und zielbewußt. Das Symbol hingegen gehört auf eine andere, psychische Ebene und wird hauptsächlich durch existentielle und emotionale Motive bestimmt. Mir scheint, daß Royce den strukturellen und funktionellen Unterschied zwischen Zeichen und Symbol in seinem Schema (siehe nächste Seite oben) sehr anschaulich dargestellt hat[42].

Der hier aufgezeigte Unterschied der Termini ,,Zeichen" und ,,Symbol" sollte in den Diskussionen beachtet werden, um diese zu vereinfachen und auf ein höheres Niveau der Sachlichkeit zu bringen.

5. Wir haben bereits beobachtet, daß im Zusammenhang mit der Frage

---

Seiendes zu vergegenwärtigen." Besondere Aufmerksamkeit haben der Unterscheidung von Zeichen und Symbol auch Thass-Thienemann, 17ff., und Bertalanffy, 35f., gewidmet. Cf. auch Fessard 291ff.

[40] Fawcett 14f.

[41] Ib. 26f. Cf. auch Tillich 1964, 208. Die Forderung der Trennung von Zeichen und Symbol hat auch Wisse, 29ff., anerkannt. In seiner Lösung schlägt er vor, das Symbol als eine untergeordnete Art der Gattung Zeichen mit einem Gradunterschied anzusehen (31), was bedeuten würde, daß das Symbol *sui generis* ein Zeichen wäre (unter direktem Einfluß von Looff 18). Dieser Lösung fehlt die Begründung, wie sie unsere Darstellung des Wesens des Symbols enthält. Eine weitere Motivierung für eine Unterscheidungslinie zwischen dem Symbol und Zeichen hat Zunini angegeben: ,,The line of demarcation between sign and symbol is that which divides the capacity of animals from that of man. Animals act in accordance with signs and configurations of signs, but they do not reach the level of symbol." (307)

[42] Royce 17.

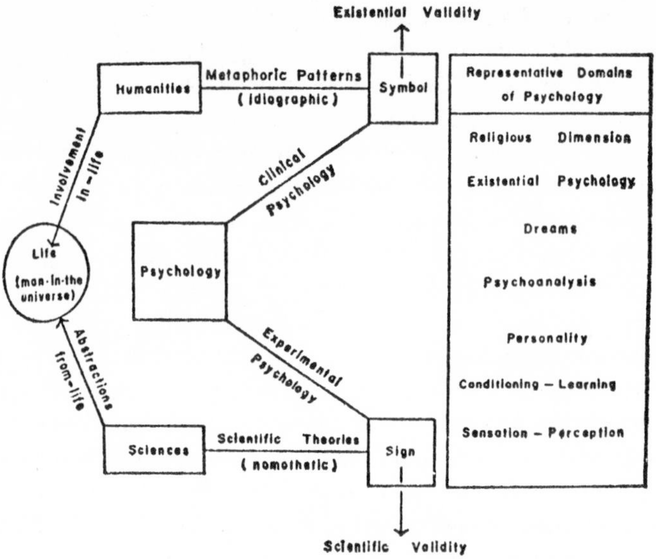

nach Zeichen und Symbolen auf die Kraft des Symbols hingewiesen wurde. Das eröffnet noch bessere Möglichkeiten, beide Erscheinungen zu unterscheiden. Es hilft auch, einen noch tieferen Einblick in das Wesen des Symbols zu gewinnen. Der Hinweis auf die Macht des Symbols ist ein sehr wichtiges Moment zum Verständnis des religiösen Symbols. Die Macht unterscheidet es seinem Wesen nach von den konventionellen, frei gewählten Zeichen, die den Erfordernissen einer Gruppe dienen. Der Unterschied ist nicht in der Notwendigkeit einer Kommunikation zu suchen. Diese besteht in allen Fällen. Im einen wie im anderen Fall hat man es mit einer kommunikativen Gruppe zu tun, deren Mitgliedern die von der Gruppe benutzten Symbole bzw. Zeichen bekannt sind. Es sind offensichtlich andere Umstände, die den religiösen Symbolen eine Kraft verleihen, die die Zeichen nicht besitzen. Welches sind diese Umstände? Die Macht des Symbols wurzelt im Wertbewußtsein. Wenn man diese Behauptung unter psychischem Aspekt betrachtet, kann man sagen, daß die Kräfte, die das Wertbewußtsein motivieren, größer sind als die Kraft der rational erkannten Wahrheit. Das kommt wahrscheinlich daher, daß im Wertbewußtsein emotionale, wenn nicht sogar biologische Motive mitsprechen[43]. Das

[43] Eine einleuchtende psychologische Theorie der emotionellen Ausbildung des Gottessymbols gibt Ferroro 112f.: ,,Il y a donc, entre Dieu et son symbole, une confusion qui est très bien expliquée par la théorie de l'*arrêt émotionnel.* Dieu n'a jamais été vu par personne; on ne peut donc en avoir qu'une image construite par l'imagination, sans l'aide des sensations, une image, pour ainsi dire, originelle: or, pour créer de toutes pièces, sans l'aide des sensations, une image assez vive, il faut un développement mental considérable et un effort assez grand. Aussi, dans la conscience du plus grand nombre des

wird besonders deutlich in rational und emotional begründeten Konfliktfällen. Es bedeutet, daß das Wertbewußtsein den Menschen in der Tiefe seiner Existenz berührt[44]. Und hier kehren wir zurück zur existentiellen Bedeutung der Religion. Das religiöse Leben ist nicht beschränkt auf Aussagen durch formale begriffliche Konstruktionen. Es äußert sich immer in umfassenden Aktivitäten, ob auf individuellem oder sozialem Bereich des Lebens. Diese Aktivitäten sind wertbezogen und damit auch existenzbezogen[45]. Ich sehe es so, daß gerade diese Wertbezogenheit dem religiösen Symbol seine Kraft verleiht. Das bedeutet aber auch zugleich, daß das religiöse Symbol als begründete Ausdrucksform des Wertbewußtseins nach erkenntnistheoretischer Meinung nicht die Fähigkeit hat, die Wahrheit auszusagen[46]. Wenn auch dem religiösen Symbol prinzipiell diese Eigenschaft fehlt, kann es dennoch vom psychischen Aspekt her die Qualität eines kognitiven Erlebnisses besitzen[47]. Im Symbolerlebnis spricht auch das Gefühl dafür mit, daß die symbolisierte Wirklichkeit die Wahrheit darstellt. Um der begrifflichen Klarheit willen müßte man in diesem Zusammenhang allerdings von Gewißheit sprechen.

---

hommes, au mot *Dieu* ne correspond-il qu'une image très vague et très peu précise. Il s'en suit que, lorsque le paysan voit une croix ou un autre symbole religieux réveillant en lui ces sentiments de crainte et de respect qui forment l'émotion religieuse, l'idée ou l'image de Dieu étant un état de conscience très peu clair et très peu précis, s'associe faiblement ou ne s'associe pas du tout à l'émotion. La sensation produite par la vue du symbole et les sentiments religieux sont seuls présents à l'esprit; ces sentiments ne peuvent donc avoir pour objet que le symbole, car la sensation du symbole est seule associée à l'émotion et la définit, tandis que l'idée et l'image de Dieu qui, dans l'acte psychique complet, devraient définir l'émotion, manquent. L'émotion s'arrête au symbole; et le symbole est adoré au lieu du Dieu qu'il devrait représenter.“ Cf. auch Ribot 393 f.

[44] Auf die existentielle Bedeutung des Symbols ist wiederholt verwiesen worden, so bei Bertalanffy 40; Kahler 53 f. Fawcett spricht klar vom ,,existencial character of symbols“: ,,The existential character of symbols has already emerged quite clearly. They operate at the level of the subject and not that of objects. They are not part of our discursive discussions of that which lies outside the self, of our intellectual manipulation of reality as made up of series of objects. They are concerned with man's subjectivity and with the subjectivity of the cosmos itself. They work intuitively and directly out of man's experience of himself as self to grasp that subjectivity which lies in the whole realm of being“ (33).

Auf die existenzielle Bindung hat auch Meslin richtig hingewiesen: ,,Parce qu'il vise, en effet, à exprimer une réalité supérieure à laquelle il relie l'homme, le symbole religieux engage, dans une certaine mesure, l'existence même de l'homme qui le vit“ (624).

[45] Leese, 1948, 397, erwähnt in diesem Zusammenhang die ,,religiöse Wertigkeit, d.h. die erlebbare Werthöhe“. Er sieht in ihr ,,das gesuchte Kriterium für die Wahrheit des religiösen Symbols“ (ib. 405).

[46] Sehr bestimmt hat sich darüber Jaspers, 1956, 151, geäußert: ,,Die *Wahrheit der Chiffre* aber kann ich nicht geradezu verifizieren, denn sie ist als ausgesprochene in ihrer Objektivität ein Spiel, das keinen Anspruch auf Geltung macht und daher auch keiner Rechtfertigung bedarf. Für mich selbst ist sie kein bloßes Spiel.“

[47] Hier ist an den weitgefaßten Begriff der Rationalität bei Langer, Susanne, 99, zu erinnern: ,,Rationality is the essence of mind, and symbolic transformation its elementary process. It is a fundamental error, therefore, to recognize it only in the phenomenon of systematic, explicit reasoning. That is a mature and precarious product.

Rationality, however, is embodied in every mental act, not only when the mind is 'at its fullest stretch and compass'.“

5.1. Die Richtigkeit der hier geäußerten theoretischen Gedankengänge kann überprüft werden, indem man sich in das sogenannte ,,Werden und Vergehen“ von Symbolen vertieft. In der Religionsgeschichte hat man es vielfach mit der ,,Wiederbelebung“ vergangener Symbole zu tun, d.h. damit, sie richtig zu begreifen. Im Laufe der Zeit haben einst aktuelle (,,lebendige“) Symbole ihre eigentliche Bedeutung verloren und sind nicht mehr verständlich. Mit anderen Worten, sie besitzen in der gegenwärtigen Situation bereits keine religiöse Funktion mehr. Die Religionsgeschichte kann ihnen ihre früheren Funktionen nicht mehr wiedergeben, d. h. sie kann sie nicht mehr ,,wiederbeleben“. Um bei dieser Metapher zu bleiben: man kann sagen, daß die religionswissenschaftliche Forschung ein Spaziergang auf dem Friedhof der toten religiösen Symbole ist[48]. Das bezieht sich im selben Maß auch auf die Geschichte der christlichen Kirche. Aber weshalb vergehen Symbole? Die Antwort ist nicht schwer. In dem Augenblick, wo das Symbol nicht mehr dem Inhalt des religiösen Erlebnisses adäquat ist, stirbt es ab. Es hat keine Bedeutung mehr, es besitzt keinen aktuellen Wert[49]. Ein Symbol ohne Wert für das religiöse Leben ist mehr kein Symbol[50]. Man weiß, daß der derzeitige Erzbischof der Kirche in Schweden Abbild und Kult des Gottes Thor kennt, der früher im alten Uppsala verehrt wurde, und eine Sammlung rationaler Erkenntnisse darüber besitzt. Er weiß, wer und was Thor ist und zu welchem religiösen Bereich er gehört. Aber das Abbild (Symbol) Thors und dessen Kult sind nicht Symbole seines religiösen Lebens. Mit anderen Worten, der Wert des religiösen Symbols von Thor ist verschwunden, denn das Oberhaupt einer christlichen Kirche des 20. Jahrhunderts hat sich in persönlicher Erfahrung eine eigene

---

[48] Ähnlich hat sich Foss, 58, geäußert: ,,Every langauge is full of 'dead metaphors'.“ Ebenso auch Bērziņš 323. Ferroro, 186, spricht vom ,,Atavisme et pathologie du symbole“.

[49] Ganz richtig verbindet Leese, 1948, 404, den Prozeß des Absterbens von Symbolen mit dem Wertbewußtsein: ,,Werden und Vergehen, Kampf und Verdrängung religiöser Symbole beruhen auf der jeweils labilen Vorzugsordnung religiös fundierter Werte, die immer mitgemeint sind [...].“ Ebenso auch Davids, Rhys 154. Jaspers findet für das Absterben eine andere Erklärung. Die Symbole seien den dynamischen Prozessen des Lebens unterworfen. Sobald sie aus dem Zustand, den er als ,,die Schwebe“ bezeichnet, zu einer statischen Erscheinung werden, sterben sie ab, d.h. sie werden zu zeichen: ,,Aber Sprache, Wirklichkeit, Unendlichkeit eignen den Symbolen nur so lange, als sie in der Schwebe ihrer Erscheinung bleiben. Sobald sie zu festen Bildern, fixierten Zeichen und damit zu Dingen in der Welt werden, geraten wir mit ihnen wieder an einen Strand, an den Strand falscher Leibhaftigkeiten, bloßer Bilder. Auch die Symbole, als verwandelte Objektivitäten, müssen in der Bewegung einer Ungreifbarkeit bleiben. Ihr Schwebesein macht allein ihre Unendlichkeit aus. Ihre Gestaltwerdung bringt sie auch auf den Weg, auf dem sie kollabieren zu festen Gebilden, die wie endliche Erkenntnisse genommen werden, aber nunmehr kein wirklicher Halt, sondern nur noch – am Realen gemessen – täuschende Illusionen sind.“ Cf. auch Meslin 624.

[50] Diesen Prozeß des Absterbens der Symbole spiegelt auch die sogenannte ,,Gott-ist-tot“-Theologie wider. Sie will sagen, daß das Wort ,,Gott“ keinen aktuellen religiösen Wert hat. Cf. zu dieser Frage die Schriften von Altizer 95ff.; Hamilton 23ff.; auch *Christianity* 315ff.; Vahanian 1961, 12ff.

religiöse Überzeugung gebildet und damit auch eine andere Welt der Symbole[51].

Das ,,Absterben" religiöser Symbole ist eine Bestätigung des oben Gesagten, daß der religiöse Wert eines Symbols und seine Funktionen in einem Wertbewußtsein wurzeln[52]. Dieser Standpunkt läßt sich nur aufrecht erhalten, wenn man innerhalb der Grenzen des empirischen historischen Materials bleibt. Dagegen ist er hinfällig, wenn man die Auffassung einer ontologisch bestimmten bipolaren Struktur des religiösen Symbols vertreten will[53]. Natürlich kann man hier fragen, wodurch die Veränderung des Wertbewußtseins hervorgerufen und bestimmt wird. Diese Frage läßt sich nicht eindeutig beantworten, denn dann müßte man zugleich auch sagen können,

---

[51] Cf. Fawcett 86 ff.: ,,Each symbolic expression in religion has enclosed within it an aspect of man's experience of the personal dimension. [...]

The power potentiality of a symbol depends upon the extent to which it corresponds to man's experience. That experience, however, constantly changes. The models which serve best in youth fall into the background in later life. The imagery which served ancient man so well may no longer speak to men in the twentieth century."

[52] Eine ausgesprochen ablehnende Haltung gegenüber der Begründung des Symbols durch das Werbewußtsein hat Looff, 71, unter Kritik an der Auffassung Leeses, eingenommen: ,,Wenn ich die Beziehung auf bestimmte Werte zum Maßstab der Wahrheit eines religiösen Symbols mache, setzt das immer ein durch eine bestimmte Werterziehung hindurchgegangenes Wertbewußtsein voraus, das dann mehr analog sich Symbole sucht und schafft, statt sich durch ein am Symbol aufleuchtendes Letztgemeintes erschüttern und in Frage stellen zu lassen. Dem einseitig religiös bestimmten Bewußtsein kann der größte religiöse Kitsch Ausdruck werden für das Unbedingt-Transzendente, wenn es darin seine geglaubte und bejahte Wertwelt wiederentdeckt. Bei einer Betonung der religiösen Wertigkeit des Symbols wird stets der mitgebrachte Glaube des Betrachters vorausgesetzt, der über die Ausdruckskraft des Symbols entscheidet."

Hierzu nur zwei Bemerkungen. Erstens hat Looff beim Gebrauch des Wortes ,,Kitsch" zur Bezeichnung des Wertbewußtseins, ausgehend von seiner religiösen Überzeugung, selbst ein Werturteil gefällt und damit bestätigt, daß religiöse Erlebnisse ein Wertbewußtsein darstellen. Zweitens scheint er nicht zu wissen, daß es sich um eine gewohnte Erscheinung in der Religionsgeschichte handelt, wenn die Anhänger der einen Religion das ,,Unbedingt-Transzendente" einer anderen Religion mit Worten belegen, die inhaltlich dem erwähnten ,,Kitsch" entsprechen. Daher berührt auch Looffs Kritik nicht das religiöse Wertbewußtsein, das seinen Ausdruck in Symbolen findet.

[53] Als Tillich seinerzeit vom ,,Vergehen" der Symbole sprach, stieß er auf die schärfste Kritik gerade aus den konservativsten Kreisen in den USA, die diesem Gedanken nicht zustimmen konnten (cf. Modernists 5). Tillich mißverstehend, hat sich ihnen auch Ahlberg, 11 f., mit seiner Äußerung ,,Gläubige ohne Glaube" angeschlossen. Die gleiche Reaktion ist auch von katholischer Seite erfolgt (Wisse 139). Wisse bekennt sich dazu wie folgt: ,,[...] ein Symbol, das zu irgendeiner Zeit wirklich existiert hat, [ist] unvergänglich, solange eben die Welt besteht" (139) und ,,das Symbol ist in sich [!], nach dem erstmaligen 'Geboren-Werden', unabhängig davon, ob es vom Menschen verstanden wird oder nicht" (139). Doch kann er nicht die Tatsache übersehen, daß Symbole verschwinden, ,,absterben". Darauf antwortet er: ,,Was als Vergehen oder Veränderung wahrgenommen wird, hat seinen Grund in Gegebenheiten auf seiten der Menschen" (210). Doch das Vergehen! Nun, der Mensch braucht und schafft sich Symbole, nicht aber Gott.

In ähnlicher Weise ist Eliade auf Irrwege geraten, wenn er meint, daß die Hierophanie, die sich einst in einem Symbol ausdrückte, nie wieder verschwindet: ,,Ein Symbolismus ist unabhängig davon, ob er verstanden wird oder nicht, mehr, er bewahrt ihn sogar, wenn er ganz vergessen ist, was jene vorgeschichtlichen Symbole beweisen, deren Sinn über Tausende von Jahren vergessen war, um dann 'wiederentdeckt' zu werden" (510).

wodurch überhaupt Veränderungen bestimmt werden. Eine Antwort auf diese Frage reicht ins Metaphysische. Anstelle einer Antwort muß man sich mit der Erkenntnis zufriedengeben, daß das Leben des Menschen in einer Welt verläuft, die ein dynamischer, ununterbrochener Prozeß von Veränderungen ist. Und in diesem dynamischen Prozeß entstehen und verschwinden auch die religiösen Symbole[54].

Literaturverzeichnis

AUU Acta Universitatis Upsaliensis. Historia religionum. Uppsala.
EJ Eranos Jahrbuch. Zürich.
LL Le Langage. Neuchâtel.
ZPhF Zeitschrift für philosophische Forschung.

Ahlberg, A., 1966, *Troende utan tro.* Stockholm.
Altizer, T., 1966, Theology and the death of God. *Theology.*
Assagioli, R., 1969, Symbols of transpersonal experiences. *The journal of transpersonal psychology.*
Bertalanffy, L., 1965, On the definition of the symbol. *Psychology.*
Bērziņš, L., 1935, Latviešu tautas dziesmas [Lettische Volkslieder]. *Latviešu literātūras vēsture* 1. Rīgā.
Bevan, E., 1938, *Symbolism and belief.* London.
Bibliographie, 1968 f., *Bibliographie zur Symbolik, Ikonographie und Mythologie* 1 f. Hrsg. M. Lurker. Baden-Baden.
Biezais, H., 1961, *Die Gottesgestalt der lettischen Volksreligion.* AUU 1.
— 1972, *Die himmlische Götterfamilie der alten Letten.* AUU 5.
— 1976, Die Stellung der Religion in den soziokulturellen Strukturen. *Dynamics and institution.* Ed. H. Biezais. Scripta Instituti Donneriani Aboensis 9. Uppsala.
Cassirer, E., 1929, *Philosophie der symbolischen Formen* 3. Berlin.
Christianity, 1967, *The new christianity.* Ed. W. Miller. New York.
Davids, Rhys, 1934, Zur Geschichte des Rad-Symbols. *EJ* 2.
Eliade, M., s. a., *Die Religionen und das Heilige.* Salzburg.
Fawcett, T., 1970, *The symbolic language of religion.* Guildford.
Ferroro, G., 1895, *Les lois psychologiques de symbolisme.* Paris.
Fessard, G., 1966, Symbole symbolisant, signes, symbole symbolisé. *LL* [1].
Fingesten, P., 1970, *The eclipse of symbolism.* Columbia.
Firth, R., 1973, *Symbols, public and private.* London.
Friedman, H., 1949, *Wissenschaft und Symbol.* München.

[54] Über das Verschwinden bzw. Absterben von Symbolen im Christentum und Judaismus sowie auch über das Entstehen neuer Symbole hat Lantis, Margaret 101, besonders 112, beachtenswerte Gedanken geäußert. Goodenough, 293 f., hat auf diese Weise ausgedruckt: „[...] that symbols have a way of dying, of apparently losing their power, and becoming merely ornaments. And they also have the power of coming to life again, as fresh associations and religious awakenings take one of the old symbols for their own. This happened when the Christians adopted the old, the universal symbol of the cross, a symbol which in pre-Christian ornament had degenerated to be only the four pointed rosette, one of many forms of the rosette. [...] For we must continue to face the problem of the 'merely decorative' as contrasted with the 'symbolic' use of forms in art; and when we contrast them in these terms, or in such terms as 'live' symbols versus 'dead' symbols, or 'active' symbols versus 'quiescent' or 'dormant' symbols in each case, we assume a theory of the nature of the contrast. Since I must have a terminology, I shall arbitrary, tentatively, and without prejudice, use the contrast 'live' and 'dead'."

Giedion, S., 1966, Symbolic expression in prehistory and in the first high civilizations. *Sign, image and symbol.* Ed. G. Kepes. London.
Goodenough, E., 1952, The evaluation of symbols recurrent in time, as illustrated in Judaism. *EJ* 20 (1951).
Goodman, P., 1973, *Speaking and language.* London.
Hamilton, W., 1966, The death of God theology today. *Theology.*
Jaspers, K., 1946, *Allgemeine Psychopathologie.* Berlin.
— 1947, *Von der Wahrheit.* Philosophische Logik 1. München.
— 1956, *Philosophie* 3. Berlin.
Kahler, E., 1960, The nature of the symbol. *Symbolism in religion and literature.* Ed. R. May. New York.
Langer, Susanne, 1951, *Philosophy in a new key.* Cambridge.
Lantis, Margaret, 1950, The symbol of a new religion. *Psychiatry* 13.
Leese, K., 1934, *Die Mutter als religiöses Symbol.* Sammlung gemeinverständlicher Vorträge und Schriften aus dem Gebiet der Theologie und Religionsgeschichte 174. Tübingen.
— 1948, *Die Religion des protestantischen Menschen.* München.
Looff, H., 1955, *Der Symbolbegriff in der neueren Religionsphilosophie und Theologie.* Kant-Studien. Ergänzungshefte 69. Köln.
Mensching, G., 1930, Analyse des Symbolbegriffs. *Christliche Welt* 40.
— 1955, Religiöse Ursymbole der Menschheit. *Studium generale* 8.
— 1977, *Topos und Typos.* Untersuchungen zur allgemeinen Religionsgeschichte 8. Bonn.
Meslin, H., 1974, Pour une théorie du symbolisme religieux. *Mélanges d'histoire des religions offert à Henri-Charles Puech.* Paris.
Modernists, 1963, Modernists are not Christians. *Lutheran news,* Nov. 4.
Moody, R., 1956, On Jung's concept of the symbol. *British journal of medical psychology* 29.
Münzhuber, J., 1950, Sinnbild und Symbol. *ZPhF.*
Parsons, T., 1968, *The structure of social action.* London.
Psychology, 1965, *Psychology and the symbol.* Ed. J. Royce.
Ribot, T., 1915, La pensée symbolique. *Revue philosophique* 49.
Royce, J., 1965, Psychology at the crossroads between the sciences and the humanities. *Psychology.*
Saussure, F., 1916, *Cours de linguistique générale.* Paris.
Schiwy, G., 1973, *Strukturalismus und Zeichensprache.* Beck'sche Schwarze Reihe 96. München.
Segerstedt, T., 1947, *Die Macht des Wortes.* Internationale Bibliothek für Psychologie und Soziologie 3. Zürich.
Seiffert, A., 1957, *Funktion und Hypertrophie des Sinnbildes.* ZPhF. Beihefte 12.
Skorupski, J., 1976, *Symbol and theory.* Cambridge.
Symbolon, 1960f., *Symbolon* 1ff. Hrsg. J. Schwabe. Basel. N. F., 1f. Hrsg. Reimbold. Köln.
Thass-Thienemann, T., 1968, *Symbolic behavior.* New York.
Theology, 1966, *Radical theology and the death of God.* Ed. T. Altizer, W. Hamilton. Indianapolis.
Tillich, P., 1928, Das religiöse Symbol. *Blätter für deutsche Philosophie.*
— 1964, *Gesammelte Werke* 5. Stuttgart.
— 1973, *Symbol und Wirklichkeit.* Kleine Vandenhoeck-Reihe 151. Göttingen.
Urban, W., 1939, *Language and reality.* London.
Vahanian, G., 1961, *The death of God.* New York.
Wisse, S., 1963, *Das religiöse Symbol.* Essen.
Zunini, G., 1969, *Man and his religion.* London.

Gottessymbol und soziale Struktur

Von RAGNAR HOLTE

Wie das Verhältnis zwischen Religion und Gesellschaft beschaffen ist, hat man in der älteren Religionssoziologie lebhaft diskutiert, wobei E. Durkheim und M. Weber zwei gegensätzliche Standpunkte vertraten. Für Durkheim waren Religion und Gesellschaft aufs Engste miteinander verwoben dergestalt, dass die Religion letzten Endes ein Produkt des kollektiven Geistes war, der den verschiedenen Gesellschaftsformen zugrunde lag. Die Religion lieferte die Kategorie der Heiligkeit und verband diese mit verschiedenen Zügen der gesellschaftlichen Struktur, die dadurch ein Gepräge der Unantastbarkeit erhielt. Die Religion dient hier also als Faktor zur Stabilisierung der gesellschaftlichen Struktur und der damit gegebenen Machtverhältnisse[1]. Weber dagegen betonte die relative Selbständigkeit der Religion gegenüber der sozialen Struktur, weshalb man die erste nicht einfach als ein Produkt der letzteren auffassen dürfe. Dagegen konnten religiöse Ideen – ebenso wie andere aus dem menschlichen Geist hervorgegangene Ideen – das äussere Geschehen beeinflussen und gestalten und damit auch zur Veränderung der gesellschaftlichen Strukturen beitragen[2].

Das Problem, mit dem Durkheim und Weber rangen und das sie auf verschiedene Weise zu lösen versuchten, ist heute noch ebenso aktuell und dringlich und kann keinesfalls als fertig durchdacht gelten. In der wissenschaftlichen Diskussion der Folgezeit dürfte Webers Anschauung es wesentlich schwerer gehabt haben, sich zu behaupten, als die Durkheims. Webers Auffassung schien allzu eng mit dem heute verlassenen Standpunkt der idealistischen Philosophie und Geschichtswissenschaft verknüpft. Auch war es nicht schwer, zahllose Belege für die These Durkheims von der Religion als einem gesellschaftlich stabilisierenden Faktor beizubringen. Dennoch hat man auch gegen Durkheims These Einwände erhoben. Seine Antwort erwies sich als allzu eindeutig und einseitig, um ein getreues Bild der vielschichtigen Frage Religion und Gesellschaft zu geben. Man hat u. a. auf jene Fälle hingewiesen, in denen religiöse Ideen tatsächlich und nachweisbar zu Veränderungen der sozialen Struktur beigetragen oder den Anstoss dazu gegeben haben[3].

Mein heutiges Thema, Gottessymbol und soziale Struktur, betrachte ich als ein wichtiges Teilproblem dieses grösseren Fragenkreises. Unter Gottessymbolen verstehe ich dabei die Bilder oder die bildlichen Ausdrücke

---

[1] Cf. Durkheim 21 ff., 462 ff.

[2] Cf. Weber 118 ff.

[3] Für die spätere Diskussion siehe z. B. Demerath besonders 150 ff. Die religionsphilosophische Seite des Problems wird u. a. von Hick, 31 ff., diskutiert.

der Sprache, mit deren Hilfe sich die Menschen den Gott/die Götter zu veranschaulichen suchen. Dabei gehe ich – im Anschluss an die Einleitungsvorlesung H. Biezais' – von dem bipolaren Charakter der Gottessymbole aus, dass nämlich ein Unterschied zwischen dem Symbol und dem Symbolisierten besteht. Ferner fasse ich mit Biezais diese Bipolarität in erster Linie als psychologisch auf, das heisst: auch wenn wir die Grenze der „subjektbezogenen Wirklichkeit" nicht überschreiten, in der „das Subjekt in seiner psychischen Aktivität den Inhalt seines Erlebnisses durch etwas Anderes [...] indirekt ausdrückt"[4], so müssen wir an dem prinzipiellen Unterschied zwischen Symbol und Symbolisiertem festhalten. Auf die Frage, ob man das Recht hat, den Erlebnisinhalt, der durch das Gottessymbol vermittelt werden soll, auf eine vom Subjekt unabhängige ontologische Wirklichkeit zurückzuführen, gehe ich nicht ein. Für den hier verfolgten Zweck ist die Beantwortung dieser Frage nicht notwendig, die wenigstens teilweise von ausserwissenschaftlicher Art sein dürfte.

In vielen Religionen spielt ja das plastisch geformte (in Stein gemeisselte, in Holz geschnitzte, in Erz gegossene), das auf eine Fläche eingeritzte oder das gezeichnete und gemalte Götterbild eine zentrale Rolle im religiösen Kult. Bei diesen Religionen bezöge sich unser Thema vor allem auf das Verhältnis dieser Kultbilder zur sozialen Struktur. Andere Religionen sind kritisch gegenüber solchen Kultbildern oder lehnen sie vollständig ab, aber bei der Bezeichnung Gottes oder der Anrede, mit der man sich an Gott wendet, ist ihre Sprache voll von bildhaften Ausdrücken wie Vater, Herrscher u. s. w. Hier konzentriert sich unser Thema mehr auf die Frage, wie die Wahl sprachlicher Symbole für Gott von der sozialen Struktur beeinflusst wird oder eventuell diese beeinflusst.

Die Sprache selbst ist ja ein Produkt der Gesellschaft und dient zum Ausdruck menschlicher Erfahrungen und zu ihrer Vermittlung an die Mitmenschen. Je enger Religion und Gesellschaft miteinander verwoben sind, desto natürlicher fungiert die Sprache als Ausdruck und zur Vermittlung von Erfahrungen und Glaubensvorstellungen vom Wesen Gottes/der Götter, von seinem/ihrem Handeln und seinen/ihren Eigenschaften. Die religiöse Erfahrung ist dann nämlich ein Teil der gesellschaftlich bedingten menschlichen Erfahrung.

In vielen von der Religion geprägten Gesellschaftsformen haben die Gottesvorstellungen ausgesprochen antropomorphen Charakter: die dem Gott zugeschriebenen Eigenschaften unterscheiden sich prinzipiell nicht von den innerhalb der Gesellschaft als ideal-menschlich gewerteten Eigenschaften, sodass auch Menschen mit den von der Religion gepriesenen Eigenschaften als göttlich betrachtet werden können. Solche göttlichen Eigenschaften können z. B. gesellschaftlich-menschliche Züge wie Fruchtbarkeit, Machtvollkommenheit oder Jagd- und Kampftüchtigkeit sein. Diese Auffassung

---

[4] Cf. oben S. XVII.

lässt sich nicht nur in der von Durkheim untersuchten australischen Religion nachweisen, sondern auch z. B. in der altnordischen und in der klassisch griechischen und römischen Religion.

In höher entwickelten Religionen begegnet uns oft eine deutliche Tendenz, Gott/die Götter und die religiösen Phänomene stärker zu transzendieren (wobei der Plural Götter vielleicht überflüssig ist, da dieser Grad der Transzendenz wohl den Monotheismus voraussetzen dürfte). Man stellt Gott als qualitativ vom Menschen verschieden und als über diesen erhaben dar, was aber eine intime Verknüpfung von Religion und Gesellschaft nicht zu beeinträchtigen braucht.

In der Antike steht die Religion Israels mit ihrer Tendenz zum Transzendieren der Gottheit im Gegensatz zu den Religionen benachbarter Völker. Ein Ausdruck dafür ist das Bildverbot (2. Mos. 20,4–5). Während etwa in dem von den Propheten ständig bekämpften Baalskult das gemeisselte oder geschnitzte Götterbild eine zentrale Rolle spielte, gab es in Salomos Tempel in Jerusalem zwar die Abbildung der vier Engel, die den Cherubenthron Gottes trugen, Jahwe selbst aber wurde nicht abgebildet, man stellte sich ihn unsichtbar thronend vor. Eine strikte örtliche Festlegung Gottes auf den Tempel lehnt man in Israel ausserdem durch die dem König Salomo zugeschriebenen Worte ab: Siehe der Himmel und aller Himmel Himmel können dich nicht fassen – wie soll es denn dies Haus tun, das ich gebaut habe? (1. Kön. 8,27) Der leere Cherubenthron symbolisiert aber höchst greifbar die Gegenwart einer unsichtbaren, prinzipiell allgegenwärtigen Gottheit. Durch eben diese Eigenschaften stellt sich die Gottheit als radikal anderen Wesens und als erhaben über den Menschen und die menschliche Gemeinschaft dar. Zugleich aber vermittelt der Thron Assoziationen zu der menschlich-sozialen Funktion politischer Machtausübung. Epitheta der politischen Machtsphäre gibt das Alte Testament Gott ganz selbstverständlich bei, man nennt ihn Herrn, Herrscher, König u. s. w. Religiöse und politische Gemeinschaft fallen im alten Israel zusammen. Der irdische Herrscher steht unter dem Schutz des himmlischen Herrschers, er ist dem letzteren aber auch Rechenschaft schuldig und kann von ihm verworfen werden (das Schicksal Sauls). Das Königtum von Israel wird durch die Religion zugleich legitimiert und relativiert, man denke auch an die ständige, schneidende Kritik der Propheten an den Königen, wie sie ihre Macht missbrauchen.

Das Christentum tritt in vieler Hinsicht das Erbe Israels und seiner Gottesauffassung an, aber es bestehen auch bedeutsame Unterschiede. An den Vorstellungen von der Erhabenheit, Unsichtbarkeit und Allgegenwart Gottes hält man natürlich fest, sie werden noch dadurch verstärkt, dass seine Gegenwart nun nicht mehr an den Tempel von Jerusalem oder an einen anderen Kultplatz gebunden ist (Joh. 4,21–24). Das Verhältnis wird aber durch die Stellung der Person Jesu kompliziert. Da man sich die Gottheit in Jesus Christus inkarniert vorstellt und ihn folglich mit göttlichen

Eigenschaften begabt denkt, eröffnen sich dem Christentum trotz allem bessere Möglichkeiten als dem Judentum, das Wesen Gottes durch die bildende Kunst zu veranschaulichen.

Das Christentum lehrt ja die Dreieinigkeit Gottes. Das alttestamentliche Bildverbot hat man im Verlauf der Kirchengeschichte immer wieder diskutiert, wobei bildfeindliche und bildfreundliche Richtungen miteinander in Konflikt gerieten[5]. Im grossen Ganzen darf man sagen, dass bildliche Darstellungen Christi als legitim betrachtet wurden, sie sind also für das Christentum bezeichnend und stehen in klarem Gegensatz zum Judentum. Aber wie verhält es sich mit Gott-Vater, der ersten Person der Gottheit? Seine Darstellung lässt sich nicht durch die Inkarnationslehre begründen, die schon im ältesten Christentum die Darstellung Jesu zuliess. Vor dem 12. Jh. gibt es praktisch auch kaum Bilder, die Gott-Vater darstellen, aber von dieser Zeit an sind sie in dem immer reicheren Bildschmuck der Kirchenwände und -fenster nicht ungewöhnlich[6]. Diese Tendenz zur anthropomorphen Darstellung der ersten Person der Gottheit verstärkte sich deutlich, als die eher stilisierende Darstellung des Mittelalters in die Renaissancekunst mit ihrem lebhaften Interesse für den Menschen und mit ihrer Betonung des menschlichen Körpers in der Kunst übergeht. Als einen Höhepunkt dieser Entwicklung darf man vielleicht Michelangelos Gemälde in der Sixtinischen Kapelle der Peterskirche von Rom auffassen, wo er den Schöpfer Gott als älteren, bärtigen Mann darstellt, der nicht nur göttliche Macht sondern auch physische Kraft ausstrahlt. In späteren Phasen der christlichen Kunst sind wohl die Bilddarstellungen von Gott-Vater wieder seltener geworden. Im Judentum dagegen wären sie in allen Epochen auch als Ausnahme undenkbar gewesen.

Zusammenfassend muss man daher sagen, dass jene Dimension der göttlichen Transzendenz, die im Bildverbot des Alten Testaments ihren Ausdruck findet, im Christentum wesentlich gemildert ist. In anderer Hinsicht dürfte aber die Transzendierung im christlichen Bereich gewachsen sein, ich denke hier an das Verhältnis der Gottesauffassung zur sozialen Struktur, ein für unser Thema zentraler Aspekt. Mit Ausnahme von einigen kleineren Gruppen hat man im Christentum die religiöse Gemeinschaft als prinzipiell von der politisch-sozialen Gemeinschaft unterschieden und als über diese erhaben betrachtet. Womit nicht gesagt ist, dass man gemeint hat, die Religion habe keine sozialen und politischen Folgen. Während aber das alte Israel ein theokratischer Staat war und die Messiaserwartung eine ausgesprochen politische Bedeutung hatte, unterscheidet man im Christentum normalerwise zwischen dem Reich Gottes (dem Reich Christi) und den irdischen Reichen, und man erklärt, das erstere „sei nicht von dieser Welt" (Joh. 18,36). Dessen ungeachtet verwendet man auch im christlichen Be-

---

[5] Im 16. Jh. hat der reformierte Zweig der Reformation die Bildfeindlichkeit vertreten.

[6] Cf. Sachs 153.

reich politische Epitheta als Gottesnamen, und man erhebt Gott auch hier bildlich auf einen (himmlischen) Thron. Wenn auch der Thron als Kultgegenstand im Christentum nicht mehr vorkommt, so bezeichnet man doch zuweilen den Altar als den Gnadenthron.

In Religionen mit einem Kodex von für heilig gehaltenen Schriften verbindet sich die Tendenz, die Gottheit zu transzendieren, oft mit der Lehre, der Inhalt dieses Kodex sei göttliche Offenbarung. Man folgert dann gerne daraus, dass die in diesem Kodex vorkommenden Aussagen über das Wesen Gottes, über seine Eigenschaften und sein Handeln absolut und unantastbar seien. Sie sind prinzipiell über die soziale Struktur erhaben und werden von dieser nicht beeinflusst, weshalb sie sich bei Veränderungen der sozialen Struktur nicht verändern dürfen. Besser geschulte Vertreter dieser Religionen geben jedoch zu, dass Gottessymbole und soziale Strukturen tatsächlich voneinander abhängig sind. Man gesteht offen zu, dass die religiöse Sprache ihre Terminologie weitgehend von gewöhnlichen menschlichen und sozialen Zusammenhängen ableitet. Wie diese Begriffe als Aussagen über Gott gebraucht werden können, erklärt man mit einer Symboltheorie, wie sie im christlichen Bereich schon in der Urkirche und im Mittelalter entwickelt wurden (z. B. Augustinus und Thomas von Aquino)[7].

Im Christentum ist in diesem Zusammenhang der Gedanke der Ebenbildlichkeit von entscheidender Bedeutung. Wenn der Mensch zum Ebenbild Gottes erschaffen ist (1. Mos. 1,27), erscheint es natürlich, dass die Aussagen über diesen Gott teils aus Erfahrungen des Menschen und der menschlichen Gemeinschaft stammen und teils moralische Implikationen enthalten, wie die Menschen leben sollen und die menschliche Gemeinschaft aussehen soll. Wenn die sozialen Verhältnisse sich verändern und die moralischen Erfahrungen und Einsichten der Menschen sich entsprechend wandeln, während die in einer heiligen Schrift niedergelegten Gottessymbole als unveränderlich betrachtet werden, entsteht ein Konflikt. Im Folgenden werde ich diesen Konflikt im christlichen Bereich untersuchen, da die christliche Religion mein Forschungsgebiet ist. Ähnliche Konflikte lassen sich aber sicher auch in anderen Religionen nachweisen.

Um auf den anfangs berührten Gegensatz zwischen Durkheim und Weber zurückzukommen, möchte ich betonen, dass man sich vor zwei Extremen hüten muss. Es lässt sich nicht leugnen, dass die Religion, also auch das Christentum, oftmals die herrschende soziale und politische Ordnung religiös legitimiert hat. Dagegen hat sie in anderen Zusammenhängen auch den Anstoss zur Kritik an dieser Ordnung und zu Bemühungen um soziale Reformen und zuweilen sogar zur Revolution gegeben. Im letzteren Falle ist es aber sicher nicht so zugegangen, dass christliche Menschen unabhängig von sozialen und politischen Zusammenhängen bestimmte religiöse

---

[7] Für Augustinus siehe Holte 329 ff. Für Thomas siehe Lyttkens 244 ff.

Ideen konzipiert haben, die sie dann sekundär auf die soziale und politische Wirklichkeit angewendet haben. In beiden genannten Funktionen spiegelt das Christentum soziale Erfahrungen, aber Erfahrungen verschiedener Art.

Als das Christentum in die Welgeschichte eintrat, fehlten ihm alle Verbindungen mit den religiösen und politischen Instanzen, in dem besetzten Israel so gut wie im römischen Staat. Seine Anhängerschaft bestand fast ausschliesslich aus Menschen ohne religiöse, wirtschaftliche oder politische Macht. Das Christentum als eine Religion der Armen wird in manchen Abschnitten des Neuen Testaments besonders betont, vor allem in der Evangelientradition des Lukas und im Jakobusbrief. Diese Lage änderte sich radikal, als das Christentum unter Konstantin zu einer anerkannten Religion im römischen Reich wurde, um dann zur Staatsreligion erhöht zu werden. In der früheren Situation trug das Christentum dazu bei, bei den Menschen, die sozial unterlegen waren, das Selbstgefühl und das Bewusstsein ihrer Menschenwürde zu stärken. Im späteren Falle erhielt es solche Formen, dass es das Vakuum, das die zerfallende römische Staatsreligion hinterliess, auszufüllen vermochte. In beiden Fällen handelt es sich um soziale Erfahrungen und Bedürfnisse: einerseits das Bedürfnis der Ausgestossenen und Verachteten, elementaren Respekt und Anerkennung zu erlangen, und die Erfahrung, dass der Glaube an einen Gott, der diejenigen liebt und auserwählt, die im Auge der Welt nichts sind, das ermöglicht (1. Kor. 1,26–28). Andererseits das Bedürfnis der politischen Macht, ihre Stellung göttlich zu legitimieren, und die Erfahrung, dass dies mit Hilfe des Christentums geschehen kann, sofern man andere Züge des Neuen Testaments hervorhebt. Der römische Staatsbürger Paulus hatte ja gelehrt, dass die Obrigkeit von Gott eingesetzt sei (Röm. 13), und er hatte auch sonst einer Über- und Unterordnung das Wort geredet (zwischen Herren und Dienern, zwischen Mann und Frau u. s. w.: 1. Kor. 11, Eph. 5–6).

Man kann daher sagen, dass das Christentum durch seine gesamte Geschichte hindurch sozial betrachtet zwei verschiedene Gesichter aufweist, und dass es sich in beiden Gestalten an Hand der Bibel legitimiert hat. Im Mittelpunkt der Botschaft des Neuen Testaments steht die Verkündigung der Einheit der ganzen Menschheit, der Gleichwertigkeit aller Menschen als Geschöpfe Gottes, die von der Schöpfungsabsicht Gottes abgefallen und durch Christus erlöst sind. In diesem Sinne kann Paulus sagen: „Hier ist nicht Jude noch Grieche, hier ist nicht Knecht noch Freier, hier ist nicht Mann noch Weib; denn ihr seid allzumal *einer* in Christus Jesus" (Gal. 3,28). Daneben gibt es aber im Neuen Testament (nicht zuletzt bei Paulus) Stellen, welche die Fortdauer der patriarchalischen Ordnungen vorauszusetzen scheinen (siehe oben).

Wie lässt sich das vereinbaren? Schon die Theologen der alten Kirche erkannten klar die Spannung zwischen der zentral religiös motivierten Verkündigung der Gleichheit im Evangelium und der dort vorausgesetzten patriarchalischen Struktur der Gesellschaft. In der Regel deutete man diese Spannung so, dass eine Gesellschaft, in der die Menschen gleichberechtigt nebeneinander leben, der eigentlichen Schöpfungsabsicht Gottes entspreche – und damit einer idealen Ethik. Mit einer vom Stoizismus entliehenen Terminologie sprach man von einem absoluten Naturrecht. Die Struktur der Über- und Unterordnung mit einer gewissen daraus folgenden Zwangsmacht ergab sich dagegen zwangsläufig aus dem Abfall der Menschen von Gottes Schöpfungsplan, der dazu führte, dass sie egoistisch nach Macht und eigenem Vorteil auf Kosten anderer strebten. Nach stoischer Terminologie sprach man hier von einem relativen Naturrecht[8].

Der Ethik, die den sozialen Ordnungen zugrunde liegt, erkennt man also nur relative Gültigkeit zu. Die ideale Ethik dagegen zeigt, wie die Menschen eigentlich zusammenleben sollten, und Jesus hat sie den Menschen in seiner ethischen Belehrung (z.B. in der Bergpredigt und in seiner Verkündigung des Reiches Gottes) erneut vorgestellt. Diese ist in religiöser Hinsicht – vor Gott – absolut gültig.

Müsste sich dann nicht die ideale Ethik wenigstens nach und nach durchsetzen und auch die sozialen Verhältnisse prägen? Die Beantwortung dieser Frage zeigt das Christentum, wie es sich im Verlauf der Geschichte entfaltet, von zwei ganz verschiedenen Seiten. Die Antworten weisen nämlich in zwei verschiedenen Richtungen.

Eine Richtung der Tradition, für die sich die anerkannten Kirchen häufig entschieden haben, betrachtet die ideale Ethik als ausschliesslich auf das geistliche Gebiet beschränkt. Die sozialen Strukturen, von denen in der Bibel die Rede ist, sind unauflöslich mit den Lebensbedingungen dieser Erde verbunden und müssen bis zum jüngsten Tag bestehen[9]. Damit weicht man also hier von der in der frühchristlichen Kirche insgemein vertretenen Auffassung ab, dass die gesellschaftliche Ordnung ethisch nur relativ gültig ist und der eigentlichen Absicht Gottes mit der Schöpfung nicht entspricht. Die gesellschaftliche Rangordnung hat man innerhalb dieser Tradition bisweilen sogar als eine unveränderliche Ordnung der Schöpfung bezeichnet[10].

Die entgegengesetzte Traditionsrichtung sieht im Evangelium eine Botschaft der Befreiung der Bedrückten, der Überwindung der destruktiven Kräfte, die das Menschenleben verheeren, sie meint daher, dies müsse auch Folgen für die sozialen Bedingungen der Menschen haben. Man muss

---

[8] Für die historische Entfaltung des Verhältnisses Christentum – soziale Struktur muss man immer noch den Einsatz von Troeltsch hervorheben. Er hat auch die Bedeutung der Unterscheidung zwischen absolutem und relativem Naturrecht bei den Kirchenvätern betont. Cf. 144ff. Für Augustinus siehe z.B. De civitate Dei XIX,14ff. (CC 48). Die Unterordnung der Frauen führt er jedoch, von dieser Grundauffassung abweichend, auf Gottes Schöpferwille zurück: De Genesi ad litt. XI,35 (CSEL 28).

[9] Diese Auffassung hat u.a. Luther vertreten. Cf. Luther 11,251ff. Cf. Duchrow 486ff.

[10] So z.B. Brunner 313ff. Von dieser Auffassung nehmen so gut wie alle moderne theologische Ethiker Abstand.

die altchristliche Einsicht, dass die soziale Rangordnung ethisch nur bedingt gültig ist, ernst nehmen, sie muss im Licht der idealen Ethik kritisiert und nach Möglichkeit in bessere Übereinstimmung mit dieser gebracht werden.

Träger dieser Auffassung waren oft religiöse Minoritäten, welche die anerkannten Kirchen kritisierten, man denke etwa an die radikalen Strömungen der Reformationszeit oder an Gruppen der Auswanderer nach Nordamerika im 18. und 19. Jh. Aber auch in der institutionalisierten Kirche wirkt sich diese Kraft aus, – wenn auch in langsamerem Takt. So gab z.B. die christliche Kirche den Anstoss zur Abschaffung der Sklaverei. Hier war Schweden übrigens seiner Zeit voraus: zu Anfang des 14. Jhs. wurde die Sklaverei sukzessiv in allen Provinzen abgeschafft, – mit einer in unserem Zusammenhang bedeutsamen Begründung: Da Christus alle Menschen durch die Taufe freigekauft habe, dürfe niemand als Knecht verkauft werden[11].

Die Lebenskraft einer Religion dürfte in hohem Masse davon abhängen, ob sie den Menschen zu einer existenziellen Deutung ihrer Lebenslage verhelfen kann. Die Gotteserfahrung muss mit einer Ich-Erfahrung verbunden sein, die das Selbstbewusstsein und das Erlebnis der eigenen Menschenwürde unterstützt. Das kann aber unmöglich jenseits der gesellschaftlichen Zusammenhänge geschehen. Die Gotteserfahrung muss dem Menschen auch dazu verhelfen, seine soziale Rolle zu finden und sie muss ihm die Identifikation mit anderen Menschen im sozialen Rahmen ermöglichen. Wenn die Religion und ihre Symbole mit einer gesellschaftlichen Struktur verbunden sind, die sich nicht mehr als Rahmen der eigenen sozialen Situation deuten lässt, so kann die Religion vielleicht noch eine Zeitlang kraft ihrer äusseren Glaubensautorität weiterleben, aber auf längere Sicht ist sie zum Absterben verurteilt. Dies dürfte einer der wichtigsten Gründe sein, weshalb der Weg des Religionshistorikers – um wiederum Biezais' Einleitungsvortrag zu zitieren – weitgehend ,,ein Spaziergang auf dem Friedhof der toten religiösen Symbole ist"[12]. ,,Symbole, die einstmals Ausdruck tiefer religiöser Erlebnisse waren, haben im Lauf der Zeit ihren Sinn verloren und sind deshalb unverständlich geworden." Wir können hinzufügen: auch Symbole, in die wir uns mit unserer Phantasie hineindenken können, haben dennoch vielfach ihre existenzielle Funktion für uns verloren.

Durch den im 18. Jh. einsetzenden Prozess der Demokratisierung, der die Gesellschaftsstruktur in der ganzen traditionell christlichen Welt immer durchgreifender gewandelt hat, ist für das Christentum in dieser Hinsicht eine radikale Veränderung eingetreten. Dabei ist es übrigens charakteri-

---

[11] Dass in anderen Ländern die Kirchen auch viel später die Sklaverei bisweilen unterstützt haben, stimmt damit gut überein, was obt über den zwei verschiedenen Gesichtern des Christentums gesagt wurde.

[12] Oben S. XXVI.

stisch, dass das Christentum in so gut wie allen Phasen dieses Demokratisierungsprozesses sein doppeltes Gesicht gezeigt hat. Christen die von der Verkündigung der Gleichheit vor Gott im Neuen Testament ausgingen, haben die Meinung vertreten, dass diese auch im Staatswesen Folgen haben müsse, und deshalb den Prozess der Demokratisierung unterstützt. Andere Christen, die sich auf die patriarchalischen Züge des Neuen Testaments stützten, haben die Gleichheit auf das religiöse Gebiet begrenzen wollen und folglich der Demokratisierung entgegengearbeitet.

Auf Grund des Demokratisierungsprozesses hat sich unser Problem folgendermassen verändert: Vor dem Beginn desselben war die Religion oft die einzige Möglichkeit für die Menschen, einen politischen Protest zu äussern, den man aber nicht direkt und klar aussprach, sondern der indirekt darin zum Ausdruck kam, dass man sich die religiöse Umwertung weltlicher Machtverhältnisse zu eigen machte und aus dem Glauben, von Gott geliebt zu sein, ein erhöhtes Selbstgefühl gewann. Dies Bewusstsein in einen direkten sozialen Prozess umzusetzen, hätte vielfach bedeutet, sich der repressiven Gewalt des patriarchalischen Staates unmittelbar auszusetzen. Unter diesen Umständen konnte sich der Protest nicht in Form einer ausdrücklichen Forderung von sozialen Reformen äussern, sondern er hat den Menschen vor allem die Kraft gegeben, dem Druck der sozialen und politischen Verhältnisse standzuhalten. Seit dem Beginn des Demokratisierungsprozesses ist diese Maskierung des sozialen Protestes bei weitem nicht mehr im gleichen Masse erforderlich, – jetzt fordert man soziale und politische Reformen direkt.

Dieser Übergang vom indirekten zum direkten sozialen Protest zeigt sich sehr deutlich bei der Auswanderung nach Nordamerika im 18. und 19. Jh. Unter den Auswanderern gab es viele, deren Religiosität mit der Ablehnung der autoritären politischen Systeme in ihren Heimatländern verbunden war. Dort hatten sie im allgemeinen nicht die Möglichkeit gehabt, ihren Protest offen auszusprechen, was sie in der neuen Heimat aber taten. Hier wollte man einen Staat gründen, in dem der vollkommene Menschenwert aller gemäss der Gleichheitsverkündigung des Evangeliums verwirklicht werden sollte. Die neu zu begründende Demokratie sollte, wie man es zuweilen etwas naiv ausdrückte, das Land zum „Kingdom of God in America" machen[13].

Ein bezeichnendes Beispiel aus unserem Jahrhundert liefert der Freiheitskampf der Neger in den U.S.A. Paradoxalerweise gab es ja in dem Staat, der sich prinzipiell auf den vollkommenen Menschenwert und die Gleichberechtigung aller gründete, eine umfangreiche Gesetzgebung zur Segregation. Widersetzte man sich dieser Gesetzgebung – sei es in Reden oder durch Handlungen – so löste dies die repressive Gewalt des Staates

---

[13] Cf. das Buch von Niebuhr, besonders 33 ff. Für das Verhältnis Christentum – soziale Struktur seit dem 19. Jh., siehe Latourette, besonders 1, 207 ff.; 3, 200 ff.; 5, 515 ff.

aus, weshalb es lange dauerte, ehe die Schwarzen es wagen konnten, offen ihr volles demokratisches Recht zu fordern. Der soziale Protest war zunächst maskiert, lässt sich aber in der religiösen Formulierung leicht erkennen. Die negro spirituals der Schwarzen handeln fast durchweg von einem Thema: von der Knechtschaft des alttestamentarischen Gottesvolkes in Ägypten und von seiner Befreiung. Man denkt dabei natürlich an das eigene Volk und seine Lebensbedingungen in einem von Weissen beherrschten Land, und das Volk weiss sehr wohl, dass es überhaupt nur durch den Sklavenhandel nach Amerika gekommen ist. Erst in einer späteren Phase der Befreiungstheologie sprechen die Schwarzen ausdrücklich vom eigenen Volk und dessen Forderung an den amerikanischen Staat und sie bringen das weitgehend von der Religion getragene Selbstbewusstsein durch Devisen wie ,,Black is beautiful" zum Ausdruck[14].

Inwiefern betrifft nun die Veränderung der sozialen Struktur die Gottessymbole selbst? Wie schon gesagt, kómmen in den biblischen Texten weitgehend Gottessymbole aus der sozialen und politischen Sphäre vor, die wegen ihres Ursprungs in den sozialen und politischen Strukturen ihrer Entstehungszeit patriarchalische Assoziationen erwecken. Die Symbole stammen z.B. aus der Späre des politischen Alleinherrschers und seiner Stellung gegenüber den Untertanen: Gott ist der Herr (kýrios), der König (basileús), der Allherrscher (pantokrátor). Hierzu sei bemerkt, dass die Bezeichnung Gottes als Allherrscher, als allmächtig, nicht philosophisch zu deuten ist (Gott als erste Ursache aller Dinge u. dgl.), wie man es später oft getan hat, der Ausdruck stammt vielmehr von dem Traum des irdischen Herrschers, sein Reich über die ganze bewohnte Erde ausdehnen zu können. Bei dem Namen ,,Herr" stellen sich ausserdem Assoziationen zu engeren sozialen Strukturen ein, bei denen der Hausvater oder der Vormann im Verhältnis zu den ihm untergebenen Dienern oder Sklaven (doúloi) gemeint ist. Gott wird schliesslich als Vater bezeichnet, mit Assoziationen zur Struktur der Familie und dem Verhältnis Eltern – Kinder, aber auch weitere soziale Strukturen klingen an: den Titel ,,Vater" hat man vielfach auch auf politische Herrscher auf verschiedenem Niveau übertragen. In den Jesus-Worten der Evangelien dominiert das Epithet Vater (patér) als Bezeichung Gottes, im Verhältnis zu ihm ist Jesus der Sohn im wahrsten Sinne, wenn auch alle, die zum Volke Gottes gehören, seine Kinder oder Söhne (hyioí) sind. Jesus Christus wird nie der Name Vater beigelegt, sonst kann aber Christus in der christlichen Überlieferung bezeichnenderweise so gut wie alle Epitheta Gottes erhalten. Ansätze dazu liegen schon im Neuen Testament vor. Christus ist ausserdem der Bräutigam im Verhältnis zu seinen Anhängern, welche die Braut sind. Im Alten Testament

---

[14] Cf. z.B Cone 25ff. Martin Luther King war wohl der erste, der den sozialen Protest der Schwarzen offen aussprach. Die moderne ,,Black theology" tut das aber in einer bedeutend aggressiveren Weise.

war dies Symbol Jahwe im Verhältnis zu seinem Volke Israel vorbehalten. Man muss beachten, dass auch dies Symbol einen patriarchalischen Anklang hat, da in ihm die Unterordnung der Ehefrau gegenüber ihrem Mann vorausgesetzt wird.

Nun mag es zunächst erscheinen, dass der Gebrauch von Gottessymbolen dieser Art in doppeltem Sinne wirken muss: *teils* formt er die Haltung des Gläubigen Gott/Christus gegenüber nach dem Modell des Verhältnisses von Untergebenen/Unterdrückten zu Vätern und Obrigkeitspersonen verschiedener Art, *teils* gibt sie der Stellung dieser Väter und Obrigkeitspersonen eine religiöse Legitimation. Dann übersieht man aber einen Kernpunkt in der Verkündigung Jesu, wie er in den Evangelien und den auf sie gegründeten Episteln hervortritt: nämlich die totale Umwertung und Umkehrung der im gewöhnlichen Leben gültigen Rangordnung. Die Ordnung im Reiche Gottes wird hier als der diametrale Gegensatz der in sozialen und politischen Zusammenhängen gültigen dargestellt. Was die Welt gering schätzt und verachtet, hat Gott erwählt (Luk. 1,51–53; 1. Kor. 1,26–28). Nicht der ist der Grösste, der als Herr über die anderen auftritt, sondern der sich zum Diener und Sklaven anderer macht (Luk. 9,46–48; 22,24–26). In diesen Kategorien deutet Jesus auch sein eigenes Werk, und wer ihm folgen will, muss sich diesen Bedingungen beugen (Luk. 22,27; Joh. 13,1–15; Phil. 2,1–11). Gerade diese Hauptlinie der Evangelien ist es ja, die einem bald maskierten, bald offenen sozialen Protest als Inspirationsquelle hat dienen können. Psychologisch gesehen dienen hier die Machtsymbole denjenigen Gruppen als Schutz und Legitimation, denen im sozialen Leben dieser Schutz und diese Legitimation am meisten abging.

Auch für die Gottessymbole ergibt sich aus dem Prozess der Demokratisierung eine durchgreifende Veränderung. Der entscheidende Punkt, der darin lag, dass die Gottessymbole weitgehend aus der politisch und sozial gültigen Struktur stammten, aber zugleich so gebraucht wurden, dass sie diese von innen her auflösten, wird jetzt nicht mehr wie früher evident. Zugleich gerät auch jene Tradition der Auslegung, welche die Umwertung der Machtstruktur auf streng religiöse Zusammenhänge begrenzen wollte, in eine eigentümliche Lage. Zuweilen wirkt sich das so aus, dass man im Namen der Bibeltreue zu Positionen zurückzukehren strebt, die in sozialen und politischen Zusammenhängen bereits verlassen sind. So kann es passieren, dass man mit einer eigentümlichen Verdrehung des Gegensatzes, wie es in dieser Welt zugeht und wie im Reiche Christi, zwar die Demokratisierung auf weltlichem Gebiet akzeptiert, ihr aber in christlichen Zusammenhängen entgegenarbeitet, z. B. sollen Frauen zu weltlichen Berufen durchaus kompetent sein, nicht aber zum Amt des Pfarrers!

Wie schon gesagt: wenn die Religion und ihre Symbole an eine soziale Struktur gebunden sind, die man nicht mehr als Rahmen der eigenen sozialen Situation zu deuten vermag, sind die Voraussetzungen für einen persönlich fundierten Glauben nicht gegeben. Die Symbole sterben ab und verlieren ihren Wert. Einer der Gründe der zunehmenden Säkularisierung in traditionell christlichen Ländern mag darin liegen, dass das Christentum von dem Einzelnen nicht als persönlich relevant erlebt wird, weil seine Symbolsprache mit veralteten Strukturen verknüpft zu sein scheint.

Zugleich arbeiten im Christentum wie in anderen lebenden Religionen Individuen und Gruppen an einer Neudeutung, die neue Wege zu einem für die Persönlichkeit wesentlichen christlichen Glauben zeigt. Diese Neudeutung hat zuweilen zu herausfordernden Formulierungen geführt, wenn man z. B. in einer amerikanischen Religionsdebatte von Gott behauptet hat ,,she is black". Da gibt es natürlich – wie immer – an die Tradition gebundenen Individuen und Gruppen, die solche Tendenzen sofort als Irrlehren anprangern. Dabei übersieht man leicht, dass bei dieser Kombination von ,,black theology" und ,,feminist theology" etwas geschieht, was in anderen Formen schon oft in der christlichen Tradition vorgekommen ist. Dass man die Gottessymbole, sowie die Symbolwelt der Bibel im Ganzen mit den Erfahrungen des eigenen Volkes, der Gesellschaftsklasse, des eigenen Geschlechts und der eigenen Person verschmelzen kann, hat sich im Verlauf der Geschichte als die Voraussetzung für die Existenz eines lebendigen, persönlich fundierten christlichen Glaubens erwiesen. Man denke nur an die Volkskunst in Dalekarlien und in anderen schwedischen Provinzen, wo Gott und die biblischen Gestalten im Milieu des schwedischen Landvolkes auftreten, oder an das Altarbild des Domes von Linköping, auf dem Jesus als blonder nordischer Jüngling dargestellt ist. Ein anderes Beispiel sind die sechs modernen Pietà-Skulpturen in der neu erbauten Kirche von Nowa Huta bei Krakau in Polen, wo die Mutter Gottes, die ihren toten Sohn beweint, durch Namen wie Auschwitz, Maidanek und Katyn mit sechs tragischen Ereignissen aus der Geschichte des politisch unterdrückten und leidenden polnischen Volkes verknüpft sind.

Man braucht die Vertreter der black, bzw. feminist theology ja nicht so zu deuten, dass sie den bipolaren Charakter der Gottessymbole aufheben wollen. Es geht wohl nicht darum zu behaupten, dass Gott tatsächlich schwarz und weiblichen Geschlechts ist, sondern darum, der Tendenz entgegenzuwirken, dass man sich Gott als einen Mann von weisser Hautfarbe vorstellt[15]. Denken wir doch nur an die Bilder Michelangelos in der sixtinischen Kapelle. Wenn auch diese extrem antropomorphe Darstellung Gott Vaters zu den Ausnahmen in der christlichen Tradition gehören mag, so kommt sie doch den Vorstellungen im christlichen Abendland recht nahe. Wieviele Kinder – und Erwachsene – haben sich Gott nicht als den bärtigen alten Mann, natürlich von weisser Hautfarbe vorgestellt! Zugleich ist man sich aber bei einer verantwortungsbewussten Auslegung der christlichen Religion stets darüber einig gewesen, dass ein Unterschied zwischen

---

[15] Für die ,,Feminist theology" siehe besonders Mary Dalys Programmschrift, 13 ff.

dem Symbol und dem Symbolisierten besteht. Ihre Lehre war im Grunde immer, dass Gott in Wahrheit weder Mann noch Frau, weder schwarz-, rot- noch weisshäutig ist, vielmehr ist er ein Gott für alle, erhaben über alle menschlichen und sozialen Unterschiede, und doch zugleich allgegenwärtig und daher beiderseits aller menschlichen Schranken erlebbar.

Bewegungen wie „black theology" und „feminist theology" mögen uns ferner daran erinnern, dass es auch in demokratischen Ländern Individuen und Gruppen gibt, die sich unterdrückt fühlen und denen die Möglichkeit fehlt, ihre Menschenrechte voll auszuüben. Wenn diese ihre Erfahrungen mit einer Neudeutung des christlichen Glaubens verschmelzen, so erkennt man das Muster aus früheren Phasen der Konfrontation der christlichen Tradition mit neuerwachten demokratischen Bestrebungen leicht wieder. Einerseits wird die Notwendigkeit betont, mit den in der Bibel vorausgesetzten sozialen Strukturen zu brechen, und die Gefahr erkannt, dass die politisch-patriarchalischen Gottessymbole der Bibel einer patriarchalischen Gesellschaftsordnung als Stütze dienen können. Zugleich erhält man die Inspiration zu dieser Neudeutung aus der Art, wie die Bibel selbst trotz der Anwendung dieser Symbole, die von diesen gemeinte Rangordnung umbewertet und in ihr Gegenteil verkehrt.

Eigentlich ist es erstaunlich, dass die Probleme, die mit dem Überwiegen der männlichen Symbolik in der traditionell-christlichen Weise, von Gott zu sprechen, verbunden sind, erst so spät in der geschichtlichen Entwicklung zu Worte kommen. Dasselbe gilt von der Tatsache, dass christliche Theologie und Predigt durch die Jahrhunderte fast immer Sache der Männer war. Während der ganzen Zeit hat aber die Gotteserfahrung der Frauen eine entscheidende Rolle für die Weitergabe des Glaubens an neue Generationen gespielt, man denke nur an die christliche Erziehung der Kinder! Es würde sich lohnen, die sicher recht zahlreichen schriftlichen Zeugnisse vom Gotteserlebnis christlicher Frauen zu sammeln und zu untersuchen, ob es zu dem heute offen ausgesprochenen Protest der feminist theology einen entsprechenden, weniger offenen Protest in früheren Generationen christlicher Frauen gegeben hat.

Zum Schluss muss ich betonen, dass natürlich nicht alle Gottessymbole der christlichen Tradition, die von der Bibel ausgeht, mit der sozialen Struktur verknüpft sind, und dass selbst unter diesen nicht alle patriarchalische Verhältnisse der Über- und Unterordnung betonen. Symbole wie Licht, Lebensspender, Liebe u. s. w. knüpfen an allgemein-menschliche Erfahrungen an, die durch alle sozialen Veränderungen hindurch bestehen. Die Auffassung Jesu als Bruder und Mitmensch knüpft an die Idee der menschlichen Gleichwertigkeit an. Auch hat das Vorwiegen der männlichen Symbolik in der Gottesauffassung das Vorkommen von Muttersymbolen nicht verhindert u. s. w. Die christliche Überlieferung enthält in der Tat eine Mannigfaltigkeit von Gottessymbolen, die aus den verschiedensten Bereichen menschlicher Erfahrung stammen. Wie bei anderen lebenden

Religionen besteht das Problem darin, wie man in der Vielfalt der Symbole wählen soll, welche traditionellen Symbole hervorzuheben sind, welche man dämpfen oder fallen lassen sollte, und welchen Raum man der Neuschaffung von Symbolen gewähren soll. Mit diesen Fragen befasst sich vor allem die normative Theologie, die sich in allen lebendigen Religionen entwickelt. Die Religionswissenschaft beschränkt sich darauf zu untersuchen, wie dies geschieht, und festzustellen, dass die Arbeit an den Gottessymbolen eine Voraussetzung für das Weiterleben der Religion ist, um einen persönlich fundierten religiösen Glauben zu ermöglichen.

Literaturverzeichnis

Brunner, E., 1932, *Das Gebot und die Ordnungen.* Tübingen.
Cone, J., 1969, *Black theology and black power.* New York.
Daly, Mary, 1973, *Beyond God the Father.* Boston.
Demerath, N., Hammond, Ph., 1969, *Religion in social context.* New York.
Duchrow, U., 1970, *Christenheit und Weltverantwortung.* Stuttgart.
Durkheim, E., 1965, *The elementary forms of the religious life.* London.
Hick, J., 1963, *Philosophy of religion.* Englewood Cliffs.
Holte, R., 1962, *Béatitude et sagesse.* Paris.
Latourette, K., 1958f., *Christianity in a revolutionary age,* 1–5. New York.
Luther, M., 1938, Von weltlicher Oberkeit. *Werke* 11. Weimar.
Lyttkens, H., 1952, *The analogy between God and the World.* Diss. Uppsala.
Niebuhr, R., 1937, *The kingdom of God in America.* Chicago.
Sachs, H., Badstübner, Neumann, H., 1973, *Christliche Ikonographie in Stichworten.* Berlin.
Troeltsch, E., 1912, *Die Soziallehren der christlichen Kirchen und Gruppen.* Gesammelte Schriften 1. Tübingen.
Weber, M., 1964, *The sociology of religion.* London.

The Veto on Images and the aniconic God in Ancient Israel

By TRYGGVE METTINGER

The prohibition of images in the decalogue appears to belong to Israel's *differentia specifica.* Already Tacitus observed: "Profana illis omnia, quae apud nos sacra." Israel's God is the aniconic God. The ban on images may be seen as a concrete expression of Israel's understanding of the deity. Our study is thus concerned with a key element in Israel's religion. But the nature of the material at our disposal makes an almost painful contrast to the importance and scope of our subject: it is not particularly plentiful, and some of the more important texts present problems for interpretation.

Throughout her long history Israel was quite familiar with the phenomenon of cultic images, a familiarity which she acquired by contact with other cultures. A pair of O.T. texts portray the actual manufacturing of images (Jer 10,1–9; Isa 44,9–20). Another text (Judg 17,4–5) has been interpreted as indicating what made up a complete image[1]: the word *pæsæl* is taken to refer to the carved wooden image, whereas *măssekā* would represent the chased covering of precious metal (cf. Isa 30,22; 40,19[2], Jer 10,9). The term *ʾepôd* is thought to refer to a cuirass-like case, and *t*^{e}*rapîm* to a cultic mask (cf. Zech 10,2).

Biblical Hebrew has an extensive terminology for idols. Certain terms, like *t*^{e}*mûnā* and *sæmæl,* are scarcely transparent; others are what linguists call semantically motivated. To illustrate from our modern languages: the German "Handschuh", but not the English "glove", is semantically motivated, it is self-explanatory[3]. Several of the Hebrew terms for "idol" belong to this category. The word *pæsæl* normally denotes a hewn image, and is readily associated with the verb *pasăl* which is used, e.g., to describe how Moses cut the two stone tablets (Ex 34,1.4; Deut 10,1.3). Only in a few marginal cases is the word *pæsæl* used of a molten image (Isa 40,19; 44,10; Jer 10,14). The standard term for a "molten image" is *măssekā,* a word cognate with the verb *nasăk,* "pour out", which is also used for casting metal (Isa 40,19; 44,10). Similarly, the noun *ʿaṣab* is related to a verb which bears the sense "form" in Job 10,8.

These terms for "images", *pæsæl, măssekā* and *ʿaṣab,* all lead to associa-

---

[1] Alt apud Rad 1962, 229, n. 60.

[2] On Isa 40,18–20 cf. Mettinger 77 ff.

[3] On semantic motivation cf. Ullmann 83 ff. On the group of words under discussion cf. Barr 17 ff.

tions with the actual manufacturing process. *ʿaṣab* has also been associated with the verb *ʿaṣăb* II, "hurt", "grieve", having a strongly pejorative ring. This brings us to the group of markedly pejorative denotations for images. To this category belongs *hæbæl/hᵃbalîm,* "vapour", "vanity", "idols". The word *ʾᵉlîlîm* is similar in meaning, indicating that the foreign idols are "things of nought". A nuance of strong physical repulsion lies in the word *šiqqûṣ,* which perhaps represents a shaphel-formation of *qûṣ,* "loathe". The same vowel pattern is found in *gillûlîm,* a word which possibly can be related to **gel,* "ball of dung". The word *miplæṣæt* may also be mentioned; though its concrete reference in the two texts in which it occurs (1 Kgs 15,13; 2 Chron 15,16) remains obscure, it conjures up associations with *palăṣ,* "shudder", and *păllaṣût,* "shuddering".

A large part of the terminology used to denote images is thus strongly negative in tone. The very choice of words seems to show a hostile attitude towards images on the part of the traditionists, with the result that our sources are governed by an anti-image tendentiousness. As always, our task must be to bring to the study of the sources an historical sensitivity and source-critical awareness. It is important to remember that an essential portion of the traditions of Israel's history have been transmitted to us by men for whom the first two commands of the decalogue—the prohibition of other gods and of images—made up the criteria for a theological criticism of Israel's past. I am here thinking of the material in the Deuteronomistic Historical Work (Deut—2 Kgs). The source-critical problem can be formulated as follows: Is this hostile attitude towards images characteristic of the transmitted material itself? Has the ban on images been inherited from the time of Moses, or is it the result of a later development?

One example will suffice to illustrate the nature of the problem. In Judg 8,22–28 we read how Gideon had an ephod made of precious metal and set up in his city of Ophrah.

> And Gideon made an ephod of it and put it in his city, in Ophrah; and all Israel played the harlot [*zanā*] after it there, and it became a snare to Gideon and to his family.

The use of *zanā,* "commit fornication", "play the harlot", to denote faithlessness towards JHWH probably originated with Hosea (cf. Hos 1,2; 4,12–15; 9,1). It is later found in Jeremiah (2,20; 3,1.6.8) and in Deuteronomistic literature (e.g. Ex 34,15; Deut 31,16; Judg 2,17). Viewed in this larger perspective, the latter part of the verse above quoted clearly represents a Deuteronomistic criticism of an undertaking the theological questionableness of which Gideon was apparently quite unaware.

An Historical Outline

We turn now to a study of the Israelite attitude towards images in its historical perspective in order to identify, if possible, the point at which the reaction against images began. In the accounts of the period in the wilderness, a couple of incidents are of interest for our subject[4]. Num 21,4–9 tells how Moses set up a bronze serpent on a pole. It is possible that this narrative is an etiology for a Canaanite cultic object which ended up in the temple in Jerusalem, but which here is legitimized by being associated with Moses[5]. In any case, what is important for us is the fact that the Moses who in the decalogue forbids Israel to make any image of "anything that is in heaven above, or that is in the earth beneath, or that is in the water under the earth" (Ex 20,4) in Num 21 makes a bronze serpent and sets it up on a pole. The account in Numbers is free of any critical nuance. But the reaction came. In 2 Kgs 18,4 we are informed that king Hezekiah smashed the bronze serpent to pieces, "for until those days the people of Israel had burned incense to it".

The second narrative in the Pentateuch is the account in Ex 32 of how the Israelites under Aaron's leadership made a bull image of gold[6]. A number of points of contact with 1 Kgs 12,25–32[7] have led most scholars to view the chapter in its present complex form as representing a negative stance adopted towards the bull cult of king Jeroboam. Certain scholars find in this polemical situation the explanation for all parts of the narrative, and thus see the whole chapter as pure fiction. It would, however, be strange if circles hostile to Jeroboam in their polemic against him created a narrative which in point of fact accuses the entire nation of apostasy. In the end it is simpler to regard the narrative in Ex 32 as tied in one way or another to an actual event during the wilderness period.

The chapter is plagued by exegetical difficulties, and every analysis must be tentative in nature. Beyerlin has pointed out that the introductory section (v. 1–6) scarcely contains polemic against the image, but is rather neutral or even positive in its description. It is tempting to regard, with Beyerlin, these verses as the core of the tradition in this narrative[8]. Perhaps this original tradition functioned as an etiology for Jeroboam's bull cult in the tenth century, though this by no means excludes the possibility that the people actually made a bull image in the wilderness[9]. Certain difficulties in the narrative can be resolved if one sees here an expression of an early assimilation between JHWH and El, who had the bull as his symbol (the bull image thus need not be associated with Baal). Evidence for such an early assimilation is found in Num 23,8.21–22 (cf. 24,8)[10].

If the core of the tradition in Ex 32 is made up of a neutral or even positive account of how the people made a bull image in the wilderness, the

---

[4] On Ex 17,8–16, a text that I shall not discuss here, cf. Eissfeldt 206f.

[5] Cf. Rowley 113ff. esp. 137.

[6] For the literature on Ex 32 cf. Childs 553.

[7] Cf. especially Aberbach 129ff.

[8] Beyerlin 144ff.

[9] Ib., 149, leaves open the question of what actually happened.

[10] On JHWH and El cf. especially Cross 1ff.; Vaux 456ff.

later tradition branded their action a covenant violation (Ex 32, 15–20)[11]. When Moses comes down from the mountain, he smashes to pieces (*šibber*) the two tablets of the testimony, thus symbolically indicating that the people have broken the covenant with their bull image (cf. Akkad. *ṭuppa ḫepû* as a symbolic action denoting the dissolving of a contract/treaty[12]). Moses proceeds to destroy the bull image: he burns it, grinds it to powder and scatters it on the water, which he makes the people drink (v. 20). This procedure has been interpreted in widely different ways[13]. It is difficult to escape the conclusion that the account contains among other things an allusion to the ordeal which a woman suspected of adultery had to go through (Num 5,11–31). If so, the later tradition in Ex 32 is in line with Hosea's use of the verb *zanā*, "commit fornication", "play the harlot"[14].

From the Pentateuch's traditions about the bronze serpent and Aaron's bull we turn to the material in the book of Judges. When Gideon made his ephod (Judg 8,27), he was certainly unaware that this would one day be regarded as a questionable undertaking. The denunciation contained in the narrative is to be attributed to the Deuteronomists' iconoclastic ideal. A detailed depiction of the making of an image and its later fate can be read in Judg 17–18. The Ephraimite Micah used silver which his mother had dedicated to JHWH in order to make a *pæsæl ûmăssekā*. This image was then placed in a shrine which he also equipped with an *'epôd* and *t^erapîm* (17,1–5). A Levite from Judah was appointed priest (17,7–13). Both the priest and the cultic equipment were, however, taken as plunder by the Danites, and thus ended up in the town of Dan. We need not here go into the question how this narrative is related to the tradition about Jeroboam's cult at the same place[15]. What is of importance for our subject is the fact that an Israelite tribe during the period when the land was settled had in its sanctuary a cultic object which in all likelihood was an image of JHWH. Over Micah, who made the image, his mother pronounced the following words: "Blessed be my son by the LORD" (17,2); and the image was made of silver which had been dedicated "to the LORD" (17,3).

We pass on now to the period of the kingdoms and thus to the question of the attitude of the Israelite state religion towards images. According to 1 Kgs 12,25–32, the first ruler of the Northern Kingdom, Jeroboam I, had two bull images made and set up in Bethel and Dan. This account is clearly pro-Judaean in character and expresses a pointed criticism of Jeroboam's cultic installations. This critical tendentiousness presumably lies behind the plural form used in the presentation formula, "Behold your gods, O Israel,

---

[11] Cf. Beyerlin 149ff.

[12] For references see *Akkadisches*, 340f.

[13] Dussaud, 245, points to the burning of the sin offering. Loewenstamm, 483ff., draws attention to the treatment of Mot in Ugarit (Cf. Gordon 49 2, 30ff).

[14] Cf. above.

[15] Cf. Noth 133ff. On Judg 17–21 as part of the Deuteronomistic Historical Work cf. Veijola 15ff.

who brought you up out of the land of Egypt!" so that this plural, which is to be understood as numeric[16] (and not as an abstract plural) expresses a charge of polytheism[17]. According to the text, Jeroboam set up two images, one in Bethel and one in Dan. Recently, however, Motzki has provided an interesting argument for the theory that Jeroboam in fact made only a single image which was set up in Bethel; the reference in the text to a counterpart in Dan would then be a fiction intended to prepare the way for the pejorative plural of the presentation formula. Motzki bases his argument on texts which speak of a cultic image in the singular (e.g. Hos 10,5, emended text; 8,4–6; 2 Kgs 17,16) and on the fact that Hosea and Amos (with the exception of Am 8,14) are silent about Dan[18]. The plural used in the tradition about Jeroboam's cultic bulls has then penetrated the formula in the tradition about Aaron's bull (Ex 32,4.8 cf. v.1), where in fact it does not fit the account of Aaron's single bull image.

Thus we have at least in Bethel a cult associated with an image in the form of a bull or a bull calf. The cultic symbols in question is scarcely to be taken as evidencing a Baal-syncretistic worship of JHWH; rather it represents an older assimilation between JHWH and El[19]. In the Ugaritic texts we find several times *ṯr* or *ṯwr,* "bull", as an *epitheton ornans* for El. In the O.T. the assimilation JHWH—El is early attested in the Balaam oracles:

> How can I curse whom El has not cursed?
> How can I denounce whome JHWH has not denounced? (Num 23,8)

> JHWH, his God, is with him ...
> El brought him [see app.!] out of Egypt,
> he is like the wild ox's horns to him. (Num 23,21–22; cf. 24,8)

El, who is here compared with the wild ox (NB El as bull in Ugarit), is in this text associated with the exodus from Egypt, as is later Jeroboam's bull image in Bethel. That the place in which Jeroboam set up his image bears the name Beth-El, "El's house", is not without interest in this context. The clan of Jacob had of course close connections with Bethel (Gen 28,10–22; 31,13; 35,7). With this in mind, it is interesting to note that we meet the phrase *ʾᵃbîr jăʿᵃqob* as a name for the God worshipped by Jacob (Gen 49,24)—a name which certain scholars translate "Jacob's bull"[20]. Since Baal mythology otherwise plays no role in the patriarchal narratives, a possible Canaanite background should be sought in the El traditions.

These indications—they are no more than indications—lend support to two suppositions:

---

[16] Cf. Donner 47.
[17] Cf. Weippert 104.
[18] Cf. Motzki 470 ff.
[19] Cf. above no. 10.
[20] For a discussion cf. Kapelrud 43 ff. The cases where it appears as a divine designation and without a dagesh are: Gen 49,24; Ps 132,2.5; Isa 49,26 and 60,16; cf. Isa 1,24. Note also the personal name *ᶜgljw* in the Samaria Ostraca no. 41; cf. Reisner 236.

(a) The bull cult in Bethel had ancient roots from a time long before Jeroboam;
(b) The bull symbol set up by Jeroboam was primarily related not to JHWH-Baal, but to JHWH-El.

Further support for this line of thinking would be found in Hos 8,6 if, for the M.T.'s *kî mijjiśra'el,* we adopted the proposed emendation, *kî mî šôr 'el,* "for who is the bull El"; but it is not to be denied that the transmitted text appears to provide at least as good sense in the context[21].

What, then, was the relation between the bull image and the deity with which it was associated? Was the cultic object a direct symbol for the deity? Or how are we to conceive the matter? Hosea's polemical cry, "A god he is not!" (Hos 8,6) suggests that the image at his time was regarded as a symbol for the deity. The conception then current was apparently that the deity was represented in the bull image[22]. It is, however, not for that reason certain that Jeroboam I and his contemporaries more than one and a half centuries earlier understood the image in this way.

When Jeroboam's bull image is seen in a larger ideo-historical context, a new perspective becomes apparent. The purpose of Jeroboam's cultic program is said to be to put a stop to his people's pilgrimages to the central sanctuary of the Southern Kingdom. "You have gone up to Jerusalem long enough," the text has him say (1 Kgs 12,28). Undoubtedly the Judaean traditionists here give expression to the Deuteronomistic principle of recognizing only the JHWH-cult observed in Jerusalem. But this is not the whole truth[23]. With the historical situation at the time of Jeroboam's new regime in view, it is a highly plausible supposition that his cultic politics were formed in deliberate competition with Jerusalem, and that his intention was to provide a convincing alternative to the Solomonic temple in Jerusalem for the pious people of his realm[24].

The cultic legitimacy of Jerusalem was the result of David's transfer of the ark to that city (2 Sam 6). The ark was, of course, the most important cultic object from the pre-monarchic period[25]. Even before the period of the kingdoms, a theology of divine presence was connected with the ark. As often as the ark was taken up, Moses said, "Arise, O LORD," and when it was placed down he said, "Return, O LORD" (Num 10,35–36). The same idea is attested in 1 Sam 4,6–7: the Philistines, on learning that the ark had come into the Israelite camp, said, "A god has come into the camp." In both these texts, language is used which stresses the close connection between JHWH and the ark, while at the same time the conceptual distinction between the god and his cultic symbol is maintained.

In time, the ark found a place in a temple in Palestine, in Shiloh and

---

[21] Cf. Wolff 182.
[22] Cf. ib. 181.
[23] Contra Debus 35 ff.
[24] Cf. especially Zimmerli 1974, 248 ff.
[25] For a survey of the research on the ark cf. Schmitt 13 ff.

later in Jerusalem. Already in Shiloh we encounter the tradition of the ark's connection with the cherubim: the ark is here associated with the divine designation, "the LORD of hosts, who is enthroned on the cherubim" (1 Sam 4,4 cf. 2 Sam 6,2)[26]. In the Jerusalem temple the ark is similarly linked with the cherubim. When it is brought into Solomon's temple, it is placed "underneath the wings of the cherubim" (1 Kgs 8,6). These cherubim were part of a contrivance which is described in more detail in 1 Kgs 6,23–27, and which has been illuminated in an interesting way by the iconic art of the ancient Near East[27]. Solomon's cherubim were 10 cubits, or nearly 4.5 metres, high. The cherubim of the Priestly tradition's Tent of Meeting faced each other (Ex 25,20); by way of contrast, those of Solomon's temple stood parallel to each other. Each cherub touched with its outer wing one of the building's walls. The inner wing of each touched that of the other in the middle of the building. M. Haran is probably correct in thinking that this pair of inner wings constituted JHWH's throne[28]. This interpretation is supported by Ezek 10,1, which shows that the cherubim were part of a throne contrivance (cf. also Ezek 1,22–26). The ark, which was only 1½ cubits in height (cf. Ex 25,10), made up the footstool (Ps 99,5; 132,7; 1 Chron 28,2). JHWH was thought to sit unseen in royal majesty over the cherub throne and the ark. The divine epithet, "he who is enthroned on the cherubim," is to be understood from this background. It is against this background as well that we are to understand the statements that the ark's role as throne and footstool has been taken over by Zion and Jerusalem (Jer 3,16–17; Lam 2,1; cf. also Ezek 43,7).

If Jeroboam's intention was to provide an alternative to the most important cultic object of the Southern Kingdom, then the bull image (or images?) ought to be seen as analogous to the empty cherub throne in the Jerusalem temple. The comparative material from the iconic art of the ancient Near East provides further support for this understanding. As Obbink has observed, there are examples where the deity is represented as standing on the back of a bull[29]. The male figure above the bull then symbolizes the god. But the animal itself is only the god's pedestal or socle animal. Similarly, Jeroboam's bull image is thus only the visible pedestal over which JHWH stands unseen. We are confronted by the Northern Kingdom's counterpart to the empty divine throne in the Holy of Holies of the Jerusalem temple. In spite of Eissfeldt's attempt to introduce another interpretation[30], the view above outlined has quite rightly won general ac-

---

[26] The same designation of God, *jôšeb hăkkᵉrubîm*, is also found in 2 Kgs 19,15; Isa 37,16; Ps 80,2; 99,1; 1 Chron 13,6. Cf. also 2 Sam 22,11 and Ps 18,11.

[27] For an excellent discussion cf. Keel 1977, 15ff.

[28] Cf. Haran, 30ff., 89ff., esp. 35f.

[29] Obbink 268f. For illustrations cf. Welten 102, Keel 1977, Abb. 97ff. and cf. no 109ff.

[30] Eissfeldt, 190ff., holds that we have to do with a cultic standard, crowned by a bull image, in Ex 32 and 1 Kgs 12.

ceptance among scholars[31]. We must therefore avoid concluding too much from the "presentation formula" with which Jeroboam introduces his cultic object: "Behold your God, O Israel, who brought you up out of the land of Egypt" (1 Kgs 12,28)[32]. We have every reason to reckon with an original distinction between socle animal and the unseen deity above it.

If it is correct to draw an analogy between the cherub throne with the ark in the temple in Jerusalem and Jeroboam's bull (or bulls), the question arises how the former cultic symbol escaped the theological censure to which the latter was obviously subjected[33]. Various factors might be mentioned. The fact that the former cultic symbol was hidden in the Holy of Holies protected it against the false interpretations inevitable in a degenerate popular cult. Its very form—a cherub throne with the ark—did not invite the same Baalistic misunderstandings as a bull image; for the bull was not only El's, but also Baal's animal. Moreover, we may suppose that the notion of a throne in Jerusalem was for a long period sufficiently alive to guarantee that the cultic symbol as such was not confused with the unseen deity who sat above it. Just the same, the ark-theology could not in the end remain uninfluenced by the spreading iconoclastic tendencies associated with Hosea and the Deuteronomistic movement. G. von Rad has shown in a classic article how the ark in the Deuteronomistic theology lost its traditional character of a numinous symbol for God's presence and, via a process of rationalization was reduced to a mere container for the tablets of the Law (Deut 10,1–5; 1 Kgs 8,9)[34].

When were Images Prohibited?

When then was the prohibition of images which we meet in the decalogue formulated?

The classical ark-theology has its centre in the notion of the aniconic God. The throne is empty: the place of the image is occupied by the unseen God. The official Jerusalem cult was imageless in the sense that it lacked a direct symbol for JHWH. The cherub throne with the ark can not be regarded as such a symbol. Nor can Nehushtan (2 Kgs 18,4). The absence of images is here early a fact. Our question, however, is when this absence took programmatic form as a prohibition of images. Often a dogma is first formulated as an answer to a crisis. Might this perhaps be the case here as well?

The answer to our question must do justice to two factors. On the one hand, we find that a man like Jehu, who in his zeal for JHWH had Baal's temple in Samaria destroyed (2 Kgs 10,18–28), took no action against Jeroboam's bull cult:

---

[31] Cf. Weippert 103, n. 55 (lit.).

[32] Jeroboam himself certainly used the singular.

[33] For the following cf. Zimmerli 1974, 258f.

[34] Cf. Rad 1961, 109ff.

> But Jehu did not turn aside from the sins of Jeroboam the son of Nebat, which he made Israel to sin, the golden calves that were in Bethel, and in Dan. (2 Kgs 10,29)

Jehu's position was thus characterized by activity against Baal syncretism, but neutrality towards the bull cult. The same position was apparently that of Elijah and Elisha. Nor does Amos, who was active in Bethel where Jeroboam had set up his bull image, seem to have reacted against it. Even if Am 5,26 is authentic—and this is disputed—a genuine Israelite cult symbol is not the issue; besides, it contains a key term for an image, *ṣælæm,* which does not appear in the texts prohibiting images[35].

On the other hand, in the richly developed metaphorical language used by the prophets to describe JHWH, there is a striking reserve towards the use of the bull as a metaphor for JHWH[36]. And above all: the formula "the sins of Jeroboam the son of Nebat" is used time and time again by the Deuteronomists to brand the cultic symbol of Jeroboam with their condemnation[37]. Behind this polemic in the Deuteronomistic Historical Work seems to lie the formulated prohibition of images. Compare the formulation: "And they forsook all the commandments of the LORD their God, and made for themselves molten images [*măssekā,* sing.!] of two calves ..." (2 Kgs 17,16; cf. Ex 34,17). It may be added in parenthesis that we are not here dealing with an isolated phenomenon. The Deuteronomistic censure not only turned against artistically created symbols, but even against more "formless" cultic objects such as the originally legitimate masseboth[38]. And we have already seen how the new theological signals influenced the classical ark-theology.

That Hosea played a very significant role in the development of an iconoclastic theology is clearly shown by the sources[39]. This prophet gives expression to a clear and conscious criticism of "Samaria's calf" (Hos 8,5), by which the prophet means the cultic symbol which Jeroboam I had erected in the national sanctuary in Bethel (cf. Hos 10,5)[40]. Two things deserve special attention. First, the original distinction between JHWH and the bull seems to have become increasingly blurred in the popular consciousness. Hosea's declaration, "A god he is not!" (Hos 8,6) is directed against just such a confusion of the pedestal animal and the deity. Second, though originally related to JHWH-El, the bull image had in the course of time become associated with Baal. Hosea's struggle was in fact a full-scale attack on the Baalization of JHWH. His struggle against Baal becomes *eo ipso* a struggle against the bull image in Bethel.

---

[35] For a discussion of the syntax in Am 5,25–27 cf. Erlandsson 76ff.

[36] Cf. Hempel 1924, 74ff., esp. 100f.

[37] On this formula cf. Debus, esp. 93ff.

[38] Compare Gen 28,18.22; 31,13; 35,14; Ex 24,4; Isa 19,19f. with Deut 16,22 and Lev 26,1.

[39] Cf. Hos 3,4; 4,17; 8,1–7; 10,1–8; 10,10; 13,2; 14,9.

[40] Cf. the discussion in Wolff 179f.

From Hosea the line can be traced to Deuteronomy and Josiah's iconoclastic reform. It is a well-known fact that there are numerous connections between Hosea and Deuteronomy, connections which lead us to assume an influx of northern traditions into Judah after the fall of Samaria in 722/721 B.C.[41]. One of these points of contact is the plemic against images to be found in both Hosea and Deuteronomy. In both writings we find the image described as the work of craftsmen (*mă‘aśē ḥarašîm:* Hos 13,2; Deut 27,15). In both, images are described as man-made gods (*mă‘aśē jedê 'adam:* Hos 14,4; Deut 4,28; 31,29)[42]; the same statement is attested in Isa 2,8 and Mic 5,12, i.e. from the period between Hosea and Deuteronomy.

The actual polemic against images can thus be traced back to Hosea in the eighth century, though scarcely earlier. To judge by the evidence, it began with this prophet, received its peripeteia in Deuteronomy and the Deuteronomistic Historical Work, and its finale in Deutero-Isaiah (e.g. Isa 40, 18–20; 41,6f.; 44,9–20)[43].

We may here pause and summarize before proceeding further. From the pre-monarchic period we have the traditions—which in all probability were originally neutral—about the bronze serpent and Aaron's bull; the polemic in the latter narrative appears not to be original. We may here include the stories of Gideon's ephod and Micah's image as well. The official Jerusalem cult was undoubtedly aniconic, but the absence of images had scarcely taken on the character of a command in a fixed prohibition. The ark had not yet been rationalized into a mere container for the tablets of the testimony. In the Northern Kingdom the bull image in Bethel (and in Dan?) escaped prophetic criticism for one and a half centuries. Jehu's reforms did not alter this fact, nor do Elijah and Elisha seem to have expressed misgivings. First in the eighth century the prophetic polemic against images is formulated by Hosea immediately in its full force.

What conclusions may we draw about the dating of the prohibition of images? In my view there exist two primary possibilities: (a) If the prohibition came early and goes back to the wilderness period, then for reasons unknown to us it long lay inactive, only to be revived by Hosea. (b) The second alternative is that Moses never took a position on the question of images, that the prohibition is rather the product of prophetic polemic against them. If so, the prophets have here preceded the Law. The fact that Hosea makes no reference to a prohibition inherited from the time of Moses—which would have given his iconoclastic declarations a

---

[41] Cf. especially Alt 250ff.; Weinfeld 366ff.

[42] Cf. also some other passages in the Deuteronomistic literature: 1 Kgs 16,7; 2 Kgs 19,18; 22,17; Jer 1,16; 25,6–7; 32,30; 44,8. Note also Ps 115,4; 135,15.

[43] On these passages cf. Preuss 192ff. On the polemic against images cf. also Rad 1970, 229ff.

special weight—means that the second alternative (b) must be regarded as the simplest explanation of the available material[44].

The prohibition has been transmitted in a variety of forms (Ex 20,3–6; Deut 5,7–10; Ex 20,22–23; 34,17; Lev 19,4; 26,1; Deut 27,15). Which form is the oldest? In perfect agreement with the observations made above, we may suppose that the oldest form of the command is the one which is directed against molten images of silver or gold (*măssekā*), or more precisely, against the bull images; this is found in Ex 34,17: "You shall make for yourself no molten gods (*ʾælohê măssekā*)."[45]

The later, classical form of the command in the decalogue (Ex 20,3–6; Deut 5,7–10), is, as Zimmerli has shown, a complex one[46]. In Ex 20, v. 5–6 are an interpretative addition. This is apparent from the fact that the plural suffixes in v. 5 ("you shall not bow down to *them* or serve *them*...") do not refer back to the (singular) image in v. 4 but rather to the other gods in v. 3. Furthermore, the expression "bow down and worship" in v. 5 was never used with an image as object, but is rather a Deuteronomistic expression for an illegitimate relation to strange gods. The core of the prohibition in Ex 20 is found in v. 4a: *loʾ tăʿaśæ lᵉka pæsæl,* "you shall not make for yourself a graven image". The addition of v. 5–6 has placed the prohibition under the shadow of the first command—quite in agreement with the intentions behind the prophetic polemic against images as it is found, for example, in Hosea. Ex 20,4b is, according to Zimmerli, a still later addition.

Theological Motifs

We have now discussed the origin and different forms of the prohibition of images. What remains is undeniably the most difficult question in this context, but just as undeniably one of the most interesting: what ideological motifs are connected with the prohibition of images[47]? We have already touched on this question with the observation that the historical force behind the "dogmatization" which banned images is to be found in the prophetic struggle against the Baalization of JHWH. The prohibition is thus one expression of the reaction against Canaanite culture and religion which found its most extreme form in the Rechabites' stubborn fight for nomadic ideals and their consequent refusal to live in houses, take up agriculture, or drink wine (Jer 35,6–7). When the prohibition is seen in this perspective, the question becomes little more than academic whether the ban was di-

---

[44] A question that needs to be discussed anew is the date of the *first* commandment, cf. Golka 352 ff.

[45] Cf. Mowinckel 264 f. Note that *măssekā* is used to denote a bull image in Ex 32,4.8; Hos 13,2; Deut 9,16; Ps 106,19 f.; 2 Kgs 17,16.

[46] Cf. Zimmerli 1969, 234 ff. For the later discussion cf. Halbe 123, n. 73 (lit.).

[47] A broad treatment is found in Bernhardt 69 ff. Cf. also Keel 1977, 37 ff.

rected against images of foreign gods or representations of Israel's God. It is directed against both, the intention being to prohibit all cultic images. Its place in the decalogue is thus quite appropriate: it forms the transition from the prohibition of other gods to the commands regarding the divine name and the sabbath, both of which refer to the JHWH cult.

Our question can, however, be put at a deeper level. The prohibition is of course not to be understood in an exclusively negative sense, as a safeguard against syncretism. It may also be understood as positively expressing the distinctive character of Israel's understanding of the deity.

Attempts to thus penetrate to the ideological roots of the prohibition of images have at times pointed to the refusal of Israel's God to allow himself to be manipulated by magical means, to his *Unverfügbarkeit*[48]. An image mediates revelation. The static presence in an image, an object charged with power at human disposal, was for Israelite religion something foreign. The prohibition of images would thus be parallel in effect to the third commandment, which was intended to protect the divine name from magical misuse. But this interpretation of the prohibition is debatable[49]. If JHWH's *Unverfügbarkeit* played such a role, Israel's God would never even have revealed his name. The magic of the Near East shows us that the name even more than a representation placed the being in question at human disposal. A general reference to the well-known Egyptian execration texts, directed against foreign princes, will here suffice. But that is not all. The notion of JHWH's *Unverfügbarkeit* scarcely suits what the texts themselves imply about God's active presence in such cultic objects as the ark (cf. 1 Sam 4,4–9).

Comparison with the third commandment is thus not particularly enlightening. Still, the texts themselves—admittedly in a pair of quite late references—provide direct indications of great interest for our purposes. One such text is Ex 20,4b. Here Israel is forbidden to make any image "of anything that is in heaven above, or that is in the earth beneath, or that is in the water under the earth". This statement gives the prohibition its maximal scope, since the triple division describes the world in its entirety. While the religions of Israel's neighbours had gods in heaven, on earth, and in the underworld with their respective images, for Israel not only the earth but also heaven is incapable of offering anything to be compared with God. Here we approach what is perhaps the deepest motif in the prohibition of images: to safeguard the border between God and the world, to accentuate his transcendence.

The other text is Deut 4,9–20, which contains an extended interpretation of the prohibition. The command here finds its motivation in JHWH's method of revealing himself on Horeb: "Then the LORD spoke to you out

---

[48] Cf. for instance Zimmerli 1969, 245f.; Rad 1962, 230.

[49] As was pointed out by Keel 1977, 37.

of the midst of the fire; you heard the sound of words, but saw no form; there was only a voice" (v. 12; cf. v. 15 and Ex 20,22–23). Other nations resort to images for their contact with the deity; Israel is pointed to God's word. To this motivation based on the Sinai theophany, however, another is implicitly added in v. 16–18. Here Israel is admonished not to make any image, "the likeness of male or female, the likeness of any beast that is on the earth, the likeness of any winged bird that flies in the air, the likeness of anything that creeps on the ground, the likeness of any fish that is in the water under the earth". One can scarcely escape the impression that we are here confronted with the same vocabulary as in the Priestly account of the creation in Gen 1 (*zakar ûn^{e}qebā, b^{e}hemā, ræmæs*). This text, too, understands the prohibition of images as an expression of the Creator's transcendence over what he has created[50].

Our journey through the O.T. texts has reached its end. As a souvenir we may take with us the insight that the prohibition of images was probably formulated quite late, but that the official cult was early aniconic: over the cherub throne and the ark, the God of Israel was enthroned in unseen majesty. The place usually occupied by the image is empty. There is thus in Israelite religion a vacuum, a vacuum which tends to be filled. The roles played by the word of God, the name of God, and man as the image of God in the O.T. should be studied in this larger perspective as functions in a structure of which the notion of the aniconic god is the very centre[51].

Translated by Stephen Westerholm.

Bibliography

FRLANT	Forschungen zur Religion und Literatur des Alten und Neuen Testaments
ThB	Theologische Bücherei
VT	Vetus Testamentum
VT Suppl	Vetus Testamentum. Supplementum
ZAW	Zeitschrift für die alttestamentliche Wissenschaft
ZAWBeih	Zeitschrift für die alttestamentliche Wissenschaft. Beiheft
ZDPV	Zeitschrift des Deutschen Palästina-Vereins

Aberbach, M., Smolar, L., 1967, Aaron, Jeroboam, and the golden calves. *Journal of Biblical literature* 86.

Ahlström, G., 1970s, An Israelite god figurine from Hazor. *Orientalia Suecana* 19–20.

— 1975, An Israelite god figurine, once more. *VT* 25.

---

[50] Cf. Rad 1964, 61 f.; Schmidt 1968, 82; 1973, 25 ff.

[51] For further observations on the problems discussed in this paper cf. Ahlström 1970s, 54 ff.; 1975, 106 ff., Blais 1 ff.; Carroll 51 ff.; Dus 268 ff.; Gutmann 161 ff.; Hempel 1 ff.; Kruyswijk 1 ff.; North 151 ff.; Ouellette 504 ff.; Schrade 1 ff.; Soggin 179 ff.; Vischer 764 ff.

Akkadisches 1965, *Akkadisches Handwörterbuch* 1. [Hrsg.] von W. von Soden. Wiesbaden.

Alt, A. 1964, Die Heimat des Deuteronomiums. Alt, A., *Kleine Schriften* 2. München.

Barr, J., 1968, The image of God in the Book of Genesis—a study of terminology. *Bulletin of John Ryland's library* 51.

Bernhardt, K.-H., 1956, *Gott und Bild.* Theologische Arbeiten 2. Berlin.

Beyerlin, W., 1961, *Herkunft und Geschichte der ältesten Sinaitraditionen.* Tübingen.

Blais, G., 1971. *Interdit des images dans l'Ancien Testament.* "Lizentiatsarbeit" Fribourg (vide Elenchus 54/1973, 331).

Carroll, R., 1977, The aniconic god and the cult of images. *Studia Theologica* 31.

Childs, B., 1974, *Exodus. A commentary.* London.

Cross, F., 1973, *Canaanite myth and Hebrew epic.* Cambridge, Mass.

Debus, J., 1967, *Die Sünde Jerobeams.* FRLANT 93. Göttingen.

Donner, H., 1973, "Hier sind deine Götter, Israel!" *Wort und Geschichte.* Festschrift Karl Elliger. Alter Orient und Altes Testament 18. Ed. H. Gese und H. Rüger. Neukirchen.

Dus, J., 1965, Ein richterliches Stierbildheiligtum zu Bethel. *ZAW* 77.

Dussaud, R., 1921, *Les origines cananéennes du sacrifice israélite.* Paris.

Eissfeldt, O., 1940s, Lade und Stierbild. *ZAW* 58.

Erlandsson, S., 1968, Amos 5: 25–27, ett crux interpretum. *Svensk exegetisk årsbok* 33.

Golka, F., 1978, Schwierigkeiten bei der Datierung des Fremdgötterverbotes. *VT* 28.

Gordon, C., 1965, *Ugaritic textbook.* Analecta Orientalia 38. Roma.

Gutmann, J., 1961, The "second commandment" and the image in Judaism. *Hebrew Union College annual* 32.

Halbe, J., 1975, *Das Privilgerecht Jahwes. Ex 34,10–26.* FRLANT 114. Göttingen.

Haran, M., 1959, The ark and the cherubim. *Israel exploration journal* 9.

Hempel, J., 1924, Jahwegleichnisse der israelitischen Propheten. *ZAW* 42.

— 1957, *Das Bild in Bibel und Gottesdienst.* Sammlung gemeinverständlicher Vorträge 212. Tübingen.

Kapelrud, A., 1973, *'abîr/'ăbbîr. Theologisches Wörterbuch zum Alten Testament* 1. Ed. G. Botterweck and H. Ringgren. Stuttgart.

Keel, O., 1973, Das Vergraben der "fremden Götter" in Genesis xxxv 4b. *VT* 23.

— 1977, *Jahwe-Visionen und Siegelkunst.* Stuttgarter Bibelstudien 84 f. Stuttgart.

Kruyswijk, A., 1962, *"Geen gesneden beeld ..."*. Diss. Amsterdam.

Loewenstamm, S., 1967, The making and the destruction of the golden calf. *Biblica* 48.

Mettinger, T., 1974, The elimination of a crux? *VTSuppl* 26.

Motzki, H., 1975, Ein Beitrag zum Problem des Stierkultes in der Religionsgeschichte Israels. *VT* 25.

Mowinckel, S., 1930, Wann wurde der Jahwäkultus in Jerusalem offiziell bildlos. *Acta Orientalia* 8.

North, C., 1958, The essence of idolatry. *Von Ugarit nach Qumran.* Festschrift O. Eissfeldt. ZAWBeih 77. Ed. J. Hempel. Berlin.

Noth, M., 1971, Der Hintergrund von Richter 17–18. Noth, M., *Aufsätze zur biblischen Landes- und Altertumskunde* 1. Ed. H. Wolff. Neukirchen.

Obbink, H., 1929, Jahwebilder. *ZAW* 47.

Ouellette, J., 1967, Le deuxième commendement et le rôle de l'image dans la symbolique religieuse de l'Ancien Testament. *Revue Biblioque* 74.

Preuss, H., 1971, *Verspottung fremder Religionen im Alten Testament.* Beiträge zur Wissenschaft vom Alten und Neuen Testament 92. Stuttgart.

Rad, G. von, 1961, Zelt und Lade. Rad, G., *Gesammelte Studien zum Alten Testament*. ThB 8. München.
— 1962, *Theologie des Alten Testaments* 2. München.
— 1964, Aspekte alttestamentlichen Weltverständnisses. *Evangelische Theologie* 24.
— 1970, *Weisheit in Israel*. Neukirchen.
Reisner, G., Fisher, C., Lyon, D. 1924, *Harvard excavations at Samaria 1908–1910*, 1. Cambridge, Mass.
Rowley, H., 1939, Zadok and Nehushtan. *Journal of Biblical literature* 58.
Schmidt, W. 1968, *Alttestamentlicher Glaube und seine Umwelt*. Neukirchen.
— 1973, Ausprägungen des Bilderverbots? *Das Wort und die Wörter*. Festschrift G. Friedrich. Ed. H. Balz, S. Schulz. Stuttgart.
Schmitt, R., 1972, *Zelt und Lade als Thema alttestamentlicher Wissenschaft*. Gütersloh.
Schrade, H., 1949, *Der verborgene Gott. Gottesbild und Gottesvorstellung in Israel und im Alten Orient*. Stuttgart.
Soggin, J., 1966, Der offiziell geförderte Synkretismus in Israel während des 10. Jahrhunderts. *ZAW* 78.
Ullmann, S., 1967, *The principles of semantics*. Oxford.
Vaux, R. de, 1978, *The early history of Israel* 1. London.
Veijola, T., 1977, *Das Königtum in der Beurteilung der deuteronomistischen Historiographie*. Annales Academiae Scientiarum Fennicae B 198. Helsinki.
Vischer, W., 1956, Du sollst dir kein Bildnis machen. *Antwort*. Festschrift Karl Barth. Zollikon.
Weinfeld, M., 1972, *Deuteronomy and the Deuteronomic school*. Oxford.
Weippert, M., 1961, Gott und Stier. *ZDPV* 77.
Welten, P., 1977, Götterbild, männliches. *Biblisches Reallexikon*. Ed. K. Galling. Tübingen.
Wolff, H., 1965. *Dodekapropheton 1. Hosea*. Biblischer Kommentar 14,1. Neukirchen.
Zimmerli, W., 1969, Das zweite Gebot. Zimmerli, W., *Gottes Offenbarung*. ThB 19.
— 1974, Das Bilderverbot in der Geschichte des alten Israel (Goldenes Kalb, Eherne Schlange, Mazzeben und Lade). Zimmerli, W., *Studien zur alttestamentlichen Theologie und Prophetie 2*. ThB 51.

The Symbol of the Centre and its religious function in Islam

By JAN HJÄRPE

A modern catechism for English-speaking Muslim children contains a map showing Mecca as the Centre of the inhabited world[1]—just as the old Arab geographers, e.g. Ibn Ḥawḳal, begin their descriptions of cities and countries with "the mother of cities" (cf. Sura 42: 7/5), Mecca[2]. Eliade cites the feeling of *a-homogeneity in space* as a basic religious experience[3]. Separate parts of a room, different places, regions and directions have different emotional values in the eyes of the individual. There is a ritual orientation in the world. In this context we may speak of a Centre, the *Origo* in the religious orientation in the world. This concept is an essential feature of Islam. To be valid the prayers must be performed facing the *ḳibla,* which is the Kaʿba in Mecca[4]. The animal to be slaughtered stands with its head towards the *ḳibla*[5], the dead is buried with his face towards Mecca. The *ḳibla* determines the orientation of the mosques, and thus indirectly, town plans throught the Muslim world. Mecca is also the goal of the Pilgrimage.

In bygone days the Muslim traveller carried an astrolabe to find the *ḳibla* with the help of the stars[6]; today a special compass is used. The *ḳibla*, the direction for ritual acts, is towards the Centre of the world, the Kaʿba in Mecca, or, to be exact, towards the north-western wall of the Kaʿba building between the western corner and the gilded spout for the rainwater from the roof[7].

Mecca's unique position and the sanctity of the Kaʿba are well evidenced in the Koran[8]: "Behold! The first temple (*bayt*) that was founded for mankind, was that in Bakka, blessed, and a guidance to the worlds. In it are evident signs, the place of Abraham (*maḳām Ibrāhīm*), and he who enters it is safe. And it is incumbent on the humans before God to make the pilgrimage to the temple, everyone who is able to do it." (Sura 3: 96/90 f.)

The difference between an object as a *religious symbol* and a neutral and

---

[1] Cf. Toto 69.
[2] Cf. Ibn Hawḳal 17 f. and 23 ff.
[3] Cf. Eliade 1957, 13 f.
[4] Cf. Wensinck 1965, 260 f. The Koranic rule is found in Sura 2: 142/136, 148/143–150/145.
[5] Cf. Bousquet 213.
[6] Cf. Arnold 114.
[7] Cf. Wensinck 1965, 260, and Wensinck 1974, 318.
[8] The most important passages in the Koran concerning the Kaʿba and Mecca are: 2: 144/139, 149/145, 150/145, 217/214, 3: 96/90–97/92, 5: 97/98, 22: 29/30, 33/34, 27: 91/93, 28: 57, 29: 67, 42: 7/5, and 107: 3.

profane object is the ritual behaviour: it attracts rituals and observances which are justified and explained by religious belief. The term Symbol of the Centre has been used freely by Eliade and his followers[9]. My use of the term does not imply acceptance of Eliade's interpretation of the phenomenon, i.e. the significance and function which he attributes to it. The Centre, in this case, is a specific object, the Kaʿba, and, to a certain extent, the city of Mecca as a whole, in their character of *focus* in the ritual geography of Islam. In what way is the Kaʿba (and Mecca) as the Centre of the Muslim world a *symbol*? What is the value of the symbol today? In short: What is the religious function of the Symbol of the Centre in Islam in the 1970's?

"Orientalist" is an invective in the mouth of a Muslim. The interest of the Western Orientalist in regard to the Kaʿba, and the ritual of the Pilgrimage, was primarily to search for their "original", i.e. pre-Islamic, significance[10]. Such studies provoke the repugnance of the Muslim who happens to read them. He maintains, perhaps rightfully, that the orientalist who uses this method cannot discern the real meaning and function of the phenomenon, i.e. its meaning for, and function among, those who profess and practice the religion today. Speculations on the possible "solar character" of the pre-Islamic rites, or whether they constituted "rainrituals", are of no interest in this connexion. We may also disregard the folklore about the Kaʿba, insofar as such material does not in one way or another occur in contemporary sources[11]. In Islam today these legends play a very insignificant role. They are often explicitly repudiated.

Source material:

(*a*) Modern guide-books (*manāsik*) for pilgrims to Mecca. Here we often find interpretations of the significance of the different rites, and prayers and precepts indicating the meaning of the different objects and modes of behaviour for the believer.

(*b*) Tracts and booklets from the Islamic *daʿwa* (mission); information, apologetics and propaganda addressed to Muslims and non-Muslims in the west.

(*c*) Accounts by pilgrims of their experiences and reactions.

(*d*) Muslim publications, speeches, articles etc. which illustrate the role of the Kaʿba and of Mecca.

(*e*) Material which gives information on events in Mecca: Islamic papers, journals, the publications of the Hajj Research Centre (created in 1975) of the Abdulaziz University, official statistics etc.

Comparative material from earlier times is to be found in abundance in Sir Richard Burton's famous *Pilgrimage to al-Madinah and Meccah*. Burton's

---

[9] Cf. Eliade 1952, 4ff.; Eliade 1949*a*, 19, 30ff.; Eliade 1957, 23f.

[10] Cf. e.g. Chelhod 204f. and 209ff.

[11] Myths and legends about the Kaʿba, cf. Chelhod 232.

own thorough observations are derived from his activity as a spy in al-Ḥidjāz in the 1850's.

The sanctity and unique status of Mecca and of the Kaʿba is indicated by the right of asylum: "He who enters it is safe" (Sura 3: 97/91, cf. 28: 57 and 29: 67). al-Ḥaram is inviolable, but its right of asylum is not without limitations. It is not valid for unbelievers who attack Muslims (Sura 2: 191/187), and a criminal who seeks refuge there must not be offered food, so that he must soon surrender[12]. The inviolability also holds good for flora and fauna. Plants and animals (with certain exceptions) are protected within the Ḥaram of Mecca[13]. The ritual slaughter during the Pilgrimage is performed not at the Kaʿba (as the Koran implies: Sura 22: 33/34) but in Minā. One result of the ban on the killing of animals is the abundance of pigeons at the Mosque of Mecca. Folklore has many legends about these pigeons[14].

Due to the religious importance of Mecca strangers have settled there[15]. Mecca has become a Muslim world in miniature. All ethnic groups and nationalities in Islam are to be found there[16]. Saudi Arabia is now one of the world's major countries of immigration and severe restrictions on illegal immigration have recently been initiated[17]. Mecca is now a large city. In 1853 Burton estimated the population as 30–40,000[18], excluding pilgrims, while now the number is reported to be 301,000[19]. Many gather in Mecca, devotees invariably congregate around the Kaʿba, night and day, not only to perform the rites of *ḥadjdj* and *ʿumra,* but for prayer and devotion. Zaki Badawi says (in 1978): "The sound of their pleading voices and the patter of their hurrying feet fills the heart with awe. No place on earth inspires such a profound experience."[20]

The Kaʿba's role as an object of devotion is also indicated by the fact that pictures of the temple actually serve as "devotional icons", in homes and in mosques. We can even see a tendency for a stylized image of the Kaʿba to replace the crescent as the symbol of Islam, i.e. the Symbol of the Centre tends to become the symbol of the religion as a whole. We may also note that the *imām* of the Kaʿba (at present Shaykh Abdulaziz b. Abdullah) is a personage of importance, leading diplomatic delegations etc. During a world tour he visited Great Britain in March 1978[21], and at the Asian Islamic Conference in Karachi 6–8 July 1978 he led 1,5 million persons in the Friday prayers[22].

As goal for the Pilgrimage Mecca is more important than ever before. At the *ḥadjdj* in 1807 Ali Bey estimated the number of pilgrims at 83,000[23], and

---

[12] Cf. *Hajj* 17.
[13] Cf. Wensinck 1974, 322.
[14] Cf. Burton 2, 174 f.
[15] Cf. Makky 23.
[16] Cf. *Hajj* 124 ff.
[17] Cf. *Impact* 8: 14, 4.
[18] Cf. Burton 2, 229, note 1.
[19] Cf. *Whitaker's* 933.
[20] *Hajj* 18.
[21] Cf. *Impact* 8: 3, 5 and 8: 4, 15.
[22] According to a notice in *Impact* 8: 14, 4. The number may be exaggerated.
[23] Statistics for the 19th century, cf. Burton 2, 188.

the maximum number recorded in the 19th century was 160,000. Between 1957 and 1962 there were 140–180,000 pilgrims *per annum*[24]. In 1964 the number (excluding residents in Saudi Arabia) was 260,000, and in 1969 375,000[25]. Now we find still higher figures: In 1976 719,040 individuals obtained visas for pilgrimage[26], and in November 1977 the Saudi Arabian officials issued permits to 739,319 persons[27]. To this figure we must add the pilgrims already residing in Arabia, who do not need visa. In all, about 1,5 million persons perform the pilgrimage (*ḥadjdj* and *ʿumra*) each year[28].

There are several factors behind this enormous increase in numbers: health services which reduce the risk of epidemics to a minimum, modern communications (2/3 of the pilgrims arrive by air)[29], security on the roads, and, of course, the moderate cost of travelling[30]. We may also consider the Pilgrims' service developed under the active supervision of the Saudi Arabian government, and the careful administration of all the details associated with the Pilgrimage[31]. Several Muslim governments provide facilities for the pilgrims in the form of public travel agencies etc. In other cases they try to limit the number of participants, particularly because of economic implications[32]. The pilgrimage to Mecca plays a major role in the co-operation between Muslim countries in the fields of religion, economics and politics[33]. The Symbol of the Centre has become a token of the political significance of Islam.

One and one half million persons perform the prescribed rites during the short period of the *ḥadjdj*. The great problem is congestion. Soon the limit will be reached when the topography itself will prevent further increase. The authorities have discussed the possibility of blasting parts of the surrounding mountains to provide more space. Some blasting has been done (for roads etc.), but the making of substantial alterations in the topography of the Sacred City is adjudged unduly provocative.

The reverence for the symbol is indicated also by the splendour of the Mosque. The most important change in Mecca is the reconstruction of the Mosque around the Kaʿba—the Kaʿba itself of course remains intact[34]. The "Mosque [improvement] project" was begun in Mecca in 1952 (and in Medina in 1955)[35]. In Mecca more than 2,400 houses were purchased and

---

[24] Cf. Wensinck 1971, 34.
[25] Cf. Holter 201, 35.
[26] Cf. *MENA* 614; *Impact* 7: 23, 4.
[27] Cf. *Impact* 7: 23, 4.
[28] For the proportions between different nationalities, see *Hajj* 111.
[29] Cf. *Impact* 7: 23, 4.
[30] Advertisement for *ḥadjdj* and for *ʿumra* are to be found in every number of *Impact*, and in many other Muslim journals.
[31] For the actual administration of the Pilgrimage, cf. *Hajj* 59 ff. and 87 ff.
[32] In 1978 e.g. Nigeria, Pakistan and Turkey, cf. *Impact* 8: 14, 14, 8: 15, 4 and 15. See also Ali Bhutto IV.
[33] Cf. Sicard 350 ff.
[34] For detailed descriptions of the Kaʿba, cf. Wensinck 1974, 317 ff. See also Burton, 2, 294 ff., for comparative material from the 19th century.
[35] Cf. Makky 43 and *MENA* 30.

demolished to provide space for the enlargement of the Mosque and for new open places and roads[36]. New two-storey galleries were built around the old mosque, so that since 1976, when the reconstruction was completed *al-Masdjid al-Ḥarām* covers 19 hectares (earlier: 2.9 hectares). A protruding wing, 395 m in length, covers *al-Masʿā*, the way between al-Marwa and as-Ṣafā hills. The Mosque is equipped with seven minarets, 92 m in height[37]. Some changes have been made in the inner court of the mosque, including the demolition of the pavilions for the imāms of the four *madhāhib*, one of which was the old superstructure of the Zamzam well, the *maḳām Ibrāhīm* has a new *ḳubba* etc.[38].

The central parts of Mecca were considerably changed[39] by the reconstruction of the Mosque, by the new open places around it, and by the new modern buildings up to 13 storeys high which have been erected nearby. The new houses and streets have not provoked universal satisfaction among Muslim architects and town planners. They find that the constructions impair Mecca's character of a Muslim city. They have an adverse effect on the spiritual experience of the Centre of Islam, in that Mecca tends to resemble any major city of glass and concrete[40]. The symbol loses some of its impact. Material prosperity is not entirely a good thing: The devotion, the spiritual benefit of the Pilgrimage and the sojourn at the Centre is impaired by such disturbing elements as the noise from cars and aeroplanes, the smell of exhaust gases—and "the horrific music of the transistors", and "In present-day Muna what is experienced is not the environment of the Prophet, but the surroundings of Manhattan ..."[41].

The benefits of modern technology, the facilities provided for the pilgrims, and the rigorous prohibition of non-Muslims approaching Mecca, are all intended to promote the devotion, the experience of "being there". But, as the specialists of the Hajj Research Centre emphasize, the Pilgrimage must not become too easy, for the spiritual benefit will be destroyed. *Ḥadjdj* must not resemble a common picnic[42].

The great influx of pilgrims was surely the main reason for the demolition of the pavilions belonging to the imāms of the four *madhāhib* at the Kaʿba[43], but this was also an expression of ideology: It emphasizes that every form of "secterianism" contravenes the true nature of Islam. The Centre ought to stand for unity. Likewise the old antagonism against the *shīʿa* is modified—or even declared nonexistent[44].

Changes in rites and in behaviour can be studied by comparison with Burton's detailed descriptions from the pilgrimage of 1853. Since the Saudi

---

[36] Cf. Makky 45.
[37] Cf. ib. 41 f.
[38] Cf. the illustrations in Makky, 10, and Plates 6 A, 8 A; Ayyūb 345, 349.
[39] Cf. Makky 27 ff.
[40] Cf. *Hajj* 36 f. also 22.
[41] Ziauddin Sardar in *Hajj* 35.
[42] Cf. ib. 1, 24 f., 33 f.
[43] Cf. Wensinck 1974, 318.
[44] In conversations with educated Muslims I encountered the response that no antagonism ever existed between *sunnīs* and *shīʿīs*.

conquest of al-Ḥidjāz in the 1920's, the rigid principles of the ḥanbalite *madhhab* have resulted in a reformation, an eradication of many former customs associated with the Pilgrimage, above all the visits to the tombs of saints and the rites there, and to the various places which popular tradition connected with different incidents in the life of the Prophet[45]. Here the wahhābīs made a clean sweep[46]. This means, in fact, that the traditions connecting Abraham with Mecca, founded on the Koran, are more accentuated today, and the traditions about Muhammad and Mecca are less stressed, perhaps not in theory, but in practice, in ritual. The commemoration in acts (=the rites) concerns the memory of the "father of the Prophets", Abraham. When now other rites, connected with the saints and with the life of Muhammad are abolished, the psychological effect is that Muhammad is displaced by Abraham and his family at the Centre of Islam. The old popular legends connecting Adam with the Kaʿba[47] are seldom mentioned today, at least not *expressis verbis,* although they are implicit, e.g.: "There are reports which take the Hajj further back in history and associate it with man's first steps on this planet"[48].

It is possible, however, that the quotation refers to the ritual at ʿArafāt, and not to the Kaʿba and Mecca.

Muslims from all over the world gather in Mecca. They meet fellow-believers, all in the same clothing, performing the same rituals. It is often emphasized that the brotherhood, the unity and the equality of Islam are there made manifest as tangible experiences[49] which the Muslim should apply in his daily life[50]. Seyyid Hossein Nasr says: "Something of the Centre is thus [by the return home] disseminated in the periphery and through this yearly act the whole of the Muslim community is purified."[51]

The rites and the events of the Pilgrimage are followed by those remaining at home, by means of press, radio and (since 1973) TV[52], and by the narratives of those who return. The social status of the *ḥādjdjī* is worth the effort.

Political leaders meet in Mecca and combine political conferences with the performance of the *ʿumra*[53]. Governments send deputations to the *ḥadjdj*[54]. An official delegation of Muslims from the Soviet Union—20 religious officials—made the Pilgrimage for the first time in November 1977[55]. The visit was evidently part of the attempt to abate the antagonism of the Muslim world against the Soviet Union, and it testifies to the political

---

45 For these cult-sites in Mecca, cf. Burton 2, 248 ff., 250 ff., esp. 253 f. Not even the *mawlid* of Muhammad is observed in Saudi Arabia today.
46 Cf. Moh. Jamil Brownson in *Hajj* 122.
47 Cf. Seligsohn 14.
48 *Hajj* 15.
49 Cf. Ahsan 20; *Hajj* 86, Nasr 116.
50 Cf. *Pilgrimage* 8.
51 Nasr 116.
52 Cf. Wensinck 1971, 31; Holter 15.
53 So e.g. al-Ḳadhdhāfī and Anwar as-Sādāt in 1974 (cf. al-Ḳadhdhāfī 80 and 111) and Sekou Toure in 1978 (*Impact* 8: 13, 2).
54 Cf. Holter 203.
55 Cf. *Impact* 7: 24, 15; 8: 3, 5.

importance of the symbolic centre of Islam. The possession of al-Ḥidjāz gives Saudi Arabia considerable religio-political prestige, and the income from the oilfields allows of its exploitation. Symbolically this is indicated by the fact that nowadays Saudi Arabia, and not as previously, Egypt, supplies the Kaʿba with its *Kiswa,* the beautifully embroidered black curtain[56].

Mecca, the conference centre of the Muslim world, the meeting-place, the symbol of the supranational nature of Islam—all this is frequently re-iterated in 20th century Islam[57]. Therefore it is quite natural that *Rābiṭat al-ʿālam al-islāmī* (Muslim World League) has it headquarters in Mecca. The *Rābiṭa* intends to erect its big new printing-house "near the Kaʿba to serve the needs of *daʿwa* (mission) throughout the world"[58].

The Kaʿba and the Haram of Mecca are *not* involved in the most important and constitutive rite of the *ḥadjdj: al-wuḳūf,* "the standing", at ʿArafāt[59], in commemoration of the meeting between Adam and Eve[60] and of Muhammad's Farewell Sermon[61]. But an important rite in both *ḥadjdj* and *ʿumra* is the *ṭawāf,* the ritual circumambulation of the Kaʿba[62]. The *ṭawāf* is performed anti-clockwise seven times, with the corner of the Black Stone as the starting-point. Circumambulation anti-clockwise is normally considered the more unusual form of the phenomenon in the world of religions; the Hindu *pradakṣiṇam* is performed clockwise[63] with the Centre to the right, but circumambulation in the opposite direction is to be found in tantric Buddhism and in the Tibetan Bön-religion. We may also note that in the Christian liturgical tradition the priest turns with his heart towards the altar, i.e. with the Centre to the left.

It is almost a dogma, since Mannhardt, to interpret ceremonial circumambulation as a solar ritual[64]. I have found no indications whatsoever of a connexion between *ṭawāf* and the sun, at least not in contemporary material. Insofar as any interpretation of the rite is given, it is called an act of obedience towards God[65], or expressing honour to Abraham's God[66]. The rite, like the whole ritual of the Pilgrimage, is regarded as instituted by Abraham. The centre which is circumambulated is Abraham's temple[67].

The *ṭawāf* of departure is the concluding rite in both *ḥadjdj* and *ʿumbra,* performed immediately before the pilgrim leaves Mecca[68]. Expressions of

---

[56] Cf. Wensinck 1974, 317.

[57] See e.g. *Hajj* 122, an-Nāṣir, the concluding paragraph, Baljon 80; Ahsan 20.

[58] *Impact* 8: 8, 15.

[59] Cf. Sardar in *Hajj* 31; Makky 40. For the ritual there, cf. Ayyūb, 167 ff., Kamāl 68 ff.

[60] Cf. Burton 2, 188 f., Sardar in *Hajj* 31; Wensinck 1960, 604.

[61] For Muhammad's sermon and his "standing" on the mount, see Ibn Hishām 968 ff.; cf. Makky 40.

[62] Ritual and prayers for the ṭawāf: cf. Ayyūb 135 ff. Kamāl 35 ff. (transl. 43 ff.), see also Buhl 583 f.; Burton 2, 161 ff.

[63] Cf. Bolle 129.

[64] Cf. d'Alviella 658.

[65] Cf. *Hajj* 31.

[66] Cf. ib. 16.

[67] The most important passage in the Koran connecting Abraham with the Pilgrimage is Sura 22: 26/27–37/38. On Abraham and Ishmael as the builders of the Kaʿba, see Sura 2: 127/121., cf. Hjärpe 386 f.

[68] Cf. Ayyūb 148 f.

strong emotional involvement follow the performance of this rite[69]. Between the eastern corner and the door of the Kaʿba extends the part of the north-eastern wall known as *al-Multazam,* where the visitors press breast and face against the wall, their arms above their heads[70], beseeching "the good things of this and the other world"[71]. This rite can perhaps be termed "glissade"[72], but to call it magic would be wrong. Often it is the expression of a strong emotional experience[73].

Maḳām Ibrāhīm is a stone north-east of the Kaʿba. Tradition says that Abraham stood on this stone when building the temple[74]. The Zamzam well, east of the Kaʿba, is by tradition the source which saved the life of Ishmael when he and his mother Hagar searched for water in the barren valley. Its water was formerly considered miraculous, curing all manner of ills[75]. One seldom finds such statements today, or at least not in print. The connection between the family of Abraham and the Pilgrimage is accentuated by other ceremonies: *Saʿy,* the "course" between aṣ-Ṣafā and al-Marwa[76] commemorates Hagar's search for water[77]. The "stoning of Satan" in Minā[78] recalls Abraham's rejection of Satan's temptation to disobey God's command to offer his son. The implication of the ceremony is that the pilgrim renounces evil, and is ready to fight against temptations[79]. The rite of slaughtering in Minā[80]—which coincides with the celebration of *ʿĪd al-aḍḥā* throughout the Muslim world[81]—derives from the legend of Abraham's sacrifice (Sura 37: 102/100–107) and commemorates his obedience[82]. The significance of the rite is stated to be the manifestation of willingness to renounce, to sacrifice one's property (or even one's life). It is also said to remind the pilgrim of his duty to help the needy[83]. The rite is a repetition, says Eliade, it "repeats an act performed at the beginning of time by a god, a hero, or an ancestor"[84]. The *ḥadjdj* (and also the *ʿumra*) is a "repetition" in two stages: The norm and model for the Pilgrimage is Muhammad's Farewell *ḥadjdj*[85]. To perform the ritual at the Centre is to follow in the footsteps of the Prophet[86]. *But* the vital and conclusive *aition* thereof are the traditions about Abraham. The pilgrim "feels outside his time and space, back in the era of Abraham and

---

[69] Cf. e.g. Burton 2, 284, note 2.
[70] Cf. Ayyūb 151; Kamāl 43 f. (transl. 51 f.); Wensinck 1974, 318; Burton 2, 166, 169.
[71] Ayyūb 151; cf. Kamāl 43 f. (transl. 51 f.).
[72] Cf. Eliade 1949, 196 ff.
[73] Cf. Burton 2, 173, 176.
[74] Cf. *Hajj* 20.
[75] Cf. Chelhod 233; Wensinck 1974, 321.
[76] The rules for *as-saʿy:* cf. Ayyūb 152 ff., see also Kamāl 53 ff. (transl. 56 ff.); Burton 2, 288 f.
[77] Cf. *Hajj* 30, 40.
[78] The rules for *ar-ramy,* cf. Ayyūb 191 ff. See also Burton 2, 203, 219, 222, note 1, 291.
[79] Cf. Makky 40, *Hajj* 16, 32.
[80] The rules for the slaughter: cf. Ayyūb 205, 231 ff. See also Burton 2, 217 ff., 291.
[81] Cf. *Muslim* 7 ff.
[82] Cf. Ḥamīdullāh to Sura 37: 102, 107; *Hajj* 32.
[83] Cf. Ahsan 20, 25; Makky 41. Notice also as-Sādāts "sacrifice", his visit to Jerusalem at the *ʿĪd* in 1977 and the allusions to Abraham's sacrifice in his speech in the Israeli parliament (as-Sādāt 310, 333).
[84] Eliade 1949*a*, 22.
[85] Cf. *Hajj* 55.
[86] Cf. ib. 35, 117; *Pilgrimage* 8.

the sacred family"[87]. The connection between Abraham and the Kaʿba is seen as an essential factor. We can, for instance, point to the famous Ṭaha Ḥusayn affair in the 1920's. He was guilty of the enormous heresy of doubting the historicity (from a strict scholarly point of view) of Abraham's visit to Mecca. This caused his dismissal from his post as a university teacher[88].

Many have testified that the Pilgrimage, nay, already the mere sight of Kaʿba, can provoke extremely strong feelings. It is described as a deep religious experience, a source of spiritual joy, a "rebirth"[89]. Burton mentions that at the Kaʿba he witnessed a case of a *malbūs* (a person in a state of religious ecstacy or frenzy)[90]. S. H. Nasr says that "the pilgrimage means to journey from the surface to the centre of one's being for, as so many Sufis have said, the heart is the spiritual Kaʿba."[91]

Hjalmar Sundén states that in psychological terms the Kaʿba can be regarded as a Mother symbol. The pre-Islamic cult of the three goddesses at the Kaʿba has disappeared, but the Kaʿba itself is preserved. The temple itself can in the patriarchal religion of Islam satisfy the unconscious (subconscious) longing for the "Mother": "Thus the Pilgrimage to the Kaʿba appears in depth-psychological perspective as an extraordinarily important factor for the establishment of the psychical balance which, according to many observers, is a characteristic of Islam's devotees."[92]

The Black Stone—never mentioned in the Koran—is regarded as the remnant of Abraham's and Ishmael's Kaʿba[93]. Sometimes it is associated with the "covenant" between God and the children of Adam (cf. Sura 7: 172/171). In old Islamic folklore this "covenant" and its connection with the Kaʿba was expressed in terms of a myth: The Kaʿba has eaten the parchment on which the contract was written[94]; thus the Kaʿba is the witness of the covenant. Such stories are not told today, but the point remains, in a demythologized form: The Black Stone is, says S. H. Nasr, a symbol of this original covenant, a symbol of the burden which God imposed on Man, the responsibility, the faculty to choose obedience or disobedience[95]. The Kaʿba is regarded as "the very symbol of monotheistic belief", says Zaki Badawi[96].

The Kaʿba, and Mecca, is the Centre of Islam's "topographical religiosity". The *Symbol* of the Centre in Islam is, on the one hand, the tangible object, the City and the temple, and on the other the ritual behaviour concerned with the Centre, i.e. *ṭawāf, ḳibla* etc. The symbol is *efficacious,* it has psychological effects, it provokes and expresses emotions, spiritual

---

[87] *Hajj* 24; cf. Makky 21 ff.; *Hajj* 15.
[88] Cf. Ahmad 45 ff.; Wessels 4, note 21.
[89] Cf. *Hajj* 9, 18, *Pilgrimage* 6; Burton 2, 152, 161.
[90] Cf. Burton 2, 175.
[91] Nasr 117.
[92] Sundén 458.
[93] Cf. *Pilgrimage* 4.
[94] Cf. Chelhod 205.
[95] Cf. Nasr 26, 41.
[96] *Hajj* 15.

experiences, feelings of fellowship, of duties towards God and fellow-believers; not only do these emotions visualize fundamental principles in Islam, but by the experience of the Symbol these ideas are integrated in the personality of the individual (or rather: of millions of individuals!), with social and political consequences for his actions. The fact that the Centre is invariably remembered as the *ḳibla,* the direction of the daily ritual behaviour, creates a profound awareness of membership of a community transcending ethnic, national and political boundaries.

Bibliography

EI	Encyclopaedia of Islam.
ERE	Encyclopaedia of religion and ethics.
MENA	The Middle East and North Africa.
SEI	Shorter encyclopaedia of Islam.
TRE	Theologische Realenzyklopädie.

Ahmad, M., 1963, *Die Auseinandersetzung zwischen al-Azhar und der modernistischen Bewegung in Ägypten von M. ʿAbduh bis zur Gegenwart.* Hamburg.

Ahsan, M., 1977, *Islam, faith and practice.* Leicester.

Ali Bhutto, Z., 1976, *Thoughts on some aspects of Islam.* Lahore.

d'Alviella, G., 1910, Circumambulation. *ERE* 3.

Arnold, T.–Guillaume, A., 1965, *The legacy of Islam.* Oxford.

Ayyūb, Ḥ., 1973, *al-Ḥadjdj fī'l-islām.* Kuwait.

Baljon, J., 1961, *Modern Muslim Koran interpretation.* Leiden.

Bolle, K., 1969, Speaking of a place. *Myths and symbols, studies in honor of Mircea Eliade.* Chicago.

Bousquet, G., 1965, Dhabīḥa. *EI* 2.

Buhl, F., 1965, Ṭawāf. *SEI.*

Burton, R., 1893, *Personal narrative of a pilgrimage to al-Madinah and Meccah* 1–2, *Memorial edition.* London.

Chelhod, J., 1964, *Les structures du sacré chez les arabes.* Paris.

Eliade, M., 1949, *Traité d'histoire des religions.* Paris.

— 1949*a*, *Le mythe de l'éternel retour.* Paris.

— 1952, *Images et symboles.* Paris.

— 1957, *Das Heilige und das Profane.* Hamburg.

Hajj, 1978, *Hajj studies* 1. London–Jeddah.

Ḥamīdullāh, M., 1973, *al-Ḳur'ān al-madjīd* (*Le Saint Coran*). Ankara.

Hjärpe, J., 1976, Abraham, religionsgeschichtlich. *TRE* 1.

Holter, Å., 1976, *Arabisk statsreligion.* Oslo.

Ibn Ḥawḳal, A., 1872 f., *al-Masālik wa'l-mamālik.* Ed. M. de Goeje. Leiden.

Ibn Hishām, A., 1858 ff., *Sīratu sayyidinā Muḥammad.* Ed. F. Wüstenfeld. Göttingen.

Impact, 1977 f., *Impact International fortnightly, Muslim viewpoints on current affairs.*

al-Ḳadhdhāfī, M., 1975, Discourses by Muʿammar el-Qathafi. S.l.

Kamāl, A., 1964, *The sacred journey. ar-Riḥla al-muḳaddasa* [1960]. London.

Makky, G., 1978, *Mecca, the pilgrimage city, a study of pilgrim accommodation.* London.

MENA, 1977–1978.

Muslim, s.a., *Muslim festivals and ceremonies.* Croydon.

an-Nāṣir, G. [Nasser], 1970, *Falsafat ath-thawra*. al-Ḳāhira.
Nasr, S., 1975, *Ideals and realities of Islam*. London.
Pilgrimage, 1975, *Pilgrimage, hajj*. Croydon.
as-Sādāt [el-Sadat], A., 1978, *In search of identity*. London.
Seligsohn, M., 1961, Ādam. *SEI*.
Sicard, S., 1976, Contemporary Islam and its world mission. *Missiology*.
Sundén, H., 1966, *Religionen och rollerna*. Stockholm.
Toto, O., 1973, *Children's book on Islam and the last prophet of God Muhammad*. London.
Wensinck, A., 1965, Ḳibla. *SEI*.
Wensinck, A., Gibb, H., 1960, ʿArafa. *EI* 1.
Wensinck, A., Jomier, J., 1974, Kaʿba. *EI* 4.
Wensinck, A., Jomier, J., Lewis, B., 1971, Ḥadjdj. *EI* 3.
Wessels, A., 1972, *A modern Arabic biography of Muḥammad*. Leiden.
Whitaker, 1976, Whitaker's Almanack 1977. London.

The Role of the Icon in Byzantine Piety

By LENNART RYDÉN

In February 754, the bishops of the Byzantine Empire met in the imperial palace at Hiereia, a peninsula on the Asiatic side of the Sea of Marmora, not far from Chalcedon. The council had been convened by the Emperor Constantine V (741–75), who wanted the bishops to examine the scriptures and express their opinion on the "deceitful painting of likenesses, which draws away the human mind from the service which is sublime and befits the Divinity to the grovelling and material service of creatures"[1]. As the phrasing shows, the assembled bishops were not expected to discuss whether the making of icons[2] was justified or not. The emperor had already examined this question and found that there was no such justification. The purpose of the council was rather to remove unorthodox elements from the emperor's argument, to give it a theological finish and to put it into a historical context. The proceedings lasted six months. In August a *horos* (definition) was approved, which may be summarized as follows[3].

In order to separate man from God, Lucifer made man worship the creature rather than the Creator (cf. Rom. i,25). God, who wanted to save man, sent him the Law and the prophets. When man failed to return to his former state, God at last sent His own Son and Logos. Christ saved man from idolatry and taught him to worship in spirit and truth (cf. John iv,24). The Christian apostles and teachers passed on the true faith to later generations. The six ecumenical councils kept it pure. But, under the guise of Christianity, Satan again made man worship the creature rather than the Creator. He made man think that an image carrying the name of Christ was God. Thus, Satan secretly brought idolatry back.

For this reason, God has raised up our emperors, i.e. Constantine V and his son Leo, the future Leo IV (775–80), His servants and the equals of the apostles, to remove the icons and destroy the demonic fortifications raised by the devil to prevent man from knowing God.

There follows a brief history of the doctrinal controversies settled by the

---

1 Gero 1977, 71.

2 The word "icon" here stands not only for portable portraits of the saints and the other holy persons but also for such pictures made in mosaic or fresco on the walls. In Byzantine Greek, *eikôn* simply means image, without further limitation.

3 The acts of the Council of Hiereia have not been preserved, but the *horos* can be reconstructed from the proceedings of the Seventh Ecumenical Council of Nicaea (787), where it is quoted and refuted. The Greek text of the *horos* is conveniently available in *Textus* 61 ff. An English translation, with discussions, is contained in Gero 1977, 53 ff. For a summary and partial translation, cf. Anastos 178 ff.

six ecumenical councils, from Nicaea (325) to Constantinople (680). It appears from this survey that he who makes a picture of a man and calls the man in the picture "Christ" is guilty of heresy. For either he thinks that he can circumscribe Christ's divine nature together with His human and so confuses Christ's two natures, which is monophysitism, or he says that he only wants to make a picture of Christ's flesh. But, in so doing, he gives the flesh of Christ a separate existence and adds a fourth person to the Trinity, and this is Nestorianism. The pictures of Christ that the painters produce are false pictures.

What, then, constitutes a true image of Christ? This question was answered by Christ Himself on the eve of His passion, when He took bread, blessed it and said, "This is my body," and distributed wine and said, "This is my blood." The bread and wine that pass from the realm of the common to that of the holy through the blessing of the priest constitute the only true image of the body of Christ. This image does not have the form of man and therefore does not provoke idolatrous practices.

It is further pointed out that there is no prayer that could transform the icons from mere matter into something holy.

The pictures of the Virgin, the saints and the prophets do not offer the doctrinal dilemma which makes the picture of Christ unacceptable. Yet they must be rejected. The craft of idol-making, which makes what is not present seem to be present, was invented by the pagans, as they had no hope of resurrection. It would be blasphemous to apply this illusionism to the saints. "How do they dare to depict, by means of vulgar pagan art, the Mother of God, [. . .] who is higher than the heavens and is more holy than the Cherubim? Or, are they not ashamed to depict with pagan art those who will reign together with Christ [. . .]?"[4] In short, the saints, living eternally with God, do not need the art of the pagans, who try in vain to reproduce life by means of dead matter.

To support their conclusions, the bishops quote from the Old and the New Testament and from the Fathers passages that warn against idolatry and underline the spiritual character of the Christian religion.

Finally, they pronounce a number of anathemas. In the context of this symposium, the most interesting is perhaps the sixteenth anathema. Here, those are declared anathema who depict the useless forms of the saints in lifeless and dumb icons, instead of reading the saints' Lives and painting living pictures of their virtues in their own souls, thereby raising themselves to a zeal equal to theirs[5].

Evidently, Constantine and his bishops were not interested in questioning the orthodox dogma, nor in changing the ideals of the Christian way of life. Their program was "Spiritual icons yes, material icons no!" The emperor probably thought that, by convening the Council of Hiereia, he had settled

[4] Gero 1977, 79.

[5] Cf. Ib. 91; Anastos 186.

the question of icon worship once and for all. He had a strong case, and his point of view had been accepted by no less than 338 bishops. This was a very large number, especially in view of the fact that by this time Byzantium had lost substantial parts of its territory through Arab expansion and the invasion of Slavs and Bulgars on the Balkan peninsula. Yet the attempt to abolish icon worship in Byzantium failed. Why? Let us take a look at the background.

The *horos* is certainly right in submitting that, originally, there was no specific Christian art. There is no indication that such an art existed prior to the third century[6]. Nor does it seem unfair to say that pictorial art was invented by the pagans. When, in the third century, a specific Christian art began to develop, this meant that the Christians adapted themselves to a pagan society in which art in many forms played an important part[7]. The process of adaptation accelerated in the fourth century, when the Christian Church and the Roman State came to terms with each other. Instead of meeting in churches disguised as private houses, the Christians could now gather freely in large, splendid basilicas. These impressive buildings were soon decorated with scenes from the Bible, and the martyria were correspondingly decorated with scenes from the lives of the martyrs[8]. From our point of view, the most important change was that the Christians also began to make portraits of the saints and the biblical figures. This innovation took place in the latter half of the fourth century[9]. Thus, if one regards heathen culture as Satan and associates religious images with idolatry, one might agree with the Council of Hiereia that Satan seemed to have reintroduced idolatry under the guise of Christianity.

Constantine V and the bishops at Hiereia were anxious to show that they were not the first to object to the introduction of Christian religious images. In the patristic florilegium incorporated in the *horos*, they quoted Eusebius (d. *c.* 340) as already pointing out the christological dilemma which constitutes the core of the *horos*. The Empress Constantia, wife of Licinius and step-sister of Constantine the Great, had asked Eusebius for a portrait of Christ. Eusebius declined, explaining to her the theological implications of her request. What sort of image did she have in mind? he asked. Was it a portrait of the true, unchanging Christ or a portrait of the servant whose shape He put on for our sake? (Cf. Phil. ii,5 ff.) No, Eusebius said, it could not be a portrait of the former, for no one has known the Father except the Son, nor will anyone know the Son properly except the Father who begot Him (cf. Matt. xi,27). Nor could it be a portrait of the latter, since the flesh of the servant was blended with the glory of the Godhead and His mortality was swallowed up by Life (cf. II Cor., 4). How could lifeless colors and outlines depict the splendors that made the disciples on Mount Tabor

---

[6] Cf. Kitzinger 1977, 19.
[7] Cf. Ib.
[8] Cf. Mango 22.
[9] Cf. Ib. 23.

fall upon their faces and confess that the sight was more than they could bear[10]? They also refer to Epiphanius of Salamis (d. 403) who, according to the *horos,* said that the Christians should remember God in their hearts and not by setting up images in the churches or in the resting-places of the saints; nor should they set up images in ordinary houses, for a Christian should not be distracted by his eyes and the wanderings of his thoughts[11]. They further quote a dictum ascribed to Amphilochius of Iconium (d. *c.* 395), namely, that "we do not engage in depicting on tablets the bodily appearance of the saints, by means of colors, because we do not need these; rather we imitate their conduct by [our] virtues"[12]. And Theodotus of Ancyra (d. *c.* 445) is quoted as saying that "we have received [the tradition that] the appearances of the saints should not be fashioned by means of material colors; rather we have been taught to perceive their virtues, as it were living images shown forth in writings about them, so that, by means of this, our zeal should be excited to emulate them"[13]. This statement reappears almost word for word in the sixteenth anathema. On the other hand, the bishops at Hiereia did not mention Bishop Julian of Adramyttion, who plays an important part in modern discussions because, in the fourth decade of the sixth century, he expressed concern about the presence of images and sculptures in the churches in a way that foreshadows the beginnings of the iconoclastic controversy two centuries later[14].

But, in general, the attitude to the development of an anthropomorphic Christian art does not seem to have been so hostile. To the troubled Julian of Adramyttion, Hypatius of Ephesus explained that the images could be tolerated as a useful means of helping the spiritually less advanced; he added that, personally, he did not delight in looking at them[15]. It is further worth noting that neither Basil the Great (d. 379) nor John Chrysostom (d. 407) denounced pictorial art, although they spoke about spiritual and living images, as the quotations in the *horos* show[16]. Moreover, the authenticity of some of the most iconoclastic quotations, especially in the case of Eusebius, seems to be open to some doubt[17], and it is also possible that the importance of certain other passages, cited by modern scholars to demonstrate the hostility of the early Church to religious art, has been somewhat exaggerated[18]. At any rate, none of the first five ecumenical councils, from Nicaea (325) to Constantinople (553), made any pronouncement concerning images. The reason for this reticence was apparently that the rise of Chris-

---

[10] Cf. Gero 1977, 85 f.; Anastos 183 f.

[11] Cf. Gero 1977, 81; Anastos 182. Unfortunately, Epiphanius does not explain what kind of images he has in mind; cf. n. 13.

[12] Gero 1977, 83.

[13] Ib. 84. Theodotus' compatriote Nilus (d. *c.* 430) may have taken a similar attitude, cf. Thümmel 17 f. Yet, to judge from the text reconstructed by Thümmel, 21, Nilus' main point was that a church built in honor of Christ and the martyrs should not be decorated with secular art.

[14] Cf. Lange 44 ff.; Baynes 226 ff.

[15] Cf. Lange 51; Baynes 228.

[16] Cf. Gero 1977, 82 f.

[17] Cf. Murray 326 ff.

[18] Cf. Ib. 319 ff.

tian art did not constitute a problem in itself. As long as the images did not play a significant role in the religious life of the people, they were rather harmless. But, in the middle of the sixth century, this situation began to change. At that time, the number of pictures of holy persons started to increase, and the images began to appear in contexts where they had not been known before[19]. The growing importance of the image of the Virgin Mary, recently discussed by Averil Cameron, may exemplify this. The Emperor Leo I (457–74) had already put up a picture in which he and his family appeared together with the Virgin in the Virgin's church at Blachernae. Justinian I (527–65) and Theodora had been depicted in a similar way on the curtains of Hagia Sophia. But, in the reign of Justin II (565–78), the image of the Virgin appeared on bronze weights, and in the reign of Maurice (582–602), the pagan Victoria was replaced by the Virgin and Child on seals. In 610, when the future emperor Heraclius sailed from Carthage to Constantinople, the image of the Virgin adorned the masts of his ships. In 626, when the Avars laid siege to Constantinople, the gates of the Theodosian wall were provided with representations of the Virgin for apotropaic purposes[20]. In the same period, we are told of so-called *acheiropoiêta,* images "not made by hand," i.e. miraculous imprints of the face of Jesus, pictures fallen from heaven and other images of supernatural origin. During the wars against Persia, such *acheiropoiêta* were used as banners in the same way as Constantine the Great had used the labarum. This development reached its peak in the first reign of Justin II (685–95), when, for the first time, Christ was represented on the Byzantine coins.

The increasing use of the icon as an official Christian symbol reflected a change in the religious life of individuals. Icons became common in private homes and were honored in a way in which hitherto only the image of the emperor had been honored, i.e. people bowed to them and lit candles and incense in front of them. People mistrusted doctors and feared their knives, not without reason. When they fell ill, they often preferred to consult the martyrs Cosmas and Damian or the martyr Artemius or other saints who were supposed to bring cures, i.e. they went to sleep in their churches, hoping that they would appear to them in a dream and cure them. But it also happened that the sick were cured by their private icons. For instance, we are told of a woman who fell ill but was cured when she scraped away a little paint from her icons of Cosmas and Damian, mixed it with water and drank it[21].

The new attitude to the icon changed the way in which the holy persons

---

[19] For a detailed analysis of this phenomenon, cf. Kitzinger 1954, 95 ff.

[20] These examples I owe to Cameron 97. For the rest of this paragraph, and for the following, I am mainly relying on Kitzinger 1954, 95 ff.

[21] Cf. Mansi XIII, 68 A–D. At the Council of Nicaea (787), this and similar stories were quoted in order to show that the icons were as holy as the relics and the cross.

were represented. As Kitzinger has demonstrated, Christian art became more abstract. Christ, the Virgin and the saints lost something of their solidity; they became elongated, thin, transparent, more spiritual and less corporeal[22]. In church, the central figure was represented in stark isolation, not unlike a statue of a god or a goddess in a Greek temple[23].

Thus, in the second half of the sixth century, the role of the icon began to change. Before the middle of the sixth century, the icons had been regarded primarily as artistic reminders of the fact that the saints had lived and worked and suffered here on earth. Now they rather expressed the beliefs that the saints were still living and accessible to man. The icons became channels, as it were, through which men could reach and associate with the holy[24]. Thereby the icons, or at least some of them, obviously ran the risk of being mixed up with the holy itself.

This was a sore point. The Jews, who seem to have returned to a strict observance of the Second Commandment at about the same time as the use of icons expanded within the Byzantine Empire[25], seized the opportunity of accusing the Christians of idolatry and violation of the Law of Moses. The well-known hagiographer Leontius of Neapolis in Cyprus, who lived in the first half and perhaps also the third quarter of the seventh century, replied that the Old Testament was not quite so hostile to religious images as the Jews maintained[26]. In support of this view, he quoted Exodus xx.18 and Ezekiel xli.18. But his main argument is that the Christians do not worship the material of which the icons are made but the holy persons which they represent. "When I am holding Christ's lifeless image," he says, "through it I think I am holding Christ and revering Him," and, "when we Christians hold an icon of Christ, or an icon of an apostle or a martyr, in our hands and kiss it with our lips, we think in our soul that we are holding Christ or His martyr"[27]. Thus, according to Leontius, when the Christian worships an icon, the icon itself melts away, as it were, and a purely spiritual meeting takes place between the worshiper and the holy person represented in the icon.

In another passage, Leontius says, "Man, created in God's image, is an image of God, especially the man who has received the indwelling of the Holy Spirit. Therefore I rightly honor and venerate the icon of God's servants and praise the dwelling of the Holy Spirit"[28]. Here, Leontius is speak-

---

[22] Cf. Kitzinger 1977, 103 ff.

[23] Cf. Ib. 105.

[24] Cf. Brown 19; Kitzinger 1954, 137.

[25] The chronology of the change in the Jewish attitude to figurative art is discussed by Kitzinger, 1954, 130, n. 204.

[26] Leontius' defense of the religious images was part of a major apology against the Jews, now lost. The section on the images was read at the Council of Nicaea (787), and has been preserved in the acts of this council. It can be studied most conveniently in PG 93, 1597 ff.; for an analysis of Leontius' arguments, cf. Baynes 230 ff.; Lange 61 ff. Lange also discusses the relation between the version read at Nicaea and the quotations appearing in the writings of John of Damascus.

[27] PG 93, 1600 C.

[28] Ib. 1604 CD. Cf. Gen. i,27 and I Cor. iii,16.

ing of two kinds of images, on the one hand, of the saints as living images of God and, on the other, of the material images of the saints, which are justified by the fact that the Holy Spirit has dwelt in the bodies of these men[29].

It is interesting to note that, in spite of his vigorous defense of icon worship, Leontius does not mention any icon in his famous biographies of John the Almsgiver and Symeon the Fool for the Sake of Christ, although he uses the word in a metaphorical sense; in the Life of John, he even quotes the Gospel according to St. John xx,29: "Blessed are those who have not seen and yet believe"[30]. In the Life of Symeon, he applies the concept of the saints and the saints' *Lives* as living images of virtue[31] to his own role as a hagiographer, saying that he who wants to teach virtue to others ought to set up his own life as an icon of virtuous acts but, finding himself unable to do this, he confines himself to describing the virtuous achievements of other, more perfect men[32]. It would seem then that Leontius regarded a man imitating Christ as the real Christian image, an image of the first class, so to speak, and the painted icon of a saint as a second-class image equivalent to a saint's *Life* but with a different function.

In addition to these and other arguments that are supposed to demonstrate that the icons are means, not goals, Leontius also says that God has shown his approval by letting the icons work miracles[33]. He does not, however, use the Incarnation as an argument for icon worship, nor would this argument have made any impression on the Jews to whom his apology was addressed.

Instead, the argument from the Incarnation was referred to at the council in Trullo (692). The famous canon 82 of this council[34] forbade artists to use the lamb as a means of representing Christ. Christ should be represented according to His human character, the canon stated. The lamb had foreboded Christ but, after the Incarnation had taken place, it would be wrong to stick to this ancient symbol, as if the Incarnation had never occurred. Unlike Leontius, canon 82 did not defend the icons against people who called them idols. Its aim was to remove an anachronistic religious symbol and to enjoin the artists to bring out the full meaning of the Incarnation. In

---

[29] According to Kitzinger, 1954, 140f., Leontius' use of Gen. i,27 reflects "an essentially Neoplatonic belief in the divine manifesting itself in a descending sequence of reflections. By implication at least, the work of the artist becomes an extension of the divine act of creation, a concept far removed from Early Christian indictments of the artist as a deceiver." One might add that this concept of the role of the artist is also far removed from Plato's theory of art.

[30] Léontios 387, 38f.

[31] This idea, which appears as early as the writings of the Cappadocian Fathers, had become a hagiographic commonplace, cf. Lange 34ff., 90, n. 37.

[32] Cf. Rydén 1963, 121. By contrast, painted icons play a conspicuous role in the *Life of Andreas the Fool for the Sake of Christ,* cf. PG 111, 628ff. The author of this *Vita* dates Andreas and himself in the fifth or sixth centuries, although indirect evidence shows that he lived in the tenth century and that Andreas is a fictitious saint (cf. Rydén 1978).

[33] Cf. PG 93, 1601 CD.

[34] Cf. Mansi XI, 977 Eff.; Engl. transl. in Alexander 45.

fact, the canon appears to have been rather superfluous, since Christ had already been represented according to His human character for centuries. But it is interesting to note that this canon was written at the same time as the bust of Christ appeared on the Byzantine coins and in a period in which there was a reaction against the abstract style that had dominated Christian art since the middle of the sixth century[35]. In contemporary art, Christ appears as a man with the harmonious proportions of the classical ideal; at the same time he radiates something inscrutable and divine. It was toward the end of the seventh century that the prototype of the Pantokrator image was created, the best examples of which give an overwhelming impression of the meeting of the divine with the human in the body of Christ[36].

In the third decade of the eighth century, this development was interrupted by iconoclastic reaction. It all started, it is said, with Bishop Constantine of Nacoleia taking measures against icon worship in his see in Phrygia because of the ban on graven images and likenesses in Exodus xx.4–5. Other bishops in Asia Minor followed suit. Patriarch Germanos I tried in vain to bring them to reason. When Emperor Leo III himself ordered the image of Christ to be removed from above the entrance of the Great Palace in Constantinople, the iconoclastic controversy broke out. Germanos, who resigned in 730, describes the preliminaries of the conflict in the following way: "There appeared a certain bishop of Nacoleia, a small town in the eparchy of Phrygia, a man not renowned for his learning and reason, although in his folly he dreamt of demonstrating his insight. Reading the divinely inspired Scriptures, he stared open-mouthed at the bare letter and tried to introduce new false doctrines which are contrary to what has been piously proclaimed, and arm himself to rise against the traditions of the Fathers"[37]. In Germanos' account, Constantine of Nacoleia appears as a narrow-minded fundamentalist unable to read the prohibition in Exodus xx.4–5 in the light of the historical context and ignorant of the patristic tradition. Emperor Leo III was stigmatized in a similar way. The iconophile chronicler Theophanes Confessor says that Leo came from Germanicea, which implies that he was a native of Syria, "but," Theophanes adds, "as a matter of fact he came from Isauria"[38]. Isauria was a mountain district in south-eastern Asia Minor, famous for its robbers and stone-cutters. If I understand him correctly, Theophanes is saying that, physically speaking, Leo was a native of Syria, although in spiritual matters he was a rude Isaurian[39]. Thus, in the opinion of the defenders of icon worship, the icono-

---

[35] Cf. Kitzinger 1977, 120 f.

[36] Ib. 122.

[37] PG 93, 77 A. This translation differs to a certain degree from that of Gero 1973, 88.

[38] Theophanes 391,5 f.

[39] My interpretation differs from the current explanation, according to which either the words "but as a matter of fact he was from Isauria" have been interpolated or Theophanes mixed up Leo III with the Emperor Leontius (695–98), who was an Isaurian. Ib. 407,17 ff., is a similar case. There, Germanos is supposed to have told Leo that he had heard that the attack on the icons would

clastic reaction was a question of lack of education and understanding. But, uneducated or not, the iconoclasts seem to have been genuinely alarmed by the growing importance of the icons. They failed to see how this development could be reconciled with the Second Commandment. They had the feeling that Christianity was being invaded by pagan materialism, that the icons were forming an impenetrable wall between God and man.

The iconophiles did not share this feeling. According to them, the Old Testament prohibition referred to the making of idols and, in their opinion, the Christian images were portraits of real historical persons, not idols. Far from tying the mind of the Christian to material things the icon reminded him of the works of the saints and urged him to follow their example. Moreover, in their view, the icon was somehow related to its prototype, so that the veneration shown for the icon did not stay there but was transmitted to the person represented. Consequently the iconophiles could accuse the iconoclasts of showing disrespect for the saints.

The iconophiles did not try to depict God himself. In this respect, orthodox Christian art differed from the art of the pagans. But, according to Christian belief, God had appeared here on earth in the guise of a man, and they did not see why this man could not be depicted. On the contrary, to refrain from depicting him was, to their mind, tantamount to denying the Incarnation.

The answer[40] of the iconoclasts to the argument from the Incarnation, which was developed by John of Damascus and became increasingly important during the controversy, was the christological dilemma pointed out by Constantine V and the bishops at Hiereia, namely, that Christ was not only man but also God. Since he was both God and man and the divine is beyond representation, a conventional portrait cannot do justice to the figure of Christ. This argument was applied to the images of the saints as well. According to the iconoclasts, the holiness of the saints could not be represented, and the images of the saints therefore give a false impression of their prototypes. In the eyes of the iconoclasts, art was something worldly that should not be allowed to interfere with the holy.

Thus, we have reached the point where we asked why iconoclasm failed. The answer appears to be implied in what has already been said. The iconoclasts of the first generation based their opposition on the Old Testament's prohibition against the making of graven images and likenesses. But a move-

---

come in the reign of Konon, not in the reign of Leo, and Leo is supposed to have answered: "In fact, my baptismal name is Konon." This story, which also appears in the libel called *Adversus Constantinum Caballinum*, PG 95, 336 C, does not seem to have been correctly understood by modern scholars. To my mind, it is simply based on the pun Konon–*eikonon* and is typical of the way in which the iconophile authors treated their opponents.

[40] It should be borne in mind that this brief summary is based on modern reconstructions of the conflict. The exact order in which the arguments were put forward and refuted is very imperfectly known.

ment that was based on the Law and not on Grace was unlikely to meet with lasting success in a Christian society. To people who had become used to icons, iconoclasm must have seemed out of focus and hard to understand[41]. As we have seen, the iconoclasts were soon obliged to produce more up-to-date arguments. When the iconoclasts accused the Christians of having learnt pictorial art from the pagans, they were undoubtedly right. But even if pagan artistic tradition had been adopted by the Christians, the substance of their art was Christian. As Christ's second coming was delayed and Christianity acquired a history, it was, in view of the cultural background, quite natural that the Christians should create an art on their own. It is understandable that the otherworldliness of the first Christians could not be maintained indefinitely. To a modern observer, it seems remarkable that the iconoclasts of the first generation did not limit themselves to trying to put an end to apparent abuse instead of attacking the images as such[42]. On one point, however, the iconoclasts yielded. At the Council of Hagia Sophia in 815, they withdrew their accusation that icon worship was idolatry.

The christological objection, according to which the bread and wine of the Eucharist constitute the only true picture of the body of Christ, was more serious. This objection was hard to refute, as it was based on an orthodox doctrine and conformed with the fact that the Early Church had celebrated the Eucharist in a milieu void of pictures. Admittedly, there was something Early Christian, something sublime and pure about iconoclastic theory. But this was also its weak point. The iconoclasts made the religious feeling the slave of the intellect. They failed to see that there was a need for greater visualization, for something less mysterious than the bread and wine. According to the iconophiles, God had complied with this need by letting Himself be incarnated. Moreover, the Incarnation implied that God had accepted matter and abolished the dualism between the material and the spiritual worlds which had been such a problem in antiquity. The iconophiles therefore did not see why the artists should not follow God's example and on their part try to visualize the Incarnation. On the contrary, it seemed natural to them to take one further step and depict Christ enthroned in His heavenly glory. Thus, the beholder got a strong impression of Christ's presence. He had a feeling of being a part of the spiritual cosmos.

The iconophiles were of the opinion that the picture complements the word, as sight complements hearing. Hearing does not exclude sight; why then should the word exclude the picture? Rather, some iconophiles said,

---

[41] Patriarch Germanos, Letter to Thomas, Bishop of Claudioupolis, PG 98, 184 C: "But now a large number of people are in no small commotion about this matter."

[42] According to Beck, 13 ff., the iconoclasts were moderate at first and became radical only because the iconophiles over-reacted. Yet, if the original aim of the iconoclasts just was to stop excessive worship, why did Leo III remove the image of Christ from above the entrance of the palace?

the picture is superior to the word[43], just as, according to an old saying[44], sight is superior to hearing. At any rate, it is clear that the icon complements the *Vita* in more than one way. If you cannot read or if you have no time for reading a *Vita,* you can always look at the icon of the saint in question. Moreover, the *Vita* also complements the icon with regard to content. In principle, the *Vita* is a historical work. In it, the saint's life and good works are described. But, in the icon, he also appears in his present heavenly state, standing close to God and having God's ear; he enjoys *parrêsia,* as it was called. Thanks to his privileged position, he can plead the cause of the beholder before God, if the beholder asks for it. This gave the icon an appeal which at last defeated the iconoclasts' radical spirituality.

After the end of the iconoclastic controversy (843), the icons began to reappear in the churches and gradually claimed more space, according to a sophisticated, hierarchical plan. In the classical Middle Byzantine church, the holy persons looked at the visitor from the cupolas, the vaults and the walls in a way which gave him the impression of communicating with them and being integrated into their spiritual world[45]. Meanwhile, the altar was withdrawn from its previous advanced position into the apse. The chancel screen became increasingly opaque[46]. At last the iconostasis rose like a wall between the sanctuary and the rest of the church[47]. This did not mean, however, that what the iconoclasts had regarded as the only true image of Christ was superseded by the icons. It was rather that the different roles of the Eucharist and the icons become more distinct. The mysterious character of the Eucharist was further underlined, whereas the icons responded to the need for the visual, immediate and easily understandable.

Bibliography

TJhS The journal of theological studies

Alexander, P., 1958, *The Patriarch Nicephorus of Constantinople.* Oxford.

Anastos, M., 1955, The argument for iconoclasm as presented by the iconoclastic council of 754. *Late classical and mediaeval studies in honor of Albert Friend, Jr.,* ed. K. Weitzmann. Princeton.

Baynes, N., 1955, The icons before iconoclasm. Baynes, *Byzantine studies and other essays.* London.

Beck, H.-G., 1975, *Von der Fragwürdigkeit der Ikone.* Bayerische Akademie der Wissenschaften, Philosophisch-historische Klasse. Sitzungsberichte, 7. München.

---

[43] This point was especially stressed by Patriarch Nicephorus I (806–15), cf. Lange 209 f., Beck 16 ff.

[44] The most famous instance is Herodotus, *History* i.8,2, but, as Lange 15 points out, the iconophiles themselves did not refer it to the classical Greek authors.

[45] For the system of Middle Byzantine church decoration, cf. Demus 14 ff.

[46] Cf. Mathews 179.

[47] The last step in this development was taken in the fourteenth century, Lazareff, 139, or perhaps already in the twelfth, cf. Chatzidakis 344.

Brown, P., MacCormack, Sabine, 1975, Artifices of eternity. *The New York review of books,* 22, 20 Feb.

Cameron, A., 1978, The Theotokos in sixth-century Constantinople. *JThS,* 29.

Chatzidakis, M., 1973, Ikonostas. *Reallexikon zur byzantinischen Kunst,* 3, ed. K. Wessel and M. Restle. Stuttgart.

Demus, O., 1948, *Byzantine mosaic decoration.* London.

Gero, S., 1973, *Byzantine iconoclasm during the reign of Leo III, with particular attention to the Oriental sources.* Louvain.

— 1977, *Byzantine iconoclasm during the reign of Constantine V, with particular attention to the Oriental Sources.* Louvain.

Herodotus, 1927, *History,* ed. C. Hude. Oxford.

Kitzinger, E., 1954, The cult of images in the age before iconoclasm. *Dumbarton Oaks Papers,* 8.

— 1977, *Byzantine art in the making.* London.

Lange, G., 1968, *Bild und Wort.* Würzburg.

Lazareff, V., 1964, Trois fragments d'épistyles peintes et le templon byzantin. *Deltion tês christianikês archaiologikês hetaireias,* ser. 4, 3.

Léontios de Néapolis, 1974, *Léontios de Néapolis, Vie de Syméon le Fou et Vie de Jean de Chypre,* ed. commentée par A. Festugière en collaboration avec L. Rydén. Institut Français d'archéologie de Beyrouth. Bibliothèque archéologique et histologique, 95. Paris.

Mango, C., 1972, *The art of the Byzantine empire. 312–1453.* Sources and Documents in the History of Art Series, ed. H. Janson. Englewood Cliffs.

Mansi, J., 1759 ff., *Sacrorum conciliorum nova et amplissima collectio.* Florence.

Mathews, T., 1971, *The early churches of Constantinople.* University Park and London.

PG, 1857 ff., *Patrologiae cursus completus, Series graeca.* Rec. J. Migne. Paris.

Murray, Ch., 1977, Art and the early Church. *JThS,* 28.

Rydén, L. (ed.), 1963, *Das Leben des heiligen Narren Symeon von Leontios von Neapolis.* Uppsala.

— 1978, The date of the Life of Andreas Salos. *Dumbarton Oaks Papers,* 32 (in press).

Textus, 1969, *Textus byzantinos ad iconomachiam pertinentes,* ed. H. Hennephof. Leyden.

Theophanes, 1963, *Chronographia,* ed. C. de Boor. Leipzig.

Thümmel, H., 1978, Neilos von Ankyra über die Bilder. *Byzantinische Zeitschrift,* 71.

Nut – Himmelsgöttin – Baumgöttin – Lebensgeberin

Von JAN BERGMAN

Verschiedene Umstände haben gemeinsam dazu beigetragen, dass der Ägyptologe sich in einer besonders günstigen Lage befindet, wenn es um das Studium einer reichen religiösen Symbolwelt innerhalb einer alten Hochkultur geht.

Erstens zeichnet sich die alte ägyptische Kultur schon von Anfang an dadurch aus, dass sie sich für das Wechselspiel von Bild und Schrift besonders interessiert hat. Davon zeugen sowohl der dauernde Bildcharakter der Hieroglyphenschrift wie auch das Zusammenspiel von Texten und Bildern in den Ritualszenen der Tempel sowie in den Totenbüchern und Jenseitsführern.

Zweitens konnte sich die mehr als 3 000 Jahre dauernde altägyptische Kultur dank der geographischen Lage einer ungestörteren Entwicklung als die Nachbarkulturen des Nahen Orients erfreuen.

Drittens hat die für Ägypten eigene Konzentration auf das Jenseitsleben eine überaus reich entwickelte Vorstellungswelt mit Monumenten bleibender Art verbunden. Die Nekropolen waren ja als Wohnungen für die Ewigkeit gebaut.

Viertens haben die ungewöhnlich günstigen ökologischen Verhältnisse im Niltal dazu beigetragen, dass auch Dokumente und Gegenstände nicht so dauerhafter Art, vor allem Papyri und allerlei Grabausrüstungen, uns in erstaunlichem Umfang bewahrt sind.

Hier können wir natürlich nur einige kleine Einblicke in diese seltsam reiche und komplizierte ägyptische Symbolwelt geben. Beim Suchen einer für das Symposium geeigneten Symbolsphäre habe ich einige mit „Leben" zusammenhängende Vorstellungen ausgewählt. „Leben" stellt ja nicht nur ein zentrales Thema in jeder Religion dar sondern kann gerade als Hauptthema der ägyptischen Religiosität gelten, die ihre Gedankenarbeit wie auch ihre materiellen Hilfsmittel und alle hochentwickelte Kunstfertigkeit dem Zusammenhang Leben-Tod-Leben gewidmet hat.

„Leben" wird von Anfang an bis in die Spätzeit mit dem Anch-Zeichen[1], das auch in frühchristlichem Zusammenhang als „Henkelkreuz"[2] bekannt ist, wiedergegeben. Seine Ausgestaltung geben – mit bloss kleiner Varia-

[1] Über Sinn und Gebrauch des Anch-Zeichens orientieren die Artikel „Lebensschleife" in RÄRG 418 ff., „Anchzeichen" in Helck 1,268 ff. Cf. weiter die Sonderforschungen Fischer 1972, 5 ff.; 1973, 16 ff.; Baines 1 ff.

[2] Für Henkelkreuz-crux ansata, cf. Cramer, 1 ff., und Doresse 24 ff.

tion – sowohl das protodynastiche Libationsgefäss wie auch die ptolemäische Opferplatte (als zentrales Zeichen) auf unserer Taf. 1 an. Wie dieses Zeichen ursprünglich zu erklären ist, bleibt umstritten. Wahrscheinlich stellt es einen Knoten oder eine Art Gürtel dar, wozu die sogenannte Isis-Schleife (oder Isis-Blut)[3] eine ausführlichere Variante ausmacht.

Als Symbol eines gesteigerten Lebens, d.h. eines übermenschlichen, göttlichen Lebens, finden wir das Anch-Zeichen in verschiedenen Zusammenhängen und Verbindungen, natürlich auch als Amulette. Als „Herren des Lebens" tragen die Götter das Anch-Zeichen in der Hand, was später auf die Könige übergegangen ist[4]. Aus der Namensgebung im Alten Reiche hat Junker „den Lebendigen" als gewöhnliches Götterepitheton belegen wollen[5]. Im wichtigen Spruch 80 der Sargtexte, wo eine imponierende Schu-Theologie entwickelt wird[6], trägt Schu die Bezeichnung „derjenige, dessen Name Anch (Leben) ist". Dieser Gedanke wird – wie Winter trefflich ausgeführt hat[7] – in den griechisch-römischen Tempeln breit weiterentwickelt, wobei die Verbindung von Anch-, Djed- und Uas-Zeichen als Bezeichnung des Opfers originell interpretiert wird. Als Trenner von Himmel und Erde hat Schu die Entstehung von Licht und Leben ermöglicht, und als Himmelsstütze ist er der Erhalter des Kosmos, der von Licht und Leben ernährt wird. Das Morgenritual der Tempel befestigt diese kosmische Ordnung, welche in fast unzähligen schönen Sonnenhymnen lebhaft beschrieben und gelobt wird. Die innige Verbindung von Licht und Leben lässt besonders die Sonnengötter als Lebensschöpfer und Lebensspender hervortreten. Wohl bekannt sind die zärtlichen Amarna-Szenen, in denen die Strahlen des Aton, in Hände mit dem Anch-Zeichen ausmündend, dem Pharao und seiner Königin das Licht-Leben überbringen.

Absichtlich soll in der Fortsetzung nicht das Anch-Zeichen als statisches Symbol für „Leben" – etwa „das ewige Leben", das sich nicht verändert – in den Blickpunkt treten. Mehr kongenial mit der dynamischen Natur des sich bewegenden und verwandelnden Lebens dürfte ein Studium der wichtigsten Lebensprozesse sein. Das bedeutet, dass wir uns mit dem Vorstellungskomplex der Lebensgebung beschäftigen wollen, und zwar so, dass teils das Werden des Lebens, die Geburt des neuen Lebens und ihre Vorbereitung, teils das Meiden von Unterbrechungen dieses Lebens, d.h. die Überbringung von Lebensmitteln, unsere Aufmerksamkeit auf sich ziehen werden.

Wenden wir uns zuerst einem alten Kultgerät zu! Dem ganzen kultischen Handeln, das im alten Ägypten besonders reich entwickelt war und das wir in den späten Tempelanlagen in Details studieren können, könnte all-

---

[3] Cf. RÄRG s.v. Isisblut, 332f.; Westendorf 144ff.

[4] Cf. Fischer 1973, bes. 23ff.

[5] Cf. Junker 1954, 32f.

[6] Cf. de Buck 1ff.; cf. auch Bergman 1970a, 54ff., 74ff.

[7] Cf. Winter, bes. 76ff.

gemein als Ziel die Lebensgebung und Lebensbewahrung zugeschrieben werden. Ganz besonders gilt diese Charakterisierung dem funerären Kontext, wo das Leben als speziell bedroht aufgefasst wurde. Zum Grabkult gehört offenbar das protodynastische Libationsgefäss (cf. Taf. 1, Fig. 1 a–b), das vor 60 Jahren in einer thebanischen Nekropole gefunden wurde und sich jetzt im Metropolitan Museum befindet[8]. Hier hat man sowohl sinnvoll als auch handgreiflich – diese Eigenschaften sind für ein wirksames Kultsymbol nötig – die Vorstellung von Lebensgebung ausgestaltet. Dieses Kultgerät, das zum Begiessen mit Wasser bestimmt war – gleichgültig, ob es sich um Libation oder Reinigung handelte, – ist als Monogramm von zwei Hieroglyphen ausgeführt. Und zwar ist dies die Verbindung von Anch-Zeichen – hier in einer archaischen, detaillierteren Form dargestellt – und von ,,Ka-Zeichen" (was mit ,,Geist, Persönlichkeit" aber auch mit ,,Nahrung" wiedergegeben werden kann). Hayes hat vorgeschlagen, hierin eine originelle Namensschreibung zu sehen, besonders da ein Beamter namens Anch-Kait(?) in der Regierung des Königs Den (1. Dynaste) belegt ist. Wenn auch die Möglichkeit einer solchen Deutung nicht zu verneinen ist, dürfte es dennoch klar sein, dass der primäre Sinn der besonderen Ausgestaltung des Gerätes gerade derjenige der Lebensgebung ist. In der vorliegenden künstlerisch ausgeformten Zusammenstellung der beiden Zeichen dienen die beiden Arme des Ka-Zeichens offenbar dazu, den Geber/Nehmer des Lebens anzugeben. Das Wasser, das in das Gefäss gegossen wurde, sollte das Gerät ausfüllen und somit die Szene der Lebensgebung lebendig machen, um danach durch den Griff des Anch-Zeichens auszulaufen und dem Toten/dem Kultdiener diese kultisch verwirklichte Lebensgebung zu vermitteln[9]. Dabei könnte natürlich auch das Ka-Zeichen davon zeugen, dass diese Handlung besonders dem Ka des Verstorbenen/des Agierenden zugute kommen sollte.

Absichtlich habe ich in der gegebenen Interpretation die Frage des Agierenden offen gelassen. Im kultischen Interaktionsprozess sind nämlich Geber und Nehmer nicht so scharf von einander getrennt sondern – tiefer gesehen – durch ein und dieselbe wechselseitige Handlung mit einander verbunden. Wenn auch in unserem konkreten Fall Ka wohl in erster Stelle als Geber aufzufassen ist, kann er gut in einer späteren Phase – oder in einer früheren, als Bedingung der Lebensgebung – als Nehmer fungieren[10].

---

[8] Das Gerät ist z.B. Hayes 43 Fig. 31, abgebildet. Cf. weiter die ausführliche Behandlung Fischer 1972, 5ff.

[9] Fischer, 1972, 34, vergleicht mit dem später belegten Verfahren bei den sogenannten Horusstelen, z.B. der Metternichstele, deren magische Sprüche vom übergegossenen Wasser aufgesogen wurden und so dank dem Wasser ihre gezielte Wirkungskraft erreichen sollten.

[10] Mit Hinweis auf einige protodynastische Amtssiegel, welche beim Titel ,,Einfanger des Ach" (*ḏḥn̆ ꜣḫ*) die Zeichen für Ach und Ka in ähnlicher Weise zusammenstellen wie die Zeichen für Anch und Ka auf unserem Gerät kombiniert sind (cf. Kaplony 3, Taf. 78 Nr. 296, Taf. 79 Nr. 299 usw.), könnte man auch hier die Deutung ,,Einfangen des Lebens" (*ḏḥn ʿnḫ*) erwägen.

In diesem Zusammenhang sind für die Deutungsmöglichkeiten zwei Umstände besonders zu beachten, teils die Richtung des Anch-Zeichens, teils die enge Beziehung, die in Ägypten zwischen Libation und Lustration vorliegt.

Man hat beobachtet, dass in den früheren Phasen der ägyptischen Kulturentwicklung beim Darreichen des Anch-Zeichens der Griff dem Nehmer zugewendet werden konnte, während in der klassischen Zeit die Götter zwar beim Tragen das Zeichen am Henkel halten, beim Darreichen aber mit wenigen Ausnahmen den Henkel der Nase des Königs nähern, so dass das Leben eingeatmet werden kann. Wenn nun beide Richtungen in der Frühzeit möglich waren, ist somit eine doppelte Deutung bei unserem Gefäss möglich[11].

Auch die enge Beziehung zwischen Libation und Lustration[12], von der später Texte und Darstellungen deutlich zeugen, dürfte eine solche doppelte Interpretationsmöglichkeit nahelegen. Bei der Reinigung besprengt man sich oft selbst, wenn auch z. B. die Szenen, welche die sogenannte ,,Taufe des Pharao" darstellen, Götter als Reiniger-Beleber des Pharao durch einen Strom von Anch- und Uas-Zeichen auftreten lassen. In ähnlicher Weise dürfte der älteste Sohn/der Ka-Priester im funerären Kult agiert haben. Aus den vielen Reinigungstexten, die von der tiefgehenden Wirkung des mit göttlichen Kräften gefüllten Wassers reden, wählen wir folgenden aus: ,,Ich reinige dich mit diesem Wasser allen Lebens und Heils, aller Gesundheit und aller Freude" (Naville Taf. 63). Ganz in Übereinstimmung mit dem Wortlaut dieses Textes wird dieses wirksame Wasser in den Reinigungsszenen geläufig gerade mit Strahlen von wechselnden Anch- und Uas-Zeichen – etwa als ,,heiliges/machtvolles Lebenswasser" – wiedergegeben.

Mit diesen Andeutungen müssen wir uns hier begnügen und zusammenfassend feststellen, dass unser Anch-Gefäss als evidentes Symbol der Lebensgebung dasteht, wobei vermutlich Ka besonders betont wird. Wer aber als ursprünglicher Geber des Lebens gilt, sagt dieses Gefäss nicht aus. In einer Gruppe von spätzeitlichen Opferplatten aus Achmim (cf. Taf. 1 Fig. 2) – etwa 3 000 Jahre später als unser Gefäss! – können wir dank der Seitenszenen eine Antwort finden. Zu dem mit diesen Darstellungen verbundenen Thema kommen wir aber unten zurück. Wir wollen hier nur feststellen, dass das hier erscheinende zum Libationsgefäss verwandelte Lebenszeichen, aus dessen Henkel Wasser gegossen wird, mehrmals schon im Neuen Reiche zu belegen ist[13]. Anch kann vereinzelt auch personifiziert auftreten, wobei seine Hände Libationsgefässe halten[14].

---

[11] Zu bemerken ist, dass beim Schreiben des Namens Anch-kai(?) in den Amtssiegeln (cf. Kaplony 3, Taf. 73 Nr. 276 A, Taf. 74 Nr. 276B, Taf. 79 Nr. 298) das Anch-Zeichen in der entgegengesetzten Richtung dargestellt ist. Für Belege der beiden Richtungen beim Darreichen des Anch-Zeichens cf. Brunner 71.

[12] Cf. RÄRG s. v. Reinigung, 633 ff.

[13] Cf. Jéquier 1922, 137 ff.

[14] Cf. Fischer 1972, 35 Fig. 9.

Es gibt eine ägyptische Gottheit, die in unserem Zusammenhang von besonderem Interesse ist, und zwar – wie der Titel sagt – die Göttin Nut. Wenn Schu oben als "derjenige, dessen Name Anch (Leben) ist" vorgestellt wurde, lässt sich diese Tatsache gut mit Nut als der Lebensgeberin *par excellence* vereinen. Die Trennung von Himmel und Erde, die als die hauptsächliche Leistung des Gottes Schu gilt, wird geläufig mythologisch ausgelegt: es handelt sich um den Sohn Schu, der die in Coitus vereinigten Eltern Nut und Geb auseinanderbringt und so als ,,Leben" ins Licht hervortritt. Als Mutter des ,,Lebens" steht so Nut als Lebensgeberin da. Und der Sohn Schu – ob als Lebenslicht oder als Lebenshauch verstanden – ist enger mit seiner Mutter-Himmel als mit seinem Vater-Erde verbunden.

Ehe wir auf zwei Vorstellungskomplexe näher eingehen, die Nut mit den beiden wichtigen Lebensprozessen, die oben angegeben worden sind, eng verbinden, ist eine kurze Darstellung dieser Göttin am Platz, wobei solche Züge ihres Wesens besonders beachtet werden sollen, die mit den folgenden Ausführungen zusammengehören können.

Nut ist vorzüglich als Himmelsgöttin bekannt. Als solche hat sie ,,die Erde und alle Dinge in ihren Armen beschlossen", sagt ein Pyramidentext (Pyr. 782 d), wobei hinzugefügt wird, dass sie ,,den König als einen unvergänglichen Stern, der in ihr ist, gesetzt hat" (782 e). Eine alte Benennung der Nut *ẖ3b3ś* wird demnach als ,,Eine mit Tausend Seelen" gedeutet, da die Seelen der Toten als Sterne am Himmel weiterlebend vorgestellt wurden[15]. Wie die Sterne dorthin gelangen, sagt ein später Text: ,,Sie gehen in den Mund (scil. der Himmelsgöttin) ein und kommen wieder aus ihrer Scheide hervor"[16]. Nach Amduat erscheint die Sonne am Morgen ,,zwischen den Schenkeln der Nut"[17]. Nut trägt als ihre gewöhnlichste Bezeichnung ,,Nut, die Grosse, welche die Götter gebiert" oder ,,Nut, die Mutter der Götter". Eine Sondervorstellung, die ihre Fruchtbarkeit hervorhebt und die seit dem Neuen Reiche zu belegen ist, lässt Nut als ,,Mutterschwein, das seine Ferkel gebiert und wieder verschlingt" erscheinen[18]. Bekannt ist das Nutbild im Kenotaph Sethos' I. in Abydos[19], das ausdrücklich diese Funktionen der Göttin darstellt und beschreibt. Auch am Ende des Amduat liegt ein Himmelsbuch vor, das ,,Nut-buch" genannt werden kann und das auch an der Decke der Sargkammer Ramses' IV. zu finden ist[20]. Der Umstand, dass Nut sowohl als Taghimmel als auch als Nachthimmel betrachtet wird, gibt ihr eine doppelte Reihe von Schwangerschafts- und Geburtsrollen. Diese Feststellung kann einen geeigneten Hintergrund für die Behandlung des ersten Vorstellungskomplexes der Lebensgebung ausmachen.

---

15 Cf. Bergman 1970, 31 Anm. 2; 35 Anm. 1.
16 Mariette Taf. 46.
17 Jéquier 1894, 136; cf. Hornung 3,24 Z. 278.
18 Cf. Grapow 45 ff.; Bergman 1974, 91 ff.
19 Cf. Frankfort Taf. 81.
20 Hornung 1963 f., 194 f.

1. *Nut, die Lebensgeberin, als Himmelsgöttin und Mutter des Toten*

Die kurze Übersicht hat uns die Himmelsgöttin Nut als Gebärerin der Sonne vorgestellt. Dies bedeutet, dass sie neben der kosmogonischen Beziehung auf Schu vor allem als Mutter des Re dasteht. Dass diese Rolle für den Totenkult äusserst wichtig war, da der Gestorbene wünschte, ,,am Tage hervorzugehen wie Re", ist selbstverständlich. Der Wiedergeburt Res sollte der Tote dank allerlei funerären Ritualen teilhaftig sein. Das erste Ziel dieser umfassenden Zeremonien war jedoch die Osiriswerdung. Als Osiris NN sollte der Tote vor Osiris als schon Gerechtfertigter beim Totengericht in der Unterwelt vorgestellt werden. Auch für die Verwirklichung dieser Rolle war Nut für den Toten die wichtigste Gegenspielerin. Als ,,Mutter der Götter" war sie nämlich nach der erweiterten heliopolitanischen Göttergenealogie, der klassischen Götterenneade, die Mutter des Osiris, wie auch die des Seth, der Isis und der Nephthys. Sowohl für die Teilnahme am Jenseitsleben, wo Osiris die Zentralgestalt war, wie auch für die Beteiligung am Diesseitsleben, dessen Hauptvertreter Re war, machte für den Toten die innigste Beziehung zu Nut, als Vereinigung mit ihr und Geburt aus ihr verstanden, eine notwendige Bedingung aus.

Dieser Vorstellungskomplex hat in mehreren Hinsichten den Totenkult geprägt, wie vor allem Rusch aufgezeigt hat[21]. Hören wir die Zeugnisse einiger Texte! ,,Nut, breite dich über deinen Sohn. Schütze ihn vor Seth. Schirme ihn, Nut. Du bist gekommen, dass du deinen Sohn schützest. Du bist gekommen, damit du diesen Grossen schirmst" (Pyr. 777). ,,Deine Mutter Nut hat sich über dich gebreitet. Sie schützt dich vor allen schlechten Dingen. Sie schirmt dich vor allem Übel, denn du bist der Grösste unter ihren Kindern" (Pyr. 825). Diese Aussagen, die in mehreren Varianten schon in der ältesten Totentextsammlung, d. h. in den Pyramidentexten, vorliegen, behandeln nicht ausdrücklich die Geburt sondern stellen primär die Göttin als Schützerin und Schirmerin des Toten und als Garantin für sein Leben im allgemeinen dar. ,,Nut, du warst ein Ach, du warst eine Macht schon im Leibe deiner Mutter Tefnut, bevor du geboren warst. Schirme diesen NN, damit er nicht stirbt" (Pyr. 779). Dieser Text verankert die Leben schützende Funktion tief im Wesen der Göttin. Nut ist selbst schon pränatal, d. h. ursprünglich, ihrer tiefsten Natur nach, ,,der grosse Ach" (vgl. Pyr. 1), wobei Ach, der höchste Rang unter den Lebenden in der Unterwelt, sehr eng mit dem Leben in höchster Potenz verbunden ist. Hier wäre es verlockend, eine Nut-Ach-Achet-Theologie – Achet ,,Horizont" kann als feminine Form des Ach verstanden werden – zu entwickeln, von der m. E. mehrere funeräre Texte zeugen. Wir müssen uns jedoch hier damit begnügen, diesen Zusammenhang nur angedeutet zu haben[22]. Zu

---

[21] Rusch 1 ff.

[22] Cf. Englund 1978, bes. 30 f., 40. Da E. in diesem Teil ihrer Achuntersuchungen, deren Fortsetzung vorbereitet wird, *ꜣḫt*-,,Horizont" nicht näher behandelt, tritt diese Nut-Ach-Achet-Theologie, die sich indessen mit

bemerken ist weiter, dass der zitierte Passus nur die erste Strophe einer längeren Textpartie ausmacht, in der die zweite Strophe diese Natur der Göttin mit ihrem Namen verbindet und die dritte – und letzte – in folgendes Gebet ausmündet: „Verkläre diesen NN in dir, damit er nicht stirbt!“[23] Diese Verklärung, die wortgetreu mit „Ach-Machung“ wiederzugeben ist, gibt den Tiefsinn der besonderen Lebensgebung der Göttin Nut an. Es geht nicht nur um einen Wiedergewinn des gewöhnlichen Lebens sondern um die Gewinnung des neuen gesteigerten Lebens eines Ach, das Nut als „die grosse Ach“ am sichersten schenken kann.

Wenn auch die Geburt in den zitierten Texten nicht direkt hervorgehoben wird, handelt es sich jedoch offenbar tiefer gesehen um die Geburt aus Nut. Die Verklärung soll in Nut, d. h. in ihrem Leib, verwirklicht werden, und der Tote wird geläufig als ihr Sohn bezeichnet, ja, er tritt als ihr Lieblingssohn hervor. Auf dem Sarge des Teti wird sogar versichert, dass Nut den Pharao mehr als ihre eigene Mutter Tefnut liebt (Pyr. 5). Einige Texte deuten ausdrücklich diese Geburt des Pharao als Verwandlung zu einem Sterngott, der am Himmel hervortritt. Interessant ist, dass diese Stellung als „am Leibe der Himmelsgöttin Nut“ oder „in ihrem Leibe“ bestimmt wird[24]. Bei der Redaktion der Pyramidentexte fand aber eine Osirisierung statt, so dass die Osiris-Rolle des Pharao bei dieser Sohnschaft zu Nut hier vorherrschend ist. Typisch ist folgende Aussage: „Nut gibt mir ihre Arme wie das, was sie für Osiris getan hat“ (Pyr. 1090). Zur selben Zeit kann aber auch seine Re-Rolle betont werden, wenn Nut als Taghimmel gedeutet wird. Ein Sargtext stellt fest: „Nut hat dich geboren gemäss der Geburt des Re“ (CT III, 398), und derselbe Gedanke wird schon in den Pyramidentexten belegt (Pyr. 1688, 1835). Den Zusammenhang der beiden Vorstellungen gibt folgender Passus an: „Dieser NN liegt da, indem er jeden Tag geboren und empfangen wird; er ist gestern weggegangen, er ist heute wieder gekommen“ (CT IV, 88–89; cf. auch Pyr. 1703 ff.).

Dieser Vorstellungskomplex hat nun seinen konkreten Audruck in der Grabkammer gefunden. Die Placierung von Texten wie: „Ich (scil. Nut) breite mich über dich aus“ unter dem Dach charakterisiert deutlich die Decke des Grabes selbst als Himmel. Aber auch an den Wänden des Grabes treten Texte auf, die davon reden, dass Nut den Toten umschliesst, vereinigt, schützt usw. In diesem Fall gilt offenbar das ganze Grab als der Himmel/Nut. Somit befindet sich der Tote sowohl under dem Himmel/Nut – oder am Himmel/Nut – wie auch im Himmel/Nut. Nut hat sich als Grabdecke über den Toten gelegt. Hier tritt eine wichtige Mikrokosmos-Vorstellung an den Tag. Eine solche liegt aber auch im Falle des Sarges vor. Der Pyramidentext 616 kombiniert beide und stellt mit einer drei-

---

ihren bisher gewonnenen Resultaten (205 ff.) sehr gut verbinden lässt, nicht besonders hervor.

[23] Cf. Rusch 4 f.

[24] Cf. ib., 15 ff.

fältigen Namensspielerei – es werden zwei verschiedene Wörter für „Grab" gebraucht – fest: „Du wirst gegeben deiner Mutter Nut in ihrem Namen 'Grab', sie umschliesst dich in ihrem 'Sarg'; du kommst zu ihr (zum Himmel) hinauf in ihrem Namen 'Grab'." Diese konkreten Anschauungen können sowohl die grosse Frequenz der Nut-Texte wie ihre bewussten Placierungen erklären. So wird auch die sonst merkwürdige Tatsache verständlich, dass Nut in diesen Texten eine weit bedeutendere Rolle als Geb spielt, der jedoch als Unterweltrichter von grosser Wichtigkeit sein soll.

Mit dem Auftauchen einer reichen Bildausschmückung der Särge im Neuen Reiche eröffnen sich neue Möglichkeiten, diese Vorstellungen auch bildmässig zu belegen. So geben die variierenden Deckendekorationen der Gräber deutlich an, dass die Decke als Himmel anzusehen ist, wenn auch die Göttin Nut selbst hier nicht so oft in anthropomorpher Gestalt auftritt. (Die interessante Nut-Darstellung an der Decke des thebanischen Grabes 216 wird unten in einem anderen Kontext behandelt.) Mehrere Königsgräber zeigen aber stattliche Nut-Darstellungen auf, z. B. die Decke der Sargkammer Ramses' IV. Die Särge sind jedoch weit ergiebiger. Hier findet sich Nut in vielen Rollen. Als Schirmerin des Toten wird sie geläufig mit weit ausgebreiteten Flügeln zentral oben am Sarg dargestellt. Die gewöhnliche kosmische Szene, in der Nut, soeben von ihrem Gatten/ Begatter Geb getrennt, sich über ihn nackt ausbreitet, findet sich oft als Seitenszene in der Herzgegend placiert. Diese wichtige Darstellung[25] fixiert den kosmisch-mythischen Kontext der Wiedergeburt des Toten, an den die anderen Nut-Bilder anspielen.

Besonders wichtig sind die grossen Darstellungen der Göttin Nut auf der Innenseite des Sargdeckels. Diese zeugen, auch von den Texten gestützt, davon, dass auch der Sargdeckel selbst, nicht nur der ganze Sarg, mit der Himmelsgöttin identifiziert wird. Wie der Deckel breitet sich Nut, etwa in derselben Grösse wie der Tote, über diesen aus. Unter mehreren Belegen[26] wählen wir zwei aus, die sich auf unserer Taf. 2 wiederfinden. Figur 1, die summarische Abzeichnung eines schön ausgeschmückten Leidener

---

[25] Bergman, 1975, gibt einige Hinweise auf solche Darstellungen (12 ff.) und hebt ihre Verbindung mit Empfängnis und Geburt hervor.

[26] Im typologischen Atlas der Särge, Mumienkisten (usw.) von Schmidt finden wir folgende Belege, die sich leicht erweitern lassen (die beiden Nummern beziehen sich auf Seite bzw. Abbildung.): 169 (930), 173 (958), 206 (1177), 218 (1238), 226 (1302), 229 (1321), 230 (1330), 232 (1340), 233 (1344) und – jedoch mit der Göttin im Profil – 168 (923, 924), 186 (1032). Auch ihre Darstellung auf dem Sargboden ist für uns wichtig. Wenn Nut nicht nur mit dem Deckel sondern mit dem ganzen Sarg identifiziert wird als „diejenige, die den Toten umschliesst" (usw.), ist ihre Placierung auch auf dem Sargboden sinnreich. Hier sind 199 (1125) und 231 (1329) wegen der Frontalität besonders zu bemerken. Cf. weiter 140 (718), 177 (983), 183 (1014), 192 (1082), 206 (1178), 218 (1239). In diesem Fall wird Nut bisweilen von anderen Göttinnen, und zwar besonders von Amentet, der Göttin des Westens, ersetzt. Amentet dürfte hier beim Empfangen des Toten im Westen etwa als eine Sondererscheinung der Nut gelten.

Sarges, zeigt die sich über den Toten ausbreitende Himmelsgöttin *en face* und nackt. Diese beiden Darstellungsweisen, Frontalität und Nacktheit, die in der ägyptischen Kunst überhaupt selten sind, dienen dazu, den Zusammenhang mit Empfängnis und Geburt hervorzuheben[27]. Wie oben beobachtet wurde, charakterisiert die Nacktheit der Göttin gerade die kosmische Nut-Geb-Szene. Die Placierung der beiden Sonnen am Leibe der Nut deuten Empfängnis bzw. Geburt an. Zu beiden Seiten der Göttin sind die je 12 Stundengöttinnen der Nacht und des Tages dargestellt, was die kosmische Dimension noch mehr betont. Durch die Vereinigung mit der Göttin und die Geburt aus ihr sollte der Tote sicher sein, des Sonnenlaufes sowohl der Nacht als auch des Tages teilhaftig zu werden.

Figur 2 (Taf. 2) zeigt Nut dagegen bekleidet und im Profil. Die Placierung der Darstellung ist jedoch dieselbe wie in Figur 1. Die Haltung der Arme deutet eine Umarmung des Toten an. Besonders wichtig für uns ist aber die ganz merkwürdige Ausgestaltung ihres Kleides. Hier erkennen wir leicht die sogenannte Isis-Schleife, die hier wohl als eine umständlichere und dekorativere Form des Anch-Zeichens aufzufassen ist. Somit tritt hier die Himmelsgöttin Nut als das Leben selbst hervor! Eine solche Darstellungsweise ist natürlich eine ausserordentliche Stütze für die Behauptung, dass Nut auch die Lebensgeberin *par excellence* ist.

Ehe wir diesen Abschnitt über Nut, die Lebensgeberin, als Himmelsgöttin und Mutter des Toten abschliessen, um zum zweiten angekündigten Motiv überzugehen, sei auf den Tatbestand hingewiesen, dass Nut auch am Boden des Sarges, meistens als Gegenhimmel gedeutet, auftritt. So umschliesst sie auch auf diese Weise den Toten, der sich in ihr befindet.

2. *Nut, die Lebensgeberin, als Baumgöttin und Ernährerin des Toten*

Das hier zu behandelnde Motiv findet sich auch nicht selten auf Särgen dargestellt, lässt sich aber ausserdem in verschiedenen anderen Zusammenhängen belegen, was von der Popularität dieser Darstellung und der dahinterstehenden Vorstellung gut zeugt. Sehr gewöhnlich ist die betreffende Szene in Vignetten zu den Kap. 57 und 59 des Totenbuchs, aber auch auf Grabstelen, in Grabreliefs, auf Opferplatten usw. ist das Motiv oft zu finden. Während der schon behandelte Typus von Lebensgebung sozusagen *ex ovo* beginnt und das Werden des Lebens in den Blickpunkt stellt, betont der zweite Typus die Fortdauer des aus Nut geborenen Lebens. Als Geberin des Lebens ist Nut auch für dessen Fortsetzung verantwortlich. Das sich von der Empfängnis bis auf die Geburt organisch entwickelnde Leben muss auch nach der Geburt weiter wachsen. Dafür sind Lebensmittel nötig. Solche bringt Nut/die Sykomore. Sie hält das Leben am Leben.

Wenn ein Pyramidentext (Pyr. 718) sagt: ,,Der König lebt vom Baum mit süssen Früchten", ist es unsicher, ob hier die Sykomore gemeint wird.

---

[27] Cf. Bergman 1974, bes. 100ff.

Vielleicht geht es eher um die Dattelpalme. Die Sykomore wird ausdrücklich in ein paar anderen Texten erwähnt, wobei indessen andere Funktionen als das Ernähren von Bedeutung sind: sie dient als Schutz und Ruheplatz sogar für die Götter (Pyr. 1485) oder wird als ein merkwürdiger uralter Baum am Osthimmel, auf dem die Götter sitzen, beschrieben[28].

Erst mit dem Neuen Reiche lassen sich bildliche Darstellungen von der Lebensgeberin Nut/Sykomore belegen, wie es auch mit dem früher behandelten Motiv der Fall war. Auf unserer Taf. 3 finden sich vier Varianten dieses Motivs. Aus Figur 1, einer spätzeitlichen Reliefdarstellung in Äthiopien, wo bloss zwei Wasserstrahlen aus dem Baum hervorquellen, kann man keine Aussage über den Geber/Geberin ziehen. Figur 2 dagegen zeigt deutlich durch die aus dem Baum halbwegs hervorwachsende Göttinnengestalt, dass eine Göttin als Geberin von Getränk und Nahrung auftritt, und der die Lebensmittel empfangende Ba markiert, dass es um einen funerären Kontext geht. Die Göttin bleibt jedoch hier anonym. Die Göttin in Figur 4 wird eindeutig als Nut gekennzeichnet. Da sie aber hier ganz freistehend vom Baum dargestellt wird, kann man ohne Parallelmaterial nicht auf eine Identität zwischen Göttin und Baum schliessen. Figur 3 ihrerseits zeugt gut von einer solchen Identität, bezeichnet aber die Göttin als Amentet, d. h. als Göttin des Westens. Dank einer fast überwältigenden Menge von Parallelen, deren Mehrzahl der Baumgöttin – aus praktischem Grunde gebrauche ich diese oberflächliche Bezeichnung – den Namen Nut zuschreiben, ist aber ihre Identität klar.

Von grösster Bedeutung für die weite Verbreitung des Motivs und seine feste Verbindung mit Nut dürfte seine Beliebtheit in den Vignetten und den diese begleitenden Texten einiger Kapitel des Totenbuches, vor allem der Kap. 57 und 59, gewesen sein. Im letztgenannten Kapitel lesen wir: ,,Heil dir, Sykomore der Nut! Gib Wasser und Luft, die in dir sind!" Und auf der Grabstele des Ineni (Urk. IV,65) beschreibt der Tote sein Schicksal nach dem Tode so: ,,Meine Seele [...] durchschreitet ihren Garten nach ihrem Belieben. Ich verwandle mich. Ich komme hervor zum Tage. Ich erfrische mich unter meinen Sykomoren, ich ernähre mich von dem, was Nut schafft. Ich trinke Wasser nach meinem Belieben."[29] Die Vignetten zeigen die Baumgöttin Nut, die dem Toten/seinem Ba Wasser aus zwei Libationsgefässen spendet. Bisweilen wird das eine Gefäss von einer Opferplatte mit allerlei festen Nahrungsmitteln ersetzt, die eine aus dem Baum hervortretende Hand darbringt.

Zu bemerken ist der Tatbestand, dass die roten Früchte der Sykomore, welche die natürlichste Gabe der Göttin sein sollten, nur selten dem Toten

---

[28] Für diese ,,seitlich verbrannte, innen verkohlte, die richtig ausgeblutete" Sykomore, cf. Moftah, 40 ff., der hierin die ehrwürdige Hathor-Sykomore südlich von Memphis erkennen will.

[29] Wallert 86; der Passus zeigt eine Lucke, die hier nach Paralleltexten rekonstruiert ist.

dargeboten werden. Das Wasser spielt hier die Hauptrolle, was sowohl die Vignetten als auch die Texte betonen. Dies hängt offenbar von der konkreten Lage der Nekropole ab. Die Grabanlagen waren ja am Wüstenrand gelegen, wo der Durst sehr drückend war. Vereinzelte Bäume dienten durch ihre Wurzelnetze als Wassersammler[30]. Baum and Teich werden geläufig in den Grabanlagen zusammengestellt. Ob wirklich im Neuen Reiche Bäume in den thebanischen Nekropolen in solcher Menge vorhanden waren, wie es die Grabreliefs usw. darstellen, ist umstritten. Vielleicht bilden die Szenen einen Idealzustand ab, welcher nur in den Gärten auf der Ostseite des Nils zu dieser Zeit verwirklicht werden konnte und – was die Nekropolen anbelangt – der Frühzeit und dem mythischen Vorbild (vgl. die Rolle des Baumes am Osirisgrab in Abydos usw.) angehörte. Es ist somit nur natürlich, dass das Wasser die Hauptsache war, was übrigens auch für die Spätzeit das formelartige Gebet an Osiris auf den Grabsteinen bezeugt, dass er dem Toten kühles Wasser bringen solle[31].

Neben dem Wasser spielt auch die Luft eine wichtige Rolle in diesem Kontext. „Gib Wasser und Luft, die in dir sind" lautet das schon zitierte Gebet. Vielleicht steckt dahinter der Gedanke, dass das Zweigwerk die Luft aufsammelte und dem Toten vermittelte wie es das Wurzelnetz mit dem Wasser tat. Bezeichnend ist folgender Wortlaut in einem späten Osirisritual: „Seine Mutter Nut ist die Sykomore, die ihn schützt und seinen Ba in ihren Zweigen verjüngt."[32] Die Vorstellung von der Verjüngung des Ba gerade in den Zweigen könnte m. E. eine solche Deutung stützen. Auch im späten Choiakritual hat die hier behandelte Vorstellung einen Niederschlag gefunden, indem Osiris gerade auf Sykomorenzweigen gebettet werden soll. Bisweilen hält der Tote in den Vignetten die Hieroglyphe des Windes in der Hand, was ihn als Empfänger des Lufthauches auszeichnen soll. Hier wäre vielleicht an die im Neuen Reiche veränderte Richtung beim Darreichen des Anch-Zeichens zu erinnern. Beim protodynastischen Libationsgefäss dient der Griff des Zeichens funktionell als Ausgiesser bei der Wasserspende. Wenn es aber um die Luft geht, könnte beim Darbieten des Anch-Zeichens/des Lebenshauches die Luft durch das Loch des Henkels zur Nase gelangen.

Aus der ptolemäischen Zeit stammt eine Gruppe von Opferplatten, die fast ausnahmslos in der Gegend von Achmim zuhause sind[33]. Schon der Umstand, dass die darauf aufgenommenen Texte gewöhnlich die oben

---

[30] Cf. Wallert 97 f.

[31] Cf. Parrot 126 ff. In diesem Buch, das den Hintergrund des „refrigerium" in der Liturgia Gallicana zeichnen will, spielt unsere ägyptische Tradition eine hervorragende Rolle (84 ff.).

[32] Cf. Junker 1913, 51. Für die besonderen Baumtraditionen, die mit dem Osirisgrab auf dem Abaton verbunden waren – und die auch bei Plutarch erwähnt werden – sei auf die weiteren Ausführungen Junkers, 51 ff., hingewiesen.

[33] Cf. Kamal Nr. 23.160–23.172, Taf. 41–44. Ein vergleichendes Detailstudium dieser symbolreichen Opferplatten könnte weitere kleine Beiträge zu unserer Lebensgebungsymbolik geben.

zitierte Totenbuchstelle (Kap. 59; inzwischen auch ähnliche Stellen aus Kap. 60 und 62) anführen, macht diese Gruppe für uns interessant. Ausserdem zeigen mehrere unter ihnen einen lockenden Symbolreichtum auf. An einem ausgewählten Beispiel (Taf. 1 Fig. 2) wollen wir die Verwendung und die tiefere Funktion eines solchen Kultgeräts beleuchten. Typisch für die Kontinuität der ägyptischen Vorstellungswelt und Kultpraxis ist die Tatsache, dass manches hier an das protodynastische Libationsgefäss erinnert, das wir anfangs behandelten. Absichtlich haben wir auch diese beiden Kultgeräte, die von einander etwa 3 000 Jahre entfernt sind, auf dieselbe Tafel placiert.

Diese steinerne Opferplatte behält die ursprüngliche Form der geflochtenen Matte, auf welche man die Opfer legte[34]. Diese Form ist übrigens mit der Hieroglyphe für „Opfer" (*ḥtp*) identisch. Es handelt sich um ein Gefäss, in welches Wasser über die dargelegten – oder vielleicht nur abgebildeten – Opfergaben ausgegossen wurde, und zwar so – was wohl in unserem Fall das Wichtigste war – dass die dort angebrachten Texte und Bilder vom Wasser belebt wurden. Durch einen Ausguss, gebildet aus dem brotförmigen Aufsatz des *ḥtp*-Zeichens, kam so dieses lebensvolle Wasser dem Toten zugute. Dass dieses Libationsverfahren das Hauptgewicht trägt, beleuchtet gut die Ausschmückung. In der Mitte finden sich drei Libationsgefässe und dazwischen allerlei Opfergaben. Von diesen drei Gefässen zeigt das mittlere eine Sondergestalt auf. Hier erkennen wir die oben kurz erwähnte Anchi-Vase, die einfach wie ein Anch-Zeichen aussieht, das mit einer Mündung, identisch mit derjenigen der beiden anderen Gefässe, versehen ist. Diese Anchi-Vase ist nun auf unserer Opferplatte an einem Teich „gepflanzt", so dass das Wasser des Teiches – mythisch als das Urwasser Nun, als der Nil und als der Ausfluss des Osiris gedeutet – von der Anchi-Vase „aufgesogen" dem Toten zugute kommen kann. Bewusst habe ich bei der Beschreibung die beiden Verba „pflanzen" und „aufsaugen" für die Aktivitäten der Anchi-Vase gebraucht. Die beiden uns bekannten Seitenszenen – es geht um die Göttin Nut, die als Sykomore dem Toten als Lebensgeberin-Ernährerin dient – stellen ja unzweideutig auch die Zentralszene in diesen Zusammenhang hinein. Somit ist man berechtigt, auch diese Anchi-Vase als eine konkrete Erscheinungsform der Wasser spendenden Göttin Nut zu verstehen. Wie oben angedeutet wurde, stellen auch die Texte, die auf dieser Platte stehen – es handelt sich um Auszüge aus dem Kap. 59 (rechts) und dem Kap. 62 (links) – die Identifikation der Göttin/des Baumes als Nut sicher.

Merkwürdig ist nun, dass Nut/die Sykomore in der rechten Szene ganz anthropomorph, in der linken aber hauptsächlich dendromorph dargestellt wird – und dies ist fast ausnahmslos für die ganze Gruppe der Opfer-

---

[34] Für die Entwicklung der Opferplatten cf. RÄRG s. v. Opferplatte 557 ff.

Fig. 1: a

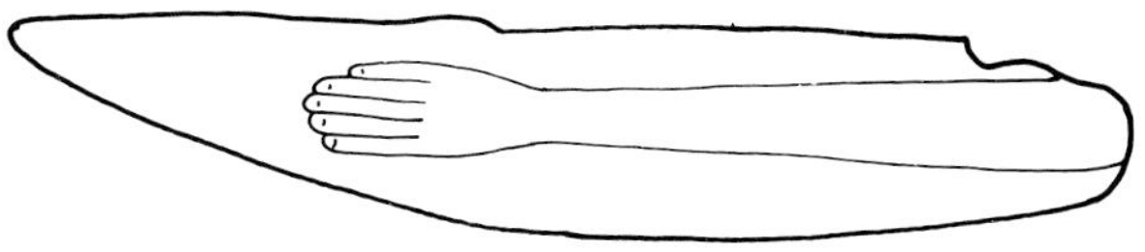

Fig. 1:b

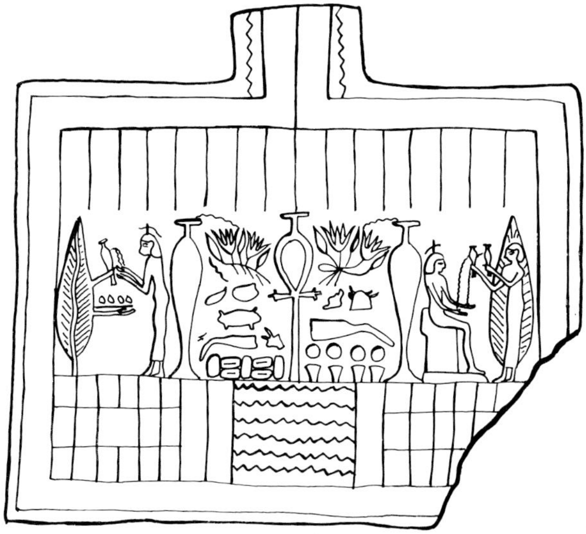

Fig. 2

Taf. 1. Kultgeräte.

Fig. 1 a–b. Protodynastisches Libationsgefäss aus der thebanischen Nekropole (Metropolitan Museum 19.2.16). Cf. Fischer 1972, 5 ff.

Fig. 2. Opferplatte aus Achmim Nr. 23.162 im Kairoer Museum (ptolemäisch). Cf. Kamal 1, 120 f., 2, Taf. 41.

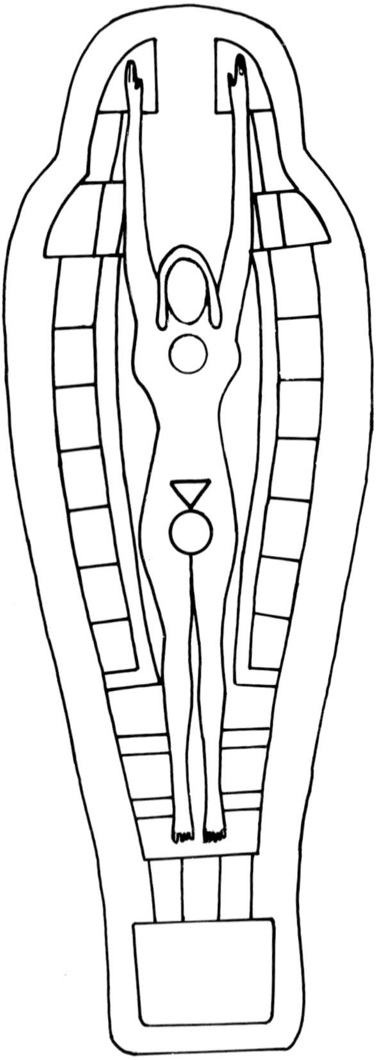

Fig. 1

Fig. 2

Taf. 2. Nut an der Sargdecke.
Fig. 1. Summarische Abzeichnung aus dem Leidener Sarg M 13. Cf. Schmidt 218 Nr. 1238. (Der Leib ist eigentlich ganz schwarz und von Sternen bedeckt.)
Fig. 2. Aus dem Kairoer Sarg Nr. 41.042. Cf. Gauthier 2, Taf. 2; cf. 1, 13 ff.

Fig. 1

Fig. 2

Fig. 3

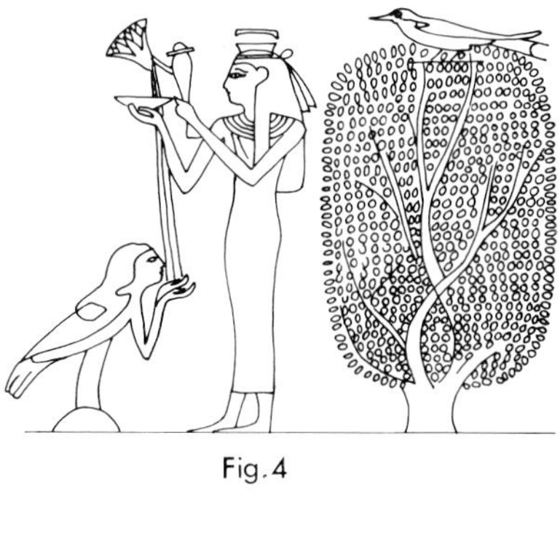

Fig. 4

Taf. 3. Nut – Baumgöttin.
Fig. 1. Relief aus Begerauieh, Nubien (ptolemäisch). Cf. Lepsius 36.
Fig. 2. Aus einem thebanischen Grab. Cf. Schmidt Titelvignette.
Fig. 3. Aus einer Mumienkiste in Marseille. Cf. Schmidt 153 Nr. 805.
Fig. 4. Aus einem Kairoer Sarg. Cf. Schmidt 153 Nr. 803. Cf. auch Englund 1974, 51 Fig. 7.

Taf. 4. Sargboden aus dem British Museum Nr. 6705 (römisch). Ich verdanke der Museumsverwaltung ein ausgezeichnetes Photo, nach dem diese Abzeichnung gemacht ist. Cf. auch Grimm Taf. 138,3

Bei der Herstellung der Abbildungen (Abzeichnungen usw.) ist mir Frau Britta Eriksson, erste Zeichnerin der Institution der Ägyptologie der Uppsala Universität behilflich gewesen. Für ihre ausgezeichnete Arbeit will ich ihr auch hier meinen besonderen Dank sagen.

platten von Achmim der Fall. Dieses Verhältnis aktualisiert ein ikonographisches Problem, und zwar den augenfälligen Variantenreichtum in den Darstellungen des Motivs Göttin-Baum. M. W. ist dieses ikonographische Thema in dieser Hinsicht einmalig in der ganzen ägyptischen Darstellungswelt, die bekanntlich von einer gewissen Stereotypie geprägt ist, da der Ägypter gern an einer idealen Darstellungsart, die aus einem gewählten Sehwinkel bestimmt ist, festhält. Deshalb wären eine gründliche Inventierung dieser Szenen und eine detaillierte ikonographisch vergleichende Analyse dieser Dokumentation wertvoll. Hier müssen wir uns damit begnügen, nur einige Feststellungen im Anschluss an die wenigen gegebenen Abbildungen (Taf. 1 Fig. 2; Taf. 3 Fig. 1–4) zu machen und ausserdem nur die wichtigsten anderen Varianten anzudeuten.

Ziemlich ungewöhnlich ist die ganz lose Verbindung, in der Göttin und Baum nebeneinander dargestellt werden, ohne dass eine Beziehung zwischen ihnen angedeutet wird (Taf. 3 Fig. 4)[35]. Eine maximal dendromorphe Ausgestaltung zeigt Figur 1 (Taf. 3) auf, wo zwei Wasserstrahlen ohne jede Andeutung einer Hand oder eines Armes aus dem Baum hervorströmen. Diese Darstellung scheint jedoch ziemlich unik und kann als missverstandene Ausgestaltung ausfallen, denn sie gehört einer entfernten äthiopischen Gegend und einer späten Epoche an. Andererseits kann die Verbindung der anthropomorph gestalteten Göttin mit dem Baum minimal sein, indem sie nur ein Baumzeichen auf dem Kopfe trägt, um ihre Baumnatur vage anzudeuten[36]. Zwischen diesen beiden Polen, dem ganz dendromorphen und dem ganz anthropomorphen, gibt es eine lange Reihe von Zwischenformen. So können nur Hände und vereinzelt (nur wenn Isis statt Nut auftritt) auch Brüste[37], mit ihren Gaben aus dem Baum hervortreten (Taf. 1 Fig. 2, links), oder aber es wächst ein Göttinnenkopf aus dem Wipfel des Baumes hervor. In einigen Fällen ist etwa die Hälfte der Göttinnengestalt im Baum dargestellt (Taf. 3 Fig. 2), in anderen sieht man fast die ganze Gestalt oben im Zweigwerk stehen. Auch die anthropomorphe Ausgestaltung kann vorherrschend sein, so dass das Zweigwerk nur die Konturen der menschlichen Gestalt hervorhebt, bisweilen ganz lose mit dieser Gestalt verbunden (Taf. 3 Fig. 3). Manchmal ist der Baum zwar ziemlich füllig dargestellt, hat aber keinen anderen Stamm als die Beine der Göttin (Taf. 1 Fig. 2 rechts). Ein Durchgehen der gesammelten Dokumentation lässt fragen, ob dieser erstaunliche Variantenreichtum vielleicht

[35] Eine solche lose Gruppierung ist überhaupt im Alten Ägypten selten zu belegen (cf. Bergman 1974, 95 ff.). Interessant ist die Darstellung Piankoff, Nr. 9, wo eine Beziehung dadurch etabliert wird, dass sowohl die Göttin als auch der Baum den Namen Nut trägt.

[36] Nach Buhl, 92, findet sich die früheste Darstellung dieser Art im Grab des Nakht. Cf. auch das Grab des Userhet (Hinweis ib. Anm. 33) und das thebanische Grab Nr. 216 (Hinweis Schäfer 24 Abb. 6).

[37] Cf. das bekannte Graffito im Grab des Thutmosis III. (z. B. Mekhitarian, 38, abgebildet). Für diese Sonderdarstellung dürfte auch der Umstand, dass die Mutter des Pharao tatsächlich Isis hiess, von Belang gewesen sein.

damit zusammenhängen könnte, dass die innere Triebkraft des Motivs gerade das Wachstum durch Ernährung ist.

Nebenbei soll ausserdem festgestellt werden, dass man keine einfachen Entwicklungslinien aufzeigen kann, die etwa von einer frühen fetischartigen dendromorphen Gestalt bis zu einer späteren, ,,höher entwickelten" anthropomorphen Darstellungsart führen. Bezeichnend ist, dass auf den ptolemäischen Opferplatten aus Achmim fast durchgehend zwei Baumszenen vorliegen, von denen die linke beinahe ganz dendromorph, die rechte aber hautpsächlich anthropomorph ist (Taf. 1 Fig. 2). Möglicherweise liegen hier verschiedene unter- und oberägyptische Sondertraditionen der Darstellungsweise vor.

3. *Verbindung der beiden Motive*

Bisher haben wir bei unserer Behandlung der beiden mit Nut verbundenen Komplexe der Lebensgebung jedes Sondermotiv für sich dargelegt und dessen Kontext und Funktion festgestellt. Hier soll nun die Frage gestellt werden, wie die beiden Vorstellungssphären sich zueinander verhalten. Die das Leben gebende Göttin ist ja dieselbe, es handelt sich um dasselbe Leben, das im funerären Kontext demselben Toten zugute kommt. Deshalb könnte man ja erwarten, dass enge Verbindungen der beiden Motive geläufig zu belegen sind. Dies ist aber nicht der Fall. Einige Begegnungspunkte können jedoch angegeben werden. Auf einigen Särgen heisst es, dass Nut dem Toten Speise und Trank gibt in einem Kontext, der eher zur Nut-Gebärerin-Sphäre gehört[38]. An der Decke des thebanischen Grabes Nr. 216 finden wir die Ernährerin Nut – sie trägt die Sykomore auf dem Kopfe und giesst Wasser aus zwei Libationsgefässen aus[39] – an einer Stelle, wo eigentlich die Himmelsgöttin als Gebärerin ihren rechten Platz hätte. Bisweilen finden sich auf Särgen Darstellungen, die je einer der beiden Vorstellungssphären angehören, in der Nähe von einander[40]. Oft trägt auch die Baumgöttin Nut die Bezeichnung ,,diejenige, die die Götter gebiert". Es sei ausserdem daran erinnert, dass die Wasserlibation der Nut mit ihrem Wesen als Himmelsozean verbunden werden könnte, einer Vorstellung, von der Sonnenschiffe und Sternenbarken, die auf dem Leib der Göttin einherfahren, zeugen. Auf einem Pariser Eimer[41] finden wir Nut/die Sykomore frontal dargestellt, was eher, wie oben betont wurde, die Gebärerin Nut kennzeichnet.

Ein Sargboden des Pollios Soter-Grabfundes aus einer thebanischen Nekropole, jetzt im British Museum ausgestellt (N:r 6705), ist für uns von besonderem Interesse, wie Taf. 4 zeigt. Den Hintergrund der Hauptfigur

---

[38] Cf. Rusch 52.

[39] Cf. Schäfer 24 Abb. 6 (cf. auch die hiermit zusammenhörende Abb. 5).

[40] Z.B. die Szenen 2 und 4, rechts, auf dem Sarg des Chonsumes in Uppsala (cf. Englund 1974, 50ff.).

[41] Abgebildet Parrot 115, 119.

bildet ein aus dem Horizont hervorwachsender Baum mit roten Früchten. Man hat diese Baumdekoration des Sargbodens, die sich in Ägypten nicht früher belegen lässt, als Einfluss des griechisch-römischen Kulturkreises erklären wollen[42]. Dass die Darstellung solche Spuren aufzeigt (z. B. Schlangenarmband, Wiedergabe des Haares und der Gewandung), ist klar. Was den Baum anbelangt, bin ich aber der Meinung, dass wir es hier mit der oben behandelten Vorstellung von Nut als Baumgöttin zu tun haben. Ich will in diesem Zusammenhang daran erinnern, dass Osiris beim Choiakfest in der Spätzeit auf einem Bett von Sykomorenzweigen ruhen sollte. Dieses rituelle Verfahren lässt sich trefflich mit dem Umstand vereinen, dass die betreffende Darstellung sich gerade auf dem Boden des Sarges befindet. Die Hauptfigur trägt keinen Namen, aber eine Reihe von Särgen aus der gleichen Zeit stellen sicher, dass es hier um Nut geht[43]. Augenfällig ist jedoch der Tatbestand, dass es sich hier nur um Frauensärge handelt. Deshalb ist es wahrscheinlich, dass die Darstellung eine durch die funerären Zeremonien mit der Göttin Nut identifizierte Frau abbildet[44]. Dieses Verhältnis könnten auch die oben angegebenen griechisch-römischen Züge unterstreichen. Wenn diese Deutung richtig ist, sollten die alten ägyptischen Nut-Züge und die modernen Kennzeichen der betreffenden Frau zusammen diese neue Identität sicherstellen. Dieses Nut-Werden dürfte eine Parallelerscheinung sein zum vereinzelt belegten Brauch, in dieser Zeit eine mumifizierte Frau als Hathor NN – nicht als Osiris NN – zu bezeichnen. Wenn man die verbreitete, tiefgreifende Symbolik bedenkt, die sich um die Göttin Nut als Lebensgeberin im alten Ägypten entwickelte und durch Darstellungen und Kultbräuche immer mehr befestigt wurde, ist es leicht zu verstehen, warum die Frauen wünschten, gerade mit dieser Göttin identifiziert zu werden[45].

Die Durchschlagskraft dieser Vorstellungwelt, in der Nut nicht nur als die Lebensgeberin *par exellence* sondern sogar als das Leben selbst hervortrat, lässt sich vielleicht noch weiter verfolgen. M. E. kann man diese Symbolik als eine Art Anch-Mystik hinter der merkwürdigen Korrespondanz zwischen der Gestalt der Toten und dem Anch-Zeichen auf der koptischen Grabstele der Rhodia[46] spüren. Um dieses aufzuzeigen, ist aber eine Sonderstudie nötig.

---

[42] Cf. Grimm, 118 Anm. 156, gibt auch einige Paralleldarstellungen an, von denen der Sargboden im Louvre (Taf. 139,1) die grösste Verwandtschaft mit dem unsrigen aufzeigt.

[43] Cf. Grimm Taf. 138 f.

[44] Cf. Parlasca 161, 166.

[45] In einem späten Louvre-Papyrus (Nr. 3148), nach dem Nut als Mutter und Sarg spricht (cf. Schott 81 ff.), sagt sie: „Deine Mutter sagt: Deine Mutter hat dich 10 Monate getragen, sie hat dich drei Jahre genährt. Ich trage dich eine unbestimmte Zeit. Ich werde dich nie gebären.“ Die letzte seltsame Aussage könnte vielleicht so erklärt werden, dass die Tote nun mit Nut für ewig vereinigt ist und so mit ihr praktisch identifiziert.

[46] Cramer, 37, (cf. auch Tafel 16 Abb. 33) liefert nur eine kurze Beschreibung dieser Stele, ohne die Verwendung des Anch-Zeichens in den von mir angedeuteten weiteren Symbolkontext einzustellen.

Literaturverzeichnis

CT Buck, A. de, The Egyptian Coffin Texts I–VII. Chicago 1935–1961.
FG From the Gustavianum collections in Uppsala, ed. S. Brunnsåker, H.-Å. Nordström. Uppsala 1974.
Pyr. Sethe, K., Die altägyptischen Pyramidentexte 1–4. Leipzig 1908–1922.
RÄRG Bonnet, H., Reallexikon der ägyptischen Religion. Berlin 1952.
Urk. Sethe, K. (uam.), Urkunden des ägyptischen Altertums. Leipzig 1903 ff.
ZÄS Zeitschrift für ägyptische Sprache und Altertumskunde.

Baines, J., 1975, ʿAnkh-Sign, Belt and Penis Sheath. *Studien zur altägyptischen Kultur* 3.
Bergman, J., 1970, *Isis-Seele und Osiris-Ei*. Uppsala.
— 1970*a*, Mystische Anklänge in der altägyptischen Vorstellungen von Gott und Welt. *Mysticism*, ed. S. Hartman, C.-M. Edsman. Scripta Instituti Donneriani Aboensis 5. Uppsala.
— 1974, Isis auf der Sau. *FG*.
— 1975, Quelques réflexions sur *nfr – nfr.t – nfrw*. *Congrès international des Orientalistes. Egyptologie* 1. Paris.
Brunner, H., 1964, *Die Geburt des Gottkönigs*. Wiesbaden.
Buck, A. de, 1947, *Plaats en betekenis van Sjoe in de egyptische theologie*, Amsterdam.
Buhl, M.-L., 1947, The goddesses of the Egyptian tree cult. *Journal of Near Eastern studies* 6.
Cramer, M., 1955, *Das altägyptische Lebenszeichen im christlichen (koptischen) Ägypten*. Wiesbaden.
Doresse, J., 1960, *Des hiéroglyphes à la croix*. Istambul.
Englund, G., 1974, Propos sur l'iconographie d'un sarcophage de la 21e dynastie. *FG*.
— 1978, *Ach – une notion religieuse dans l'Egypte pharaonique*. Uppsala.
Fischer, H. G., 1972, Some emblematic uses of hieroglyphs with particular reference to an archaic ritual vessel. *The Metropolitan Museum journal* 5.
— 1973, An eleventh dynasty couple holding the sign of life. *ZÄS* 100.
Frankfort, H., 1933, *The cenotaph of Seti I at Abydos*. London.
Gauthier, H., 1913, *Cercueils anthropoïdes des Prêtres de Montou* 1–2. Kairo.
Grapow, H., 1935, Die Himmelsgöttin Nut als Mutterschwein. *ZÄS* 71.
Grimm, G., 1974, *Die römischen Mumienmasken aus Ägypten*. Wiesbaden.
Hayes, W., 1953, *The sceptre of Egypt* 1. New York.
Helck, W., Otto, E., 1972, *Lexikon der Ägyptologie* 1. Wiesbaden.
Hornung, E., 1963 f, *Das Amduat* 1–3. Wiesbaden.
Jéquier, G., 1894, *Le Livre de ce qu'il y a dans l'Hadès*. Paris.
— 1922, Matériaux pour servir à l'établissement d'un dictionnaire archéologique égyptienne. *Bulletin de l'Institut français d'archéologie Orientale* 19.
Junker, H., 1913, *Das Götterdekret über das Abaton*. Wien.
— 1954, „Der Lebendige" als Gottesbeiname im Alten Reich. *Anzeiger der österreichischen Akademie der Wissenschaften* 12.
Kamal, A. B., 1909, *Tables d'offrandes* 1–2. Kairo.
Kaplony, P., 1963, *Die Inschriften der ägyptischen Frühzeit* 3. Wiesbaden.
Lepsius, R., 1849 ff., *Denkmäler aus Ägypten und Äthiopien*. Atlas 5. Berlin.
Mariette, A., 1872, *Monuments divers*. Paris.
Mekhitarian, A., 1954, *Ägyptische Malerei*. Genf.
Moftah, R., 1965, Die uralte Sykomore und andere Erscheinungen der Hathor. *ZÄS* 40 ff.

Parlasca, K., 1966, *Mumienporträts und verwandte Denkmäler*. Wiesbaden.
Parrot, A., 1937, *Le « Refrigerium » dans l'au-delà*. Paris.
Piankoff, A., Rambova, Natacha, 1957, *Mythological Papyri*. New York.
Rusch, A., 1922, *Die Entwicklung der Himmelsgöttin Nut zu einer Totengottheit*. Leipzig.
Schäfer, H., 1935, Altägyptische Bilder der auf- und untergehenden Sonne. *ZÄS* 71.
Schmidt, W., 1919, *Levende og Døde i det gamle Aegypten*. Kopenhagen.
Schott, S., 1965, Nut spricht als Mutter und Sarg. *Revue d'Egyptologie* 17.
Wallert, I., 1962, *Die Palmen im alten Ägypten*. Berlin.
Westendorf, W., 1966, Beiträge aus und zu den medizinischen Texten. *ZÄS* 92.
Winter, E., 1968, *Untersuchungen zu den ägyptischen Tempelreliefs der griechisch-römischen Zeit*. Wien.

The Traditional Symbolism of the Sun Dance Lodge among the Wind River Shoshoni

By ÅKE HULTKRANTZ

1. *Introductory remarks*

Of all the North American Indian religious ceremonies no one is as spectacular and as well-known as the Sun Dance of the Plains Indians[1]. The information collected on the subject since the turn of the century is quite extensive[2]. However, while there is a mass of materials on the outer features of the Dance, on behavioural and ritual aspects, there is very little information on its religious aspects, in particular the meaning of the ritual. As F. Eggan has stated, "despite all the studies of the Sun Dance we still do not have an adequate account giving us the meaning and significance of the rituals for the participants and for the tribe. One such account would enable us to revalue the whole literature of the Sun Dance"[3]. Neither is there any thorough study of the religious symbolism of any Sun Dance, although for instance G. Dorsey's monograph on the Arapaho Sun Dance observes meticulously all pertinent details (Dorsey 1903)[4].

The comparative studies of the Sun Dance dismiss the religious meaning of the Dance as unessential. The following pronouncement by such an authority as Robert Lowie is representative: the Sun Dance "does not revolve about the worship of a particular deity, the popular English name for it being a misnomer, but is a composite of largely unintegrated elements prominent in the area at large. The remarkable thing about it is the wide distribution of many objective features, while the interpretations and ostensible motives for holding it vary widely. [... Yet] the alleged aims of the ceremony vary widely. We must infer that the ceremonial behavior in the festival was older and that the assumed objectives were subsequent additions. It is also clear that the Dance was only in part a religious ceremony and in large measure served for the aesthetic pleasure and entertainment of the spectators"[5]. In a characteristic way Lowie here loses sight

---

[1] The English name, Sun Dance, is a misnomer. The gazing at the sun in the Sioux Sun Dance inspired this designation. The sun plays a role in some Sun Dances; as the Crow say, it is the "mask" of the Supreme Being. The basic import of the Sun Dance will be given below. Cf. also 57.

[2] Cf. Hultkrantz 1967 a, 29 ff.

[3] Eggan 757. Cf. also Hultkrantz 1965, 88; cf. the critical remarks, Jorgensen 177.

[4] For a forthcoming study on the Crow, cf. Miller Ms.

[5] Lowie 1954, 178, 180.

of the central perspective which joins all partakers of the Dance, the religious meaning which is the motive for its performance. This meaning may be different in different tribes, but it is there. When formulated by the dancers or believers it is as "objective" as any other ceremonial trait. Lowie's assumption that behaviour antedates objectives is just one of those behaviouristic clichés.

Lowie belonged to the team of anthropologists who seventy years ago noted down the Sun Dance ceremonials of the Plains tribes. His general views mirror the spirit in which these investigations were undertaken. It is obvious that the interest in the symbolism of the Dance[6] was minimal among these anthropologists. A new effort to appreciate this symbolism at its intrinsic value is pressing. Such an effort is possible because the material that was salvaged is—in spite of all shortcomings in our documents—partly satisfactory for analysis. Moreover, many Sun Dances are still performed, and may thus be observed in the field[7].

The following account is an attempt to view the religious symbolism of the Wind River Shoshoni Sun Dance lodge in a "meaningful" perspective. Attention is paid not only to the ideology of the Dance as such but also and foremost to the concrete elements of the Sun Dance structure which together throw further light on this ideology. A particular place in the analysis will be devoted to a new scholarly interpretation according to which the Shoshoni Sun Dance serves as a revitalization cult.

The investigation is mainly based on my own field research among the Wind River Shoshoni in Wyoming 1948–58. There is, however, additional material in printed works, such as ethnographical accounts by Lowie and Shimkin and a folkloristic book by Olden (Lowie 1919, Shimkin 1953, Olden 1923). Besides there are archival documents and other unprinted sources in public or private ownership to which I have had access. The value of these sources is very different. Some are tall tales, like Allen's impossible story of the ceremony of the Sheepeater Indians, a mountain branch of the Wyoming Shoshoni[8]. Others are most informative, as is (the Shoshoni) H. St. Clair's manuscript on the Dance (1902), published as an appendix to Shimkin's book[9], or his kinsman L. St. Clair's manuscript from 1936 which he amended and corrected for me in 1948, four years before his death. St. Clair's information goes back to Judge Ute, a Shoshoni traditionalist who died in 1927[10].

---

[6] The word "dance" should not mislead: it expresses the dominant ritual action during the ceremony. Most Indian ceremonies are labelled "dances".

[7] However, the new Indian secrecy as regards traditional religion prevents field observations in many places.

[8] Cf. Allen 9f., 70f., and comments Hultkrantz 1970a, 253ff.

[9] Cf. Shimkin 1953, 474f. St. Clair was Lowie's chief informant on the Wind River Shoshoni. Cf. Lowie 1909, 169.

[10] Cf. the Fort Washakie: death records. F. Burnett, in a letter to Professor Hebard in 1929, gives the year 1928, cf. Hebard 1933, 235.

Our classic sources on the Plains Sun Dance have been presented in a "flat" perspective, that is, in the ethnographic present, regardless if the ceremony was celebrated at the time of recording or a hundred years earlier[11]. The Wind River Shoshoni symbolism as described here refers primarily to the traditional pattern of symbols at the time of my field visits, and secondarily to the Christian symbolism at the same time. Some twenty years ago the Christian symbolic interpretation seemed superficially to supersede the traditional one. It is however less certain that this is the situation today, considering the renaissance of traditional Indian values.

2. *The Plains Indian Sun Dance*

The Sun Dance is, beside the ubiquitous vision quest, the most typical exponent of Plains Indian religion[12]. It is closely tied up with the ancient way of life peculiar to these Indians: bison-hunting on horseback, living in movable tents (tipis), a tribal organization and graded war-societies. Whatever its antecedents—there are indications that it sprang forth in old archaic society—the Sun Dance as we know it from historical records was formed inside the dynamic Plains culture that emerged in the early XVIIIth century. It became so firmly settled that it survived the downfall of the independent Plains socio-political organization and the abolition of the Plains Indian economy at the end of the last century.

Analysis of the distribution of Sun Dance traits convinced Leslie Spier that the Dance had originated among, or diffused from, the Arapaho, Cheyenne and Teton Dakota[13]. Perhaps it would be more cautious to say that the Plains form of the ceremony was modelled in these societies (for it seems to belong to a widespread cultic complex). The Dakota Dance was closely knit up with the military complex of the Plains Indians, whereas the Arapaho and Cheyenne Sun Dances strongly elaborated the religious import: the Dance as a cultic drama, a re-creation of the primeval action through which the earth was once created[14]. Now, this religious idea is manifested in ritual and symbolic details in most Sun Dances all over the Plains area, but is not always clearly recognized as such. The war complex ideology, for instance, often seems to have taken over, several recurrent features having a direct association with warfare. After the eclipse of the Plains military pattern a hundred years ago the Sun Dance scene sometimes turned into an arena for the cure of diseases—a hypertrophy of a trait that had originally been subsumed under the re-creation aspect.

I am anxious to point out that this reconstruction is not in line with the opinion of many of my American colleagues (cf. Lowie, above). It is however perfectly in harmony with the main tendencies in W. Schmidt's

---

[11] Cf. Hultkrantz 1967, 102.
[12] Cf. Wissler 1950, 222.
[13] Cf. Spier 477, 491, 494 f., 498.
[14] Cf. Hultkrantz 1973, 9 ff., and sources quoted there.

and W. Müller's interpretations[15], and it backs up Eliade's view of the meaning of ritual drama[16].

As a New Year ceremony the Sun Dance was originally held in June when a fresh new verdure covered the ground. A typical Sun Dance like the one arranged by the southern Arapaho contains the following elements (Dorsey 1903)[17]:

The man who has made the vow or been blessed by a dream (vision) to set up a Sun Dance, and the military society to which he belongs, prepare the tribe for the ceremony and select the time and place. When time is up the different bands come together, and their tipis form a big circle with the opening to the east, the sacred direction.

During four days of preparation the candidates of the ceremony are assembled in the so-called White Rabbit lodge, a tipi which has been erected to the west of the middle point of the big camp circle. Here a new fire is kindled, the sacred fetishes (a sacred wheel, a buffalo skull) are brought in, and the candidates rehearse the songs and rituals pertaining to the ceremony.

Renowned warriors from military societies, equipped with horses, lances and guns charge on a particularly selected cottonwood tree, shoot at it and make coup on it (i.e., touch it with their hand or a staff in order to count a point of honour). After prayers to the tree some other soldiers cut it down. It is dragged to the Sun Dance circle, but before reaching camp it is attacked by members of other societies in a sham battle. The latter ends with the victory of the pole-dragging soldiers. The tree is then ceremonially raised in the centre of the dance ground. Other poles are attached to the tree as roof poles, peripheral uprights and cross-pieces, and the walls are covered with willow brush. The result is an airy, circular structure with a big opening towards east. It stands ready on the fourth day, and at the same time the Rabbit tipi is taken down.

In the evening of the same day the dancers enter the Sun Dance lodge in their ceremonial outfits. For three days and three nights they fast, dance (periodically) in front of the centre pole and pray to the powers. In the early mornings they perform the "sunrise dance". The body-paint of the dancers is changed each day by the "grandfathers", or personal advisors of the dancers. The first day after the "dancing in" an altar is built on the west side of the centre pole. It is formed by prairie sods representing the first ground in the creation myth and by the buffalo skull and sacred wheel mentioned before and a ceremonial pipe, among other items. The next day is "medicine day" when the dancers might receive visions from the powers above. This day there is also a display of supernatural power,

---

[15] Cf. Schmidt 811 ff., Müller 1956, 303 ff. Cf. also Underhill 151: the development of a basic firstfruits rite.

[16] Cf. e.g. Eliade 51 ff.

[17] Cf. the summary Hultkrantz 1973, 11 ff.

and curing of the sick. On the final day each dancer may have a sip out of a bucket containing water from "the great lake in the sky". In the evening there is a great feast. The ceremony ends the next morning.

Some tribes, like the Teton Dakota and the Blackfoot, practised self-torture in their dancing in the past. The aim was to call on the powers and ask for their pity. Recently these tribes have resumed their mortifications.

3. *The Wind River Shoshoni Dance: history and phenomenology*

The Sun Dance that is performed among the Wind River Shoshoni differs in some respects from the Arapaho Sun Dance, just as both differ from other Plains Sun Dances in ritual details and symbolism. The Shoshoni Dance is clearly marginal to other Sun Dances, in this respect reflecting the peripheral location of the Shoshoni on the Plains[18]. It has moreover changed with time, depending primarily upon three factors: the re-creating force that may be attributed to visions, influences from other Sun Dances, and, in later times, pressure from the European civilization resulting in an increasing adoption of white (Christian) values.

Everything seems to indicate that the Wind River Shoshoni Sun Dance is of comparatively recent origin[19]. It had however a predecessor of considerable age, a round-dance called the "Father Dance" (*apönökar*), possibly also the "Thanksgiving Dance"[20]. In this Dance which continued until recently the people came together and shuffled around a cedar tree, while they thanked the Supreme Being (*tam apö,* "our father") for his gifts and asked him for bounty in the year to come. Similar prayer dances have existed among the Shoshoni and Paiute of the Basin area[21].

Although the Father Dance and the Sun Dance have occurred independently of each other, some elements of the former could have found their way into the Sun Dance. According to my informants a round-dance formerly took place inside or outside the Sun Dance lodge after the end of the regular Sun Dance ceremonies; some people found this being less proper, however. Informant L. St. Clair, an excellent historian, considered the preliminary dancing before a shelter (cf. below) a left-over of an original "Sun Dance". This seems however less probable.

The beginnings of the Shoshoni Sun Dance are veiled in mystery. Indeed, the Dance escaped the attention of the explorers of the last century.

---

[18] Cf. Shimkin 1953, 408.

[19] I leave aside here the whole problem of the relationship, if there ever was one, between the archaeological remains of the Medicine Wheel on Bald Mountain in the Big Horn range, other medicine wheels of the area and the ancient Sun Dance. Early on there was the idea among the whites that some sort of connection existed between medicine wheels and Shoshoni religion. Cf. Comstock in Jones 265. However, knowledgeable Shoshoni Indians refer the wheels to the Crow.

[20] Cf. Olden 37f., Lowie 1915, 817, Shimkin 1953, 433f. and Thompson Ms.

[21] Cf. Hultkrantz s.a., Mythology.

Colonel Brackett's paper on the Shoshoni from 1879 does not mention it, which however may be due to his limited knowledge[22]. H. St. Clair's manuscript from 1902 is the first authentic description[23]. As to the age of the Dance Robert and Yolanda Murphy seem to infer that it appeared only with the early reservation period[24]. Grace Raymond Hebard held the opinion that the Dance was brought to the Shoshoni by the famous Sacajawea, the pilot of Lewis and Clark, when she returned from the Comanche in 1843, for some of her descendants claimed she was the introducer of the Dance[25]. Shimkin, again, basing his conclusions on the evidence of old informants and archival data, establishes the years 1800–1820 as the probable date of the introduction of the Sun Dance[26]. My own field information and research in old documents confirms his results. Moreover, I think a forgotten notice by J. Beckwourth on "the medicine lodge" in the Shoshoni camp at Weber River in 1825 refers to the Sun Dance[27].

The man who brought the Sun Dance to the Shoshoni was apparently Ohamagweia, or Yellow Hand, a Shoshoni chief who was by birth a Comanche, and who in one or another way was related to Sacajawea[28]. It was probably an old Kiowa or Comanche form of the Dance that was introduced[29]. Certainly, there is also another Shoshoni tradition according to which the Shoshoni Dance antedates all other Sun Dances[30]. This version is however more a testimony of pious belief than a record of historical facts. Yellow Hand is said by many people to have received the Dance in a vision, and several versions of this vision have circulated on the reservation.

We do not know for sure the outlines of the original Shoshoni Dance, although Shimkin has tried to reconstruct it[31]. So much is certain that in the main it followed the general Plains pattern as illustrated here with the Arapaho Dance. It also showed some peculiarities of its own. Thus, elderly

---

[22] He writes, for instance, "Material pleasures alone are those which a Shoshoni understands." Cf. Brackett 331.

[23] It has since been printed in Shimkin 1953, 474 f.

[24] Cf. Murphy 308.

[25] Cf. Hebard 1933, 157, 201, 259 f., 275. The date for Sacajawea's arrival is not certain, and her role in the Sun Dance history is doubtful. Cf. Shimkin 1953, 410 f.; Hultkrantz 1975, 154.

[26] Cf. Shimkin 1953, 413. There is in the agency files a copy of a letter (June 15, 1937) from Mr. F. Stone, superintendent, in which he gives the date "about the year 1819" for the first Sun Dance. He does not say how he arrived at this date.

[27] Cf. *Life* 61 f.; cf. Hultkrantz 1968, 297 f., 302. According to Beckwourth the ceremony took place in the winter season. However, this is in agreement with what some informants have to tell, cf. below.

[28] This relationship was in my view different from the one postulated by Shimkin, cf. Hultkrantz 1968, 294 f., 296 n. 17. On Ohamagweia as introducer of the Dance, cf. Shimkin 1953, 409 ff.; Hultkrantz 1968, 294, 301 f.

[29] I follow here Shimkin's interpretation, Shimkin 1953, 414 ff.

[30] St. Clair Ms.: "The first Indians to dance the Sun Dance were the Shoshone Indians. This Sun Dance was founded by a Shoshone Indian." Other Shoshoni Indians corroborated this "information", and one of them asserted that the Shoshoni had exported the Dance to the Arapaho, Sioux and other Indians.

[31] Cf. Shimkin 1953, 417 ff.

informants could still in the 1940s tell us that the Sun Dance was also formerly celebrated in wintertime[32].

The general motives for the Dance to be arranged were wishes for a long life and good luck in general, and particularly success in war and cure for diseases[33]. It is difficult to judge if these goals were collectivistic, aiming at the tribe as a whole, or individualistic. In any case, they were expressed in the ceremony leader's prayer before the centre pole immediately prior to the beginning of the dancing. The centre pole was adorned with a buffalo skull, facing west, an eagle in a nest of willows and a small "Sun Dance doll" made from wood or buckskin. On the other hand, there was no altar and no buffalo skull at the foot of the pole. During the four nights prior to the proper ceremony the leader and a few other participants practised Sun Dance songs at a particular windbreak erected for the purpose. The lodge ceremony then started in the evening and lasted three nights and days[34]. The dancers jogged steadily up and down looking upon the centre post and its sacred images. Occasionally they also danced up to the centre pole. On the second full day relatives helped to construct a small booth around the place where the dancer lay down to rest, just behind his dancing position. The skin of the booth was, according to Shimkin, painted with "records of visions of war experiences"[35]; I have no such information. An interesting detail is that when the dancers received a sip from the sacred water (the event that marked the termination of the Dance) they vomited[36]. Such vomiting occurred also in the Arapaho and Cheyenne Dances. One is furthermore reminded of the sacred vomiting in the New Year rituals of the Southeastern Indians.

The great change in the Sun Dance occurred around 1890 when the Shoshoni had adapted themselves to reservation life, buffalo hunting and warfare was gone and the old religion was on the verge of becoming suppressed by the white rulers and the Christian missions. Ritual traits referring to war disappeared to a large extent, and the emphasis on blessings for success in war was replaced by prayers for good health and cure from disease. The new political organization with a tribal council (1893) instead of chieftainship and informal meetings was reflected in the creation of a Sun Dance committee. The date of the Dance was postponed from June to late July, the time when the harvest had been taken care of. Some old traits like the putting up of a Sun Dance doll and the vomiting went out

---

[32] Cf. Hultkrantz 1968, 302. My chief informant here, Nadzaip (a medicine-woman), had a brother, Morgan Moon, whose innovations as a Sun Dance leader—due to his visionary experiences—created strong counter-reactions among the Shoshoni. Cf. Shimkin 1953, 435 f.

[33] Cf. Shimkin 1953, 431.

[34] The number three is sacred west of the Rocky Mountains, the number four east of them; the Wind River Shoshoni having geographically an intermediate position keep both numbers sacred.

[35] Shimkin 1953, 425.

[36] Cf. also Olden 36; *Fremont* 9.

of use, at least temporarily, whilst others, such as the dancing up to the centre pole, became more common. Influences from other Sun Dances—particularly from the one of their eastern neighbours, the northern Arapaho, who in the 1870s had settled on the reservation—resulted in some new ritual elements. The most conspicuous change, however, was the reinterpretation of the Sun Dance symbolism into Christian concepts[37].

The reformulation of the Sun Dance in the 1880s and 1890s, and the new emphasis on health and curing, saved the Shoshoni Dance in a time when the old hunting life was gone, most Sun Dance ceremonies were forbidden by white authorities and several of them—in particular among the tribes practising torture in their Dance—became extinct. Indeed, it was during this difficult time that the Wind River Shoshoni version of the Sun Dance spread to the northern Ute (1890), the Fort Hall Shoshoni and Bannock (1901), and the Shoshoni of Nevada (1933)[38].

After the Indian Reorganization Act (1934) there was a new resurge of Sun Dance celebration on the Wind River Reservation[39]. More people than ever before took part in the Sun Dance. Since the Sun Dance was now mainly a means of achieving spiritual power—which in the old days could only be procured on solitary vision-quest expeditions—and a ritual for the removal of disease, and therefore its presumably old interpretation of a New Year's rite had become vague and even obsolete, it was possible to arrange several Sun Dances each summer[40]. For instance, one Dance is usually arranged by conservative believers, another by peyotists. The latter deviate from other sun dancers in not expecting visions of supernatural power during the Dance, and in wearing a pouch with a Peyote button around the neck.

One of the renewers of the Sun Dance in recent times has been the famous medicine-man John Trehero, now in his nineties (and no longer active). Being a descendant of Yellow Hand he reintroduced the Sun Dance doll for the ceremonies in which he or his close kinsmen took part. He also transferred the Shoshoni Dance to the Crow Indians (1941)[41].

The 1950s brought tendencies of commercialization into the Sun Dance celebration. However, the sacred character was not lost and has since been strenthened under the pressure of resurging Indian nationalism.

Looking back we may say that in modern times the Shoshoni Sun Dance has absorbed almost all expressions of earlier religious rituals, in particular the vision complex and the "shamanism"[42]. With a certain justification we

---

[37] Cf. Hultkrantz 1969, 22, 33, 36 ff.

[38] Cf. Jorgensen 19 ff., 25 f.; Hoebel 578 f.

[39] Cf. Hultkrantz 1969, 34.

[40] This notwithstanding I was informed, during my visit to the Stoney (Assiniboin) of Alberta in the autumn of 1977, that these Indians had held six Sun Dances that summer.

[41] See Voget 1948, 634 ff. There is testimony that, in spite of Shimkin's denial, dolls had been used in the time between the two World Wars by Sun Dance leaders Andrew Bazil and Morgan Moon.

[42] In Shimkin's words, the Sun Dance is "going far in socializing shamanism." Cf. Shimkin Ms., 9.

may consider the Sun Dance as the aboriginal religion of today. As such it is the core of Shoshoni traditionalism, and the ideological centre of ethnic cohesion.

4. *Shoshoni Sun-Dance ideology and the revitalization theory*

The foregoing reconstruction of the Wind River Shoshoni Sun Dance presupposes continuity in patterns and ideas up to our own time. This interpretation has recently been challenged by J. Jorgensen in a provocative book, *The Sun Dance Religion*. He suggests that the modern vigorous Sun Dance among the Ute and Shoshoni (which both belong to the Numic-speaking peripheral Plains and Basin groups) constitutes a so-called redemptive movement, and thus has little connection with the old Sun Dance. He puts this new "Sun Dance religion", as he calls it, on a par with nativistic, contra-acculturative movements (although he refuses to use a term like acculturation).

Jorgensen points out that the main motivations for the Dance are an oppressed population's need for health and happiness in a white-dominated world, and for tribal coherence against white power, furthermore the single individual's need for personal status and esteem within his community[43]. It is the ritual participant's conscious intention to gain supernatural power in the Dance. He does it in order to forward his own health, or that of others, or to help those who are mourning by injecting into them resources from the power-filled ceremony. If possible he also tries to become a medicine-man through visions during the Dance[44]. In Jorgensen's view the Shoshoni Sun Dance is not just a ceremony, it is the nucleus of a religious movement, a Sun Dance religion. He adopts the view that in the 1880s, "at a time when the Wind Rivers had lost access to the strategic resources on which they once subsisted, when their movements were restricted, and when their death rate greatly outstripped their birth rate, a few Wind River shamans began to retool the Sun Dance ritual"[45]. There was a change in focus from hunting and warfare to curing of illness and maintenance of communal unity, and "a few Shoshone shamans sought a solution to the illness, death, and petty factionalism that became pervasive in the 1870s and 1880s"[46]. Thus, the Sun Dance was reworked and crystallized into a redemptive movement[47].

Jorgensen observes that the restructuring of the Sun Dance took place when the people had lost faith in another revitalization movement, the Ghost Dance. Using D. Aberle's terminology he states that when the transformative movement the Ghost Dance failed, people turned to a redemptive movement, the new Sun Dance. According to Aberle a transformative

---

[43] Cf. Jorgensen 234 ff., 244, 246 ff.
[44] Cf. ib. 247.
[45] Ib. 18.
[46] Ib. 19.
[47] Cf. ib. 77.

movement seeks total change of social or natural order, whilst a redemptive movement seeks total change of the individual[48]. It stands to reason that in North America a movement of the latter kind should be more successful during reservation time. The Sun Dance "religion" has persisted for almost a century and will, in Jorgensen's view, continue to persist.

Is Jorgensen's picture correct? His description of the changes about 1890 are certainly to the point: this was the time when Christian symbolism began to be accepted, when references to war and hunting were dampened down and problems of tribal cohesion and, in particular, concerns of health took precedence in prayers and rituals. The gradual reduction of other ritual complexes, such as the vision quest, have given a strengthened importance to the Dance, and perhaps the visions received in the Dance. Thus the Sun Dance has become the focus of Shoshoni religious life, an observation that I was able to make during my field research[49].

However, I do not agree with Jorgensen when he defines this modified Sun Dance as a redemptive movement in the sense referred to. In the minds of the participants this "western form" of the Sun Dance is not separated from other Sun Dances. Nor is it alien to other Plains tribes, and it attracts visitors from these peoples. The Shoshoni are conscious of its supposed origin in a very ancient time, and the procedures follow basically the old Sun Dance pattern. The Sun Dance is not considered a separate "religion", but part of the old religion. At the most we may say that the old religion has been condensed into a "Sun Dance religion"[50].

If my reasoning here is correct, as I think it is, the present leaders of the Sun Dance would still today cling to a traditional, possibly cosmological interpretation of the ceremony. In the following I shall try to demonstrate that this is the case to a large extent, through three consecutive operations:

a) an investigation of Shoshoni opinion on the meaning of the Sun Dance;

b) an analysis of traditional symbolism of the cultic lodge; and

c) a short examination of the nature and function of Christian symbolism attached to the Sun Dance lodge.

5. *The meaning of the Sun Dance*

As has emerged from the foregoing the manifest meaning of the Sun Dance has changed considerably over the generations. Still, due to the conservatism of religious thought it should be possible to reveal some very old tenets still held by practitioners. The investigator has to be aware of the fact that the Shoshoni generally confuse the m e a n i n g of the Dance with the m o t i v e s behind the arrangement of individual Dances or the joining in the Dance by individual believers.

---

[48] Cf. Aberle 318 ff.

[49] Cf. Hultkrantz 1969, 27, 33.

[50] I used this expression in Hultkrantz 1969, 22.

The presumably original existential interpretation turns up occasionally. Said informant L.S.C.[51], "we dance the Sun Dance so that we may live during the winter, survive it and manage to live until next summer, when we have a new Sun Dance." The same informant also said that people pray "for strength, happiness, many animals to kill, berries and roots and good health and happiness for the people." Or as J.T. put it, he hoped for good spiritual gifts in the days to come. Closely connected with prayers for the future is the thanksgiving for past blessings. For instance, when at the sunrise rite the dancers face the east they thank the Supreme Being for the sun and its light and for the life that he bestows on the earth (L.S.C.). J.T. felt good when his grandson returned unhurt from Korea. God was good, and he wanted to thank him by sponsoring a Sun Dance for the people; "I could not thank God in any other way."

It is a common observation today, also conceded by an idealist like L.S.C., that all Shoshoni have different views of what the Sun Dance stands for[52]. L.S.C. could even see that "people enjoy meeting, it always makes you glad to see your friend and relative." He was quite aware that many interpretations are possible. Foremost among them all he stressed the curative aspect[53]. According to him the buffalo spirit of the inauguration vision[54] said the following to the hero who was granted the message to set up the first Sun Dance: "Our Father on high sent me to you to tell you that a certain power will be imparted to you. It will enable you to cure those who are sick. You may cure any sickness by faith and prayer. I shall give you that power. [...] When you have gone through [the Dance] the power will help you to extract those agents that make people sick." Other informants (T.R., P.C. and others) agreed that this was the chief message of the Sun Dance. One of medicine-man J.T.:s guardian spirits once urged its client to go into the Sun Dance and pray with the other dancers for the sick.

Some other interpretations are also given, probably spoils from the once more comprehensive program and import of the Dance. There is still a vague remembrance that the Sun Dance gives divinatory visions of war.

[51] In the following the informants will be rendered by their initial letters. Two main informants who have already been mentioned are John Trehero (J.T.) and L. Clair (L.S.C.). Of these Clair (1903–1952) was my foremost informant on the symbolism of the Sun Dance. He had, as I have indicated, written an account of the Sun Dance which however, deviated in part from what he told me. He explained that this was due to his reticence to present the true facts in the manuscript. Lynn had received his information from the knowledgeable old-timer Judge Ute, or Yutatsi (1843–1927).

[52] In her unpublished notes Miss Marion Roberts states that all dancers have different reasons for going into the Dance: some think they will recover from illness, others ask for a good harvest, and still others go in for renown. Roberts, Marion, Ms.

[53] Cf. also St. Clair Ms.

[54] L.S.C., quoting Ute (see above), embraced the tradition that the Sun Dance was first entrusted to the Shoshoni by a buffalo spirit. This tradition is at variance with another tradition according to which Yellow Hand dreamt about a human spirit he had seen as a white man in a picture.

L.S.C. told me that in the old days a person who fainted from exhaustion in the Dance was covered with a buffalo robe. When he came to he vomited white horsehair, for instance—a sure sign that the people would win a battle and catch a white horse from the enemy, or make a coup on that horse. Several features of the old ceremony indicated that it was once coupled with military purposes, such as the formal "killing" of the tree selected to become the centre post, the singing of a war song in front of the centre post during the Dance by a woman or an old man, and the fire-bringers' songs about their stealing horses from the enemy. These rites are of course now obsolete. However, wars are still topical. T.W. put up a Sun Dance in 1948 because some young Shoshoni had been drafted for military service, and he feared there would be a new war. He wanted the boys to be safe and out of danger, so he prayed for them.

Another motive for arranging or joining a Sun Dance is to attain supernatural power. Nobody prays for such power, as one does in the vision quest; if it comes, this is coincidental (L.S.C.). When in 1955 T.R. found that he recently had had bad luck and made bad medicine he decided to put up next year's Sun Dance; this way he thought he could bring about a change for the better. Many medicine-men use their powers in the Sun Dance, either in curing people, or prophesying or calling forth a soothing rain. Some are granted such power in the visions they receive during the Dance.

My chief informant on the Sun Dance and its ideology, L.S.C., made a remarkable connection between the Dance and Shoshoni eschatology. "If," he said, "I believe in the Sun Dance and go in and believe that I shall be free from my sickness, then I shall recover. If I am a good Indian and pray to the Father to help me, I have a straight road to walk after death. However, if I do not believe in the Sun Dance, and I live a no good life, I shall walk the other road and do not come to the Father." It is easy to see Christian reminiscences in this pronouncement. However, the double path of afterlife has a definite association to the old symbolism of the centre post, as we shall soon see.

It is, as we observed, necessary to make a distinction between the ideological frame, or meaning, of the Sun Dance and the causes (motives) of joining it or putting it up. Too often the issues are confused by the Shoshoni, as in the cases of T.R. and T.W., related above. In a few instances they are kept distinct, in most cases only individual motives are given. For instance, the sponsor of the Sun Dance in 1955, J.T., was urged in a vision to arrange it, no reason being provided. "I dreamt this year", said J.T., "that the eagle wanted me to put up the Sun Dance, for three nights and three days, for all my people [. . .]. The spirit pointed out to me the place of the Sun Dance lodge." Such a commandment has, certainly, some interior meaning, but it is hidden for human beings. The spirits have their reasons which man cannot grasp.

All the variety of interpretations which have been reproduced here indicate that the meaning of the Sun Dance, vaguely perceived in some statements, is mostly obscured behind individual motives (which may be considered to represent parts of this meaning). It is furthermore obvious that, although the Shoshoni may be aware of a cosmic symbolism in their Sun Dance, the idea of a cyclic renewal as a re-creation of the world is not present in their thoughts. We have to keep this in mind when the account now turns to the symbolism of the Sun Dance lodge and its particulars.

6. *Cultic symbolism*

In the following presentation only such cultic objects as I found associated with the Sun Dance lodge will be referred to. Thus, the heap of stones and the digging-stick, mentioned by Shimkin, will not be discussed. The main symbolic parts of the lodge are demonstrated in the adjoining drawing[55].

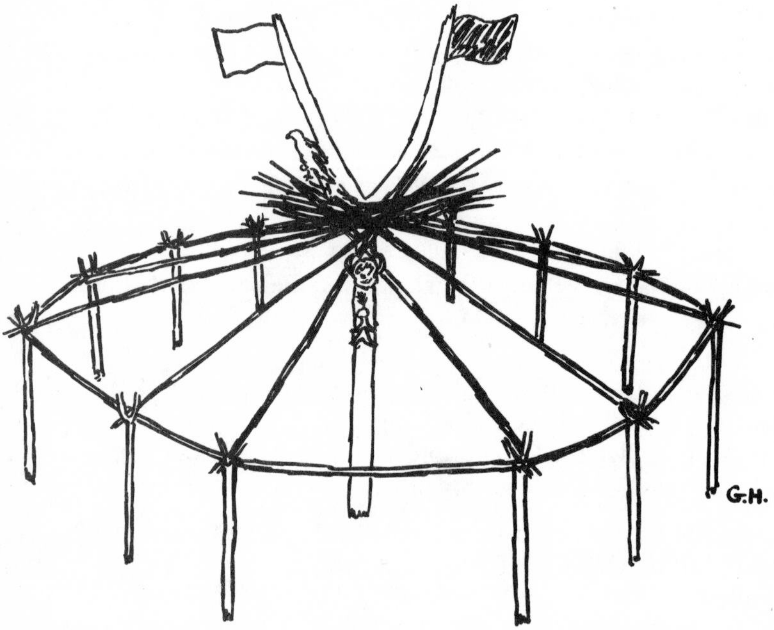

Diagram of a Wind River Shoshoni Sun Dance lodge.

6.1. The Dance lodge. The Dance lodge is called *taguwunexa,* "thirst-standing-lodge", or *taguwunögani,* "thirst-standing-house"; *taguwunö,* or thirst-standing, being the name of the Sun Dance. The name thus refers to the physical exertion, not to the sacred import of the lodge.

[55] For pictures of the Shoshoni Sun Dance, cf. Shimkin 1953, pl. 30–37; Hultkrantz 1973, pl. XVII–XXV.

This does not mean to say that the lodge is not sacred. "The Sun Dance lodge is a symbol of the world," said L.S.C. "It is round because it is the world[56]. The rafters are supposed to extend over the earth. It is the first place where the humans could pray." Here is the original idea of the lodge as a microcosmos, a sacred replica of the earth or the world, clearly expressed.

Those who take part in the preparation dance—which is sometimes performed at the place where the dancing lodge will be erected—"dance to make the ground sacred place." "After the last preliminary night's singing the ground of the Sun Dance lodge is sacred ground" (L.S.C.). This means that in principle only the dancers are allowed in the section of the lodge where dancing takes place; not even a reputed medicine-man is supposed to be there unless he is one of the dancers. Outsiders coming in to receive blessings from dancing medicine-men are often requested to take off their moccasins and, if men, their hats. Women in the process of menstruation and men who are drunk have to keep away from the lodge. L.S.C. was most upset when after a Sun Dance in 1948 mounted youths played around inside the lodge.

The normal procedure is that the lodge rots away, or that its timbers are sold to interested buyers, whites and half-breeds. This is a new custom, said N., but "it spoils the medicine": diseases return to those who have been cured during the dance. However, even today the central pole is left to decay.

6.2. The centre pole. The middle post, or "forked pole" (*wurušagar*), is the most sacred part of the lodge. Ideally it should be a cottonwood tree which is quite juicy when green; however, nowadays also a pinetree may be chosen, for cottonwood grows sixteen miles up the river, whereas pine is available up in the foothills. A cottonwood centre pole "is always cool, however much the sun shines on it; this is not the case with common cottonwood trees" (L.S.C.). Stories circulate that during the Dance the centre pole opens, and water comes out. It is spiritual water that blesses the dancers but only can be seen by some. Dancers may drink it through their whistles.

These wonderful qualities of the centre post, as well as the ceremonial felling of the tree, the shambattle around it and the circumstantial ritual at its raising, testify to its symbolic importance. N. told me that the centre pole "from way back, when the Sun Dance was given to my people," was a vehicle for prayers. "The Father above told us that we must not destroy this pole, it should be left standing to decay naturally, for all the prayers and the ailments of the sick who attended the Dance still remain on this

---

[56] The Indians represent the earth as a round disc. Cf. also Müller 1970, 203 ff. (Sioux Indians).

pole." However, my informants were careful to point out that the prayers were not directed to the centre pole as such, just as they were not meant for the sun[57]. The pole thus serves as an intermediary between man and God. Sacred power emanates from the pole. L.S.C. admonished me to observe how the medicine-man J.B., when attending to the sick in the Dance, first stroked his medicine-feathers against the centre post before he made them touch his patients.

It is obvious that the centre pole, besides being a communication channel for prayers, represents divine power. "Many sun dancers pray before the centre pole, for it stands for Christ. Before this was done they prayed there nevertheless, for it stood for Our Father above," said G.W., a man in his thirtees in 1948. Chief Dick Washakie told Grace Hebard in 1926 that the cottonwood tree of the Sun Dance hall represented God[58]. L.S.C.:s opinion was that this forked pole "is a sign for the Milky Way. The Milky Way is believed to be a great path over which travel the people who have passed to the beyond"[59]. Thus, the centre pole has the function of being a replica of God and of the "backbone of the sky," as the Shoshoni call the Milky Way (*tugungu:himp*). The cosmic associations are obvious. The centre, God, the Milky Way, the communication channel—this is the world pole, the *axis mundi* and the road to God and the powers above.

In this light the very last ritual gesture becomes understandable. When the Dance is over the dancers throw their aprons at the foot of the centre pole, and some of the spectators tie on some pieces of clothing, and also tobacco or feathers, to the pole. In the old days, N. told me, the centre pole was sometimes covered with the clothing of the participants and their relatives. They should obviously be interpreted as prayers to the Supreme Being, a kind of communicative offerings. N. informed me further that the supplicant first made a prayer to God, and then placed a dress or a blanket as an offering. The custom seems to be the same today. J.T. said that anybody who is sick—not necessarily a dancer—could "throw away [*witēin*] his disease" by laying down his clothes by the pole. The disease would, he meant, dwindle away with the clothes. On the plain outside of Fort Washakie one can still observe those lonely forked poles with clothing attached to them, the last remnants of a Sun Dance celebrated months or perhaps years before.

---

[57] Cf. L.S.C.: "The dancers pray to God to bless them through the centre pole. But I have never heard anybody pray to the centre pole or the sun; they always pray to Our Father."

[58] Chief Dick Washakie was the son of old Chief Washakie, the last tribal chief (Hebard 1930, 294).

[59] St. Clair Ms. L.S.C. explained to me that from the fork there is a bad path to the left, and a good one to the right, and in the Sun Dance you should ask God to be admitted to walk the right path. This echoes Christian teaching. However, the idea of a road of the dead which is plit in two, one for those who embraced the tribe's values and conformed to them in their lives, and one for those who lived unworthy lives and are excluded from the community in afterlife, is known from many parts of North America.

6.3. The buffalo head. A head of buffalo, *kwïc,* is fixed on the centre pole just where the forked branches come together, or slightly below. It faces west and is the centre of attention during dancing. In the old days it was painted with white clay, and sweet sage was put into its nostrils (L.S.C.). The latter custom is still extant. Another old custom, counting coup on the buffalo head by an old man before it was put in place (L.S.C.), has become obsolete.

The symbolism of the buffalo head was explained in the following way by L.S.C.: The buffalo represents the buffalo spirit of the founding vision, "the first message"; the sweet sage in its nostrils is "the symbol of the vapor" of this spirit, for "that had the smell of sweet sage." Also, the buffalo on the pole stands for food and nourishment. J.T. made the following statement: "The buffalo was created here on earth for food. He is the biggest eatable animal that has a split hoof. And all animals that have a foot like the buffalo are eatable. For that reason he represents the eatable animals on the pole." Several dancers who have been staring at the buffalo head while dancing during the potent second day, the day of visions, have experienced how the buffalo head moves, its eyes roll violently and steam stands around its nostrils. Such signs predict a vision, perhaps of the buffalo spirit itself.

The stuffed buffalo head has replaced the buffalo skull of earlier days, but the symbolism is apparently the same. It represents the most important economic resource of the heyday of Plains culture, when enormous bison herds strolled over the grounds. Its association with a ceremony that means the rejuvenation of all Nature's resources is therefore natural. If the spirit that revealed the ceremony to the people had the form of a buffalo this points to the importance the buffalo had in comparison to other animals. Indeed, there are hints that the buffalo spirit was a kind of a master of the game in Plains Indian ideology. "He is the chief of all animals," said the well-informed L.S.C.[60].

6.4. The willows. A bunch of willows (*sihö^{wi}*) or grass is attached to the fork of the centre pole. I heard that in former days the buffalo skull should have been fastened over this bunch, but I have only seen Sun Dances where the buffalo head was placed under the willows[61]. It seems more reasonable to imagine that the eagle (cf. below) had the willows as its nest, as was the case among other Plains Indians.

The willows are tied in such a way that the ends point south and north[62]. I do not know if this arrangement has any symbolic implication.

According to L.S.C. the willows are symbols of the growing food[63]. They

---

[60] Cf. Hultkrantz 1961, 208f., 216.

[61] Cf. D. Washakie in Hebard 1930, 294.

[62] St. Clair Ms.

[63] The willows that are shaken by the female choir seated close to the drummers left of the lodge entrance have the same symbolism. "It is the women's task to pick berries and roots," said L.S.C., "and the shaking of the willows is a prayer of much vegetational food."

have been produced by Mother Earth. They stand for "the branches carrying nourishment for the living." L.S.C. drew a parallel between berry bushes and willows on one side, human beings on the other: the former are more reliable than the humans, they have a duty to fulfil, and that is to feed the humans.

It strikes us that this description is not quite accurate: willows and grass may be food for buffaloes, but not for men. The original idea was possibly that the willows symbolized the new verdure that would provide the animals—horses, buffaloes, antelopes, and so on—with food. Unless, of course, the eagle-nest idea was basic.

6.5. The eagle. One of the rafters that serve as a "roof" carries at its top end an eagle, or eagle feathers. This rafter, which runs in an east-west direction from its anchorage in the centre pole, is usually called "the backbone", and is deeply forked. In the old days people caught an eagle (*pia kwina*) for each, or every second, Sun Dance. Like other Prairie and Plains tribes the Shoshoni constructed small hide-aways made from stones on mountain ridges, and caught the eagles alive there (C.S.)[64]. Nowadays the bird is usually replaced by its tailfeathers, or a stuffed bird is fetched. I have seen both alternatives used. When the Dance has ended the eagle, or eagle feathers, are brought back to a pine in the mountains.

Like the buffalo the eagle is a most sacred being. S.S.C. told me that he represents "the second message" in the Sun Dance legend, at the same time as he symbolizes peace and purity. "The second message" was handed down to L.S.C. by Judge Ute and begins in the following way: "Many years after the introduction of the Sun Dance [through the buffalo vision], when the first sun dancers had long been dead, a young Shoshoni had a nightly vision. It was an eagle that came flying from the place of sunset towards east, into the tipi of the sleeping young man[65]. The spirit said that he should make new the endurance dance." The eagle ordered some new ritual performances, prescribed that an eagle bird was appended to the "backbone" pole and that black rings should be painted on the nether part of the centre pole for the number of days the Dance should run. (Since the painting should be done by a brave warrior who at the same time recounted his war deeds this custom has become abandoned.) Finally, the eagle instructed the people to put up as many roof poles as he had tailfeathers—twelve in number—and to make whistles to be used in the dance from the bones of his shoulder wings and to use his wings as a fan in healing sick persons.

The same informant, L.S.C., remarked that the Supreme Being had selected the eagle for his second message because "he is superior to all

[64] The procedure is described in Wilson 108 ff. (Hidatsa Indians).

[65] The buffalo in the first vision arrived, on the other hand, from the rising sun, for "like the sun he gives life and food for man" (L.S.C.).

birds, and in his flight he will soar; his body is free from impurity." (On the other hand, L.S.C. underlined that the eagle is not, like the U.S. eagle emblem, a symbol of freedom.) Before the eagle is fastened to the rafter a man chosen for the task offers a prayer in which he asks the Supreme Being to bless the people "as you have this eagle to whom you have given power to fly in the sky, where there is fresh clean air, where there is no sickness"[66].

The eagle is the bird of peace. His feathers are used "for peaceful meeting." If two Indian groups come together, they hold up eagle feathers as a token of peace, said L.S.C. This is of course an echo of calumet and peace pipe ceremonies on the central and northern Plains. At the same time the custom conforms to conceptions of the eagle held all over North America. On the other hand, the Sun Dance eagle's association with the thunderbird is not as clearcut with the Shoshoni, as for instance, it is among the Oglala Sioux.

It seems that the symbolism of the eagle as expressed here is a reformulation of its role—known all over the northern hemisphere—as the heavenly bird (the messenger of God, or God himself) at the top of the world tree[67]. Such a reformulation could easily take place within the frame of the vision pattern so characteristic for the Plains Indians and for the Shoshoni. L.S.C., who was a chairman of the Sun Dance committee, had witnessed many cases where dancers had experienced visions of a spiritual eagle, groped after it with their arms and then fallen backwards or sideways, losing their consciousness. J.T. was visited in his sleep by an eagle who urged him to put up a Sun Dance. "The eagle gave me the Sun Dance." It is most probable that the so-called second message (in so far as it really contained any innovations) had a similar origin.

6.6 The flags. The forks of the centre pole are topped by two square flags. Tradition prescribes that they should be one white, the other blue. However, also other colours are possible, provided they express the opposition between light and dark. L.S.C. saw them as symbols of day and night, sky and earth[68]. In other words, the two branches of the tree are supposed to express the cosmic duality.

I noticed that at one Sun Dance the northern fork had a yellow and the southern a whitish flag, which does not conform to this interpretation; also, the centre pole had been painted yellow up to shoulder-height. The reason for this was a vision that the medicine-man T.R., one of the Sun

---

[66] St. Clair Ms.

[67] According to Dick Washakie eagle feathers could be fastened to the high forked branches of the centre pole (Hebard 1930, 294). Other observers have like myself seen the eagle lashed to the tip of a long rafter (Hart 8). Reports that the eagle was tied to the lower end of a rafter just over the entrance seem less trustworthy (Stafford 1938; this paper is apparently a copy of an anonymous manuscript preserved in the agency files at Fort Washakie).

[68] Cf. also St. Clair Ms.

Dance leaders, had had. T.R. told me he was visited by one of those spirits that had instructed the people about the first Sun Dance. The spirit, that looked like a human being, approached him from the north and said, "When you put up the Sun Dance, use yellow paint. Tell the tribe that whenever they are going to have a Sun Dance to paint it yellow."[69]

This example shows how easily symbols may change character in the Plains area. L.S.C. was aware of this: "In the eagle vision[=the second message] people were told to make the flags green and blue, since the eagle and Our Father have their abodes in the sky. Later on, since we introduced two Sun Dances [each season], the colours have been revealed in the sponsor's vision."

6.7. The manikin. The Sun Dance doll (*puēlk*) is no regular feature of the modern Sun Dance. B.S.C. remembered that before about 1918 a doll was carved for each new Sun Dance by a certain man selected for the job. It was made from wood, had feathers sticking up from the back of the head, and its cheeks were decorated with the lightning sign. According to B.S.C. this wooden doll was the spirit that imparted the first instructive vision to the founder of the Sun Dance[70]. T.R. called the doll "the spirit of the Sun Dance"[71], and L.S.C. said vaguely that "it represents creation."

What T.R. and L.S.C. said holds good for the present doll spirit as well, although its import is slightly different. As B.S.C. stressed, the doll used by Andrew Bazil in the 1920s was his personal medicine, and the same goes for the present doll which is in the possession of J.T. The latter puts it up when he himself, or a relative of his, dances and needs protection. It is then fixed on the west side of the centre pole, about 2 metres from the ground. It portrays a little Indian, 30 cm in height, made from buckskin and thus white and yellow in colour. There is a little green feather at the back of the head. The facial features are sown with a black thread, and the eyes are small black crosses. J.T. received this spirit in a vision. It is a "desert spirit" that helps when a person is strained, and J.T. called it "the great medicine-man that gives power in the Sun Dance." At the same time he regarded it as a link in the chain of Sun Dance dolls: he had, he said, received it from the old-timers. It connected him with his ancestor, Yellow Hand, who owned the first Sun Dance doll.

All the data presented here clearly show that the Sun Dance lodge and its parts has a cosmological symbolism. It could be easily demonstrated that also the paraphernalia of the dancers and the ritual actions before and during the Dance may express a similar symbolism. However, our special

---

[69] It should be added that the medicine-man M. Moon, active during the time between the World Wars, and mentioned in the foregoing, demanded all dancers to have yellow paint the first dancing day (information by L.S.C.).

[70] B.S.C. probably refers to the spirit of the picture revealed to Yellow Hand, cf. note 54 above.

[71] Cf. also Shimkin 1953, 418, 441 n. 48.

object of analysis has been the cultic lodge, and its symbolic language is unequivocal.

Compared with the preceding account of the meaning of the Sun Dance the analysis of cult symbolism brings out more readily the ulterior import of the Dance. Some statements on the meaning of the Dance seem to get along with the symbolic interpretation of the Dancing lodge, others are mixed up with the particular motives for arranging a Dance.

In addition, there is the confusion caused by the application of Christian symbolism.

7. *Christian reinterpretation*

The main lines of Christian reinterpretation of the Sun Dance were presented in an earlier paper[72]. Here I shall restrict the account to the Christian symbolism in the Sun Dance lodge, but at the same time present some more details.

One strong difference from the foregoing description will immediately catch the attention: whereas there was a fair consensus about traditional symbolism, there is not the same agreement among informants as to the Christian interpretation. Indeed, one and the same individual may even suggest different Christian symbols to denote one and the same cultic phenomenon. Thus, L.S.C. identified the centre pole as the cross, Christ and the path through life. The same persons who ascribe a traditional tribal symbolism to the dancing lodge will, as an addition to this, and as an afterthought, present a Christian interpretation. This attitude fits in with my observations of the Shoshoni tendency to conceive alternating religious configurations[73]. At the same time it bears testimony that the Christian symbolism is imposed upon the Sun Dance and does not constitute its ideological premisses.

The Christian reinterpretation represents a process that certainly took its beginning about 1890 but, since that date, has gone on incessantly. As an example could be mentioned the case of L.S.C. When studying to become a catechist in the Episcopal church this faithful guardian of Shoshoni traditions found out that Christ and his apostles were represented in the upright main poles of the Sun Dance lodge. After 1945 he and his companions made these findings public in the Shoshoni Sun Dance camp.

Here are some examples of Christian reinterpretation.

7.1. The Dance lodge is, according to Y.S., the grave of Christ. "When you get out of it you go to a renewed life, like Christ." An imaginative Idaho Shoshoni (J.R., belonging to the *hukandïka* group[74]) told me that the Dance symbolizes how Jesus hung on the cross for three days, and then

---

[72] Cf. Hultkrantz 1969, 36 ff.

[73] Cf. Hultkrantz 1969, 26 f., and literature referred to there.

[74] Cf. Hultkrantz 1975, 139 f.

was taken down. He also said that the rafters of the lodge stand for the apostles and the brush intertwined in the "wall" for the innumerable members of the people.

7.2. The centre pole is in most cases Christ or, as he is designed in this connection, "our brother". L.S.C. explained that by its fork the centre pole forms the sign for brother in the sign language: two fingers drawn out of the mouth into the air[75]. Another interpretation is that the centre pole represents the cross of Christ, for the bunch of willows forms the arms of the cross (L.S.C.)[76]. Finally it is our path through life, a conception which may have Christian patterning, as noted in the foregoing.

In contradistinction to traditional symbolism also other poles may have a symbolic value in Christian reinterpretation. The twelve main corner poles are designated the apostles of Christ. Also the twelve rafters are so called ("Jesus' brothers"). One informant, J.T., agreed with the first interpretation, but at the same time he suggested that the poles standing directly north and south of the centre pole represent the robbers of Golgotha. L.S.C. who was not very sympathetic to J.T. denied the truth of this interpretation.

7.3. The buffalo head was identified as Christ by T.W. and G.W., father and son. I did not find that other Shoshoni applied a Christian interpretation in this case. See however the paragraph on the eagle, below.

7.4. The willows may be seen as part of the cross (see above). One of Shimkin's informants held that the willows symbolize the Holy Water that Christ made in the mountains[77].

7.5. The eagle, the "second messenger" according to L.S.C., might be a representative of the New Testament (just as the buffalo, in a vague sense, might be the Old Testament) in L.S.C.'s opinion. It was his thought that the eagle vision was sent at the birth of Christ. The rafter that the eagle is resting on is, said the same informant, the Judas pole, for it is the only rafter that is forked. L.S.C. is referring here to the sign language where "talking with a forked tongue" stands for lying[78]. Judas was of course a lyer, hence the association.

7.6. There is to my knowledge no Christian symbolism attached to the flags.

7.7. The doll is a symbol of Jesus. L.S.C. admitted this interpretation although he rightly suspected that the doll then (1948) in use was made by J.T.'s wife.

8. *Conclusions*

It is now possible to arrive at some valid conclusions concerning the original idea and later religious change of the Shoshoni Sun Dance. The analysis

---

[75] Cf. Clark 82.

[76] The missionaries translated "cross" into Shoshoni "branched tree", cf. Roberts 13.

[77] Cf. Shimkin 1953, 441.

[78] Cf. Clark 234.

of the symbolism of the lodge itself provides us with means to make this evaluation, and it also helps us to judge Jorgensen's theory that the modern Dance is a revitalization movement.

First of all it is obvious that the Shoshoni Sun Dance lodge, like many other Sun Dance lodges, evinces a symbolism that stresses its character of being a renewal ceremony with cosmological implications[79]. The symbolism of the cultic lodge brings out that, whatever the motives for the arrangement of the Sun Dance, its basic ideology must once have been largely identical with that of the modelling western Algonkian tribes (Cheyenne, Arapaho). This is an important statement. It furthermore generates the hypothesis that the original idea behind all the older Sun Dance performances among the Plains tribes had the same contents.

We may here pause and make some other inferences. It seems reasonable to presuppose that the old Shoshoni way of life and its values were expressed in the original thanksgiving ceremony, the "Father Dance". When, however, this hunting and gathering existence was superimposed by the more nomadic and colourful Plains culture—with its roots in highly developed cultures farther east—the Father Dance was replaced by the Sun Dance in importance and slowly dwindled away. The Sun Dance embodied the ideas and values of the bison-hunting, warlike Plains tribes[80]. It also contained the cosmogonic and cosmological symbolism of the eastern cultures. The deep impact of the Sun Dance in Shoshoni culture is obvious to anyone studying their traditional religion. There is even a tale of rats dancing a Sun Dance in a buffalo skull, and J.T. told me he had seen one morning bears perform the Sun Dance at a creek[81]!

Our second conclusion is that the Christian reinterpretation of the symbolism of the Sun Dance lodge is accidental rather than integrative. From the outset it represented a kind of reconciliation between Christian and Shoshoni religions. The Christian symbolism was an additive element in the Sun Dance designed to make the latter more acceptable to Christian missionaries. We must remember that from the 1880s onwards missionaries and superintendents made efforts to prohibit the Plains Sun Dances, and some clergymen on the Wind River Reservation succeeded in closing the ceremony for a number of years. The religious liberalism initiated by the Government after 1934, and the proclamation of the free exertion of American Indian religions in 1978, have of course made such reasons for a Christian reinterpretation increasingly superfluous. In later years the Christian symbolism has served as an alibi for the participation in the Dance by Indians with a predominating Christian faith. There is reason to believe that

---

[79] Wissler's statement, that Plains Indian art "is strongly geometric, but as a whole, not symbolic" (Wissler 1950, 222), is apparently erroneous. Cf. Wissler 1941, 132ff., in particular 137.

[80] Cf. Hultkrantz 1949, 153.

[81] Cf. Hultkrantz 1970, 72f.

with the new religious situation the Christian reinterpretation will gradually weaken.

The third conclusion we can draw is that Jorgensen's view of the Shoshoni Sun Dance as a redemptive movement is misleading. It is true that health and curing of disease are prominent issues in today's sun dancing. However, this is not a testimony of a restructuring of the Dance, its transformation into a new religion. It only means that one of the moments of the Sun Dance mystery, the renewal of life and health, has received a central position in a daily existence no longer marked by anxieties for the survival of the tribe and the world, but by worries of the individual's fate in a multidimensional human situation.

Finally, a comparison with the modern Crow Sun Dance is rewarding. The Crow, situated in southwestern Montana, earlier had a Sun Dance which, however, on account of its close association with military life disappeared with the cessation of warfare in the 1870s[82]. In 1941 the Shoshoni J.T. introduced the Shoshoni form of the Sun Dance among the Crow[83]. The Crow Dance thus shares the peculiar traits of the Shoshoni Dance, such as the concentration on health and curing, and the back-and-forth dancing[84]. Recently the symbolism of the Crow Sun Dance lodge has been studied by Mr. F. Miller, U.S.A.[85] He was not able to find any clearcut Crow statements on the renewal-of-the-world motif[86], but the cosmic symbolism seems clear.

Miller states that to the Crow the centre pole and the circle of forked poles surrounding it are "symbols of the cosmos as a whole." The shape of the lodge provides "a visual image of the cosmos of the Crow." The centre pole is the centre of the sacred space of the lodge, and the place where power is concentrated. One of its forks represents heaven, the other earth, and their merging at the fork signifies the unity of these cosmic principles. At the base of the pole cigarettes are collected which have been smoked in prayer by dancers. "With these objects the center pole becomes

[82] Cf. Lowie 1915 a, 5.

[83] Cf. Voget 634 ff.

[84] For some reasons unknown to me Jorgensen identifies the "new" Sun Dance as a particular expression of the aspirations of the Numic-speaking peoples. The Crow are not mentioned. In this way he can easier keep the new Dance apart from the "true" Plains ceremony.

[85] Cf. Miller Ms.

[86] In a letter to me (May 10, 1978) Miller states that he was surprised by its absence. "I probed for it with a number of Crow friends, but in vain. It is all the more unusual in that the Crow do feel that the performance of the Sun Dance has a revitalizing effect on the community. I spoke with a number of dancers who said that one of the main reasons for their participation was the promotion of the general welfare of the Crow for the coming year. I also encountered a general, but rather vague, understanding that there is some danger, not clearly or specifically defined, in allowing a summer to go by without performing a Sun Dance. This in spite of the decidedly non-cyclical nature of the Sun Dance ritual itself [. . .]. The emphasis seems to be on the present moment and the potential for future events, rather than upon a primordial past which must be re-created and renewed annually. Hence, the perception of the revitalization of the community without the attendant notion, which we could expect, of re-creation and renewal of the cosmic order."

a representation both of the powers to whom the Dance is directed and of the silent and verbal offerings which invite them to sanctify the Lodge by their presence."

The buffalo head, the eagle and the buckskin doll are appended to or near the centre pole as they are in the Shoshoni Dance. They have here the same symbolic implications. The eagle is said to be very closely associated with the Supreme Being.

The cosmic symbolism of the Crow Sun Dance, an offshoot of the modern Shoshoni Sun Dance, is thus most evident. Perhaps it partly derives from the old Crow Dance, although the hiatus of 67 years between the two Dance forms seems to preclude this possibility. The parallels with Shoshoni symbolism are so intimate that the latter has probably been the chief source of inspiration. It seems however that in both Sun Dances the basic ideological structure to which the cosmic symbolism refers has fallen away as a conscious thought: the idea of the re-creation of the world. Among the Shoshoni we have no origin myth to substantiate this idea[87]. The origin legend, instanced in the foregoing, sheds no light on the cosmological interpretation. What remains of the latter is the symbolism, and its language is clear.

Bibliography

Unpublished sources

BERKELEY
University of California,
Shimkin, D., 1939. Some interactions of culture, needs and personalities among the Wind River Shoshone. Diss.

LARAMIE
University of Wyoming—Archives,
Thompson, J., In Old Wyoming.

FORT WASHAKIE
Wind River agency files,
[Anonymous] The Indian Sundance.
St. Clair, L., The so-called Shoshone Sundance, which the Shoshones call: Da-g-oo Wi-n-o-de.
Various letters; death records.

LIDINGÖ
Private archive—Å. Hultkrantz,
Hultkrantz, Å., Wind River Shoshoni field notes.
Miller, F., letter to Å. Hultkrantz, May 10, 1978
Roberts, Marion, The Shoshone Sun-Dance.

PHILADELPHIA
Temple University,
Miller, F., 1977, The Crow Sun Dance lodge: form, process, and geometry in the creation of sacred space.

---

[87] Cf. Hultkrantz 1960, 565; id. 1972, 348 f.

Published sources

AA American anthropologist
HR History of religions
APNH Anthropological papers of the American museum of national history

Aberle, D., 1966, *The Peyote religion among the Navaho.* Viking Fund publications in anthropology, 42. New York.
Allen, W., 1913, *The sheep eaters.* New York.
Brackett, A., 1880, The Shoshonis, or Snake Indians, their religion, superstitions, and manners. *Annual report of the Smithsonian Institution for 1879.* Washington.
Clark, W., 1885, *The Indian sign language.* Philadelphia.
Dorsey, G., 1903, *The Arapaho Sun Dance.* Field Columbian Museum, Anthropological series, 4. Chicago.
Eggan, F., 1954, Social anthropology and the method of controlled comparison. *AA,* 56.
Eliade, M., 1971, *The myth of the eternal return.* Princeton.
Fremont, 1952, *Fremont county and its communities.* Ed. C. Jayne. Laramie.
Hart, S., & Carlson, V., 1948, *We saw the Sun Dance.* Concord.
Hebard, G., 1930, *Washakie.* Cleveland.
— 1933, *Sacajawea.* Glendale.
Hoebel, E., 1935, The Sun Dance of the Hekandika Shoshone. *AA,* 37.
Hultkrantz, Å., 1949, Kulturbildningen hos Wyomings Shoshoni-indianer. *Ymer* 69.
— 1960, Religious aspects of the Wind River Shoshoni folk literature. *Culture in History,* ed. S. Diamond. New York.
— 1961, The Masters of the Animals among the Wind River Shoshoni. *Ethnos* 26.
— 1965, The study of North American Indian religion. *Temenos,* 1.
— 1967, Historical approaches in American ethnology. *Ethnologia Europaea* 1.
— 1967 a, North American Indian religion in the history of research, 3. *HR* 7.
— 1968, Yellow Hand, chief and medicine-man among the Eastern Shoshoni. *Proceedings of the 38th International congress of Americanists,* 2. Munich.
— 1969, Pagan and Christian elements in the religious syncretism among the Shoshoni Indians of Wyoming. *Syncretism,* ed. S. Hartman. Scripta Instituti Donneriani Aboensis, 3.
— 1970, Attitudes to animals in Shoshoni Indian religion. *Studies in comparative religion,* 4. Bedfont.
— 1970 a, The source literature on the "Tukudïka" Indians in Wyoming: facts and fancies. *Languages and cultures of Western North America,* ed. E. Swanson, Jr. Pocatello.
— 1972, An ideological dichotomy: myths and folk beliefs among the Shoshoni Indians of Wyoming. *HR,* 11.
— 1973, *Prairie and Plains Indians.* Iconography of religions, 10. Leiden.
— 1975, Haivodïka, an acculturated Shoshoni group in Wyoming. *Zeitschrift für Ethnologie,* 100.
— s.a., Mythology and Religious Concepts. *Handbook of the North American Indians,* 11. Washington (in press).
Jones, W., 1875, *Report upon the reconnaissance of Northwestern Wyoming* [...] *in the summer of 1873.* Washington.
Jorgensen, J., 1972, *The Sun Dance religion: power for the powerless.* Chicago.
Life, 1931, *The life and adventures of James P. Beckwourth.* Ed. T. Bonner. New York.
Lowie, R., 1909, *The Northern Shoshone.* APNH, 2.
— 1915, *Dances and societies of the Plains Shoshone.* APNH, 11.
— 1915 a, *The Sun Dance of the Crow Indians.* APNH, 16.

— 1919, *The Sun Dance of the Shoshoni, Ute, and Hidatsa*. APNH, 16.
— 1954, *Indians of the Plains*. New York.
Müller, W., 1956, *Die Religionen der Waldlandindianer Nordamerikas*. Berlin.
— 1970, *Glauben und Denken der Sioux*. Berlin.
Murphy, R. and Y., 1960, *Shoshone-Bannock subsistence and society*. Anthropological records, 16. Berkeley.
Olden, S., 1923, *Shoshone folk lore*. Milwaukee.
Roberts, J., 1925, Indians of the Rockies and the Pacific Coast: Shoshone and Arapaho, Wind River reservation. *Indian tribes and missions*, 4. The Church in story and pageant, 8. Hartford.
Schmidt, W., 1929, *Der Ursprung der Gottesidee*, 2. Münster.
Shimkin, D., 1953, *The Wind River Shoshone Sun Dance*. Bureau of American ethnology. Bulletin 151. Anthropological papers 41. Washington.
Spier, L., 1921, *The Sun Dance of the Plains Indians: its development and diffusion*. APNH, 16.
Stafford, C., 1938, Shoshone Indian Sun Dance. *Wyoming wild life*, 3.
Underhill, R., 1965, *Red man's religion*. Chicago.
Voget, F., 1948, Individual motivation in the diffusion of the Wind River Shoshone Sun-dance to the Crow Indians. *AA*, 50.
Wilson, G., 1928, *Hidatsa eagle trapping*. APNH, 30.
Wissler, C., 1941, *North American Indians of the Plains*. New York.
— 1950, *The American Indian*. New York.

"Christ is the Mountain"

Some observations on the religious function of symbols in the encounter of Christianity and other religions

By CARL HALLENCREUTZ

In this paper I will focus on the religious function of symbols in the encounter and interaction of Christianity and other religions. Like Livingstone once, I venture to "draw your attention to Africa". I will illustrate the problem with some observations on the religious function of the symbol of the Holy Mountain in different African contexts. These contexts are a) traditional Kikuyu religion, b) a Christian hymn from Northern Tanzania, and c) the New Year's Fiest of the independent *Nazaretha* Church among Zulu in South Africa.

1. *Symbols of power or agents of change?*

When we raise the question of the role and function of symbols in the encounter of Christianity and other religions, it may at first seem rewarding to speak of drastic confrontations between Western missions and indigenous religious structures. We can, of course, advance a number of examples of such confrontations from different periods of history. However, at a more detailed study of the history of Christian expansion the problem proves to be more qualified and involved than we first imagined.

Assessing the specific religious function of symbols in such local encounters of Christianity and other religions which took the form of drastic confrontations, I suggest that the predominant role of symbols is to integrate and enforce religious and social structures, which are seen to be mutually exclusive. In the confrontation of religions such symbols became expressions of religious and social power within the opposing structures. S. Axelson illustrates this particular problem in his study of tense relationship of Kikongo *banganga* and Western missionaries in Lower Congo from the late 15th century onwards[1].

However, this is only one aspect of the religious function of symbols in the encounter and interaction of Christianity and other religions. This encounter takes different forms and moves at different levels. Often it becomes personal and internalized among those, who within the framework of their inherited religious tradition get affected by new religious influences and let their inherited religious practises and worldview as well as their

[1] Cf. Axelson 15 ff.

ethnic loyalties be reorientated by the new religion[2]. As is increasingly made evident in studies in local Church History in Africa, Asia and Latin-America religious symbols play a significant role as agents of change in such processes[3]. Further investigations in related problems may be a relevant contribution of Studies in Mission to on-going interdisciplinary search for the religious function of symbols.

2. *Mount Kenya—God and/or abode of God*

Let us first turn our attention to the role of the Holy Mountain in traditional Kikuyu religion!

Today, when Jomo Kenyatta is mourned as a national hero of independent Kenya it is interesting to recall his significant contribution from the 1930s to East African Anthropology, which he programatically called *Facing Mount Kenya*[4]. In this study Kenyatta scholarly expounded the social, cultural and religious tradition of his own Kikuyu people. He also gave a profound contribution to the emerging Kenyan nationalism[5].

Discussing Kikuyu religion Kenyatta illustrates the role of the Holy Mountain. According to Kenyatta "religion is a dramatisation of belief and belief is a matter of social experience of the things that are most significant to human life"[6]. As "in Kikuyu life the earth is so visibly the matter of all things animate"[7], Kenyatta emphasises the symbolically involved relationship of *Kere-Ngai* (or *Kiri-Nyaga*[8]) which means the mountain of brightness and is the Kikuyu name for Mount Kenya and *Mwene-Ngai* (or *Mwene-Nyaga*) which means the possessor of brightness and is the most often used Kikuyu name for divinity or the Supreme Being in ritual and/or liturgical contexts[9].

Ngai is the creator and giver of all things. He is not visible to mortal eyes but manifests himself in natural phenomena such as the sun, the moon, the rainbow and not least in thunder[10]. *Ngai* is a distant God, though in times of crisis the Kikuyu calls upon *Ngai,* as communication with *Ngai* is established within the family at significant events in the life of an individual, such as birth, initiation, marriage and death[11].

Ngai lives in the sky yet *Kere-Ngai* is believed to be his official resting place. However, apart from Mount Kenya other mountains, such as *Kea Njahe* (the mountain of the Big Rain=Donyo Sabuk), *Kea Mbiroiro* (the mountain of the Clear Sky=*Ngong*), and (*Kea-Nyandarwa=Kinan-*

---

[2] The development of Mvemba Nzinga is one example; cf. ib., 54 ff.; 65 ff.

[3] Cf. KÅ 1978, which contains papers on Church and Colonialism in different regions read at CIHEC Conference in Uppsala, August 1977.

[4] Cf. Kenyatta, 1968, 34, on conditions when Kenyatta wrote this study.

[5] Cf. Kenyatta 1961, XVII ff.

[6] Ib., 316.

[7] Ib.

[8] Cf. Kibicho 1978, 371 f.

[9] Cf. Kenyatta 1961, 234; Leakey 1077.

[10] Cf. ib. 234 ff.

[11] Cf. ib., 243–252. Cf. Leakey 1078 ff.; Mbiti 237 ff.

gop) are seen as minor abodes of *Ngai*[12]. Big trees symbolise these holy mountains. Under such trees the traditional Kikuyu worships and makes sacrifices to *Mwene-Ngai*. Offering his sacrifice the Kikuyu turns towards *Kere-Ngai* and raises his hands to the holy dwelling place of *Ngai*[13].

A younger compatriot of Kenyatta, S. Kibicho, presses this analysis of Kikuyu theology further. He analyses different names of the godhead and draws attention also to *Githuri* (=the Great Elder) as the name of him, who lives on *Kere-Nyaga* and makes "mountains tremble and rivers flood" and to whom prayers are adressed[14]. He also specifies the different activities of *Ngai* and emphasises particularly that according to Kikuyu tradition *Ngai* is God for all men though the worship of him is conditioned by social frames of reference, family, clan, tribe etc[15]. According to Kibicho this is a significant factor in the continuity of the concept of God in Christian Churches in today's Kenya, in spite of drastic confrontations in the past between Kikuyu religion and Western missions[16].

Kibicho also ventures an interpretation of the religious function of the Holy Mountain as a symbol in traditional Kikuyu religion and world view. He draws attention to the relationship of the name of God and the name of the Holy Mountain, but following Kenyatta he does not suggest a complete identification of the symbol with what it symbolises as characteristic of the Kikuyu understanding of the relationship of God to Mount Kenya. Instead he distinguishes between two aspects of the Holy Mountain as a religious symbol. On the one hand Mount Kenya—more, perhaps, than other mountains—was a representative symbol. It witnessed to the presence and the power of the high God. On the other hand Mount Kenya was also an effective symbol. It was "imbued with the very power and presence of God". As such an effective symbol it could properly be addressed to in worship as an active manifestation of divinity[17].

The holy mountain, thus, plays a significant role as a symbol in traditional Kikuyu religion. It continues to do so also among Christian Kikuyu although Kiicho admits that the predominant missionary attitude did not ask for points of contracts for the Christian Message in traditional Kikuyu religion but assumed a relationship of radical discontinuity. To the Kikuyu, however, the concept of *Ngai* as God for all men provided a religious framework for appropriating the new religious and social influences, in the encounter with Christianity and education (*githoma*) and social progress became new values in a period of drastic disintegration of traditional structures after the British colonial expansion. Conversion to Christianity

---

[12] Cf. Kenyatta 1961, 236.
[13] Cf. ib.; Leakey 1078 ff.
[14] Cf. Kibicho 1978, 372; Kenyatta 1961, 246 f.
[15] Cf. ib.; Kenyatta 1961, 234.
[16] Cf. ib., 380 ff.
[17] Cf. Kibicho 1965, 2 ff.

actually, was called *Guthoma,* which literally means "to read" or "to become a literate"[18].

What is the religious function of the holy mountain to the Christian Kikuyu and to Christians in other parts of Africa? In order to illustrate this problem I turn to a Christian hymn to the Holy Mountain from Northern Tanzania and the New Year's Fiest of the Zulu *Nazaretha* Church.

3. *The Holy Mountain—a symbol for Christ*

The Holy Mountain, thus continues to be a living symbol for many Christians in Africa. This is a more involved fact than a mere illustration of the easy identification which African Christians can make of his own situation with Old Testament realities. As the Psalmist of old, the African Christian, too, can lift his eyes to the hills and ask "from whence does my help come" (Ps. 121,1). Nor does the religious functions of the traditional mountain symbolism in the Christian context reflect, only a local appropriation of Evangelical references, to the "rock of ages cleft for thee".

In the encounter of Christianity and traditional African religions the religious function of the mountain symbol actually is twofold. In the first place it becomes a carrier of a new religious message and gets influenced by what this message conveys. At the same time it serves as an indigenous means whereby this message can be appropriated in its religious sense. There is then a dialectic of continuity and discontinuity in the religious function of the symbol of the holy mountain—and I suggest in other symbols, too—in the encounter. The symbol takes on wider both religious and social references in the process[19]. This is illustrated very well in a Chagga-hymn to the holy mountain and to Christ[20], which however, does not seem to be very widely used and is not included in the Kiswahili Hymnal the Evangelical Lutheran Church of Tanzania (ELCT).

Among the Chagga on the slopes of Kilimanjaro in Northern Tanzania there has developed a local Christian culture, which has become a significant part of ELCT. With its impressive stature and its glacier, Mount Kilimanjaro, of course, is suggestive as a symbol to both Christian and pre-Christian Chagga[21]. As such it is praised also, in the Christian Chagga hymn, to which we have referred. It introduces its theme in unequivocal terms:

> There raises a chieftain
> bright and beautiful,
> high above all mountains.
> It is Kilimanjaro,
> which everybody can see.

---

[18] Kibicho 1978, 372ff., 383f. Cf. further Macpherson 93ff.
[19] Cf. Shorter 66ff.
[20] The hymn is published in German translation in Rosenkrantz 124f.
[21] Cf. Dundas 32ff.

Mount Kilimanjaro is believed to have been installed by God. As such it is a holy mountain and the hymn expresses the religious function of this symbol in a way which corresponds very well to characteristic features of traditional Kikuyu religion. It, thus, affirms:

> The bright appearance of Kilimanjaro
> became a sign to the Chagga
> from God, the Highest,
> who sheds light upon us
> as a bright light without an equal.
>
> The glorious glacier
> on Kilimanjaro's forehead
> testifies that God is with us.

If we focus more especially on the way in which the religious function of the symbol of the holy mountain is understood here we can note—in Kibicho's terminology—that Mount Kilimanjaro is primarily seen as a representative symbol, which witnesses to the presence and power of the high God. It does not say explicitly that Kilimanjaro is the abode of God "imbued with the very power and presence of God".

However, the hymn does not end here. It moves a step further and developes the traditional mountain-symbol by relating it to Christ. Without in any way denying the validity of what the traditional symbol signifies and communicates, it states in terms of a witness to Christ:

> It is Jesus, your son,
> Who makes visible
> what is prepared for our salvation.
> He is the Mountain
> full of eternal brightness.
> He gives us courage
> to fulfill our duties
> under your guiding hands.
>
> O Jesus, your countenance,
> which shows forth God's glory,
> excells the light of Kilimanjaro.
> In your name everything shall bow down.

It is worth noting here, that Jesus is addressed to as the son of the same divinity, to whom Mount Kilimanjaro testifies! The hymn, thus, explicitly affirms the continuity of the traditional references of the symbol of the mountain with what is contained in the revelation of Christ, the Holy Mountain. At the same time it implies that the traditional references are qualified and reorientated when they are related to the divine mysteries which Christ discloses. As a religious symbol Mount Kilimanjaro becomes secondary to Christ, in the same way as the holy trees in traditional Kikuyu worship is secondary to *Kere-Ngai*.

This development of the symbol of the holy mountain might mean that in the encounter of Christianity and traditional Chagga religion Mount Kilimanjaro as a Holy Mountain has become obsolete. This is an exclusive interpretation, which emphasises the element of discontinuity in the encounter. I doubt, however, whether that is the necessary interpretation of the hymn. Instead I suggest that the hymn reflects a reorientation and further development of the traditional symbol of the Holy Mountain, when in the encounter it becomes a carrier of the Christian message and gets influenced by what this message contains and refers to. As a representative symbol, thus, the Holy Mountain refers from itself to him who is seen to make manifest divinity in its very essence. As such Christ stands forth as the effective symbol who makes divine presence concrete and is brighter and reaches further than Mount Kilimanjaro and its glacier. This further implies that the social terms of reference of the traditional symbol are widened and that there is involved a critique of social and religious loyalities which are defined primarily in tribalistic terms[22].

The Christian Chagga-hymn to the holy mountain, thus, illustrates the religious function of the symbol within a qualified, continuous relationship of Christianity to traditional African religion. However, this is not the only way traditional mountain symbolism functions in Christian spirituality in Africa. There are also more radical, continuous relationships particularly among so called independent Church movements.

Both Kenyatta and Kibicho illustrate that this holds ture also for Kenya. Kenyatta, thus, comments on the worship of *Mwene-Ngai* facing *Kiri-Ngai* among the so called *Watu wa Nugu* or People of God, a breakaway group from the emerging Presbyterian Church of East Africa[23]. Kibicho on the other hand refers to the radical continuity with traditional *Ngai*-worship among Christian Mau Mau freedom fighters. He even quotes one of their hymns:

Pray earnestly
beseech truly,
for God is the same
one of ancient times[24].

Even so, the problem of independent church movements is particularly challenging in South Africa. As I have already mentioned I will illustrate alternative functions of the symbol of the holy mountain in Christian spirituality in Africa with some reflections on the New Year's Fiest of the *Nazaretha* Church.

---

[22] Cf. Kibicho 1978, 366f.
[23] Cf. Kenyatta 1961, 273ff.
[24] Kibicho 1978, 381ff.

4. *The royal mountain and Christ*

At a previous symposion, which dealt with new religious movements, Bengt Sundkler illustrated characteristics of independent church movements among Swazi and Zulu[25]. The *Nazaretha* Church is one of the more distinct of these movements with charismatic and/or "Zionist" features[26]. It is inspired by a rich heritage from Isaiah Shembe, prophet, church-leader and hymn-writer.

The New Year's Fiest plays a central role in the worship of the *Nazaretha* church[27]. In an extraordinary BBC series on different religions it was presented to a greater audience. This Fiest recalls the initiation of the *Nazaretha* church and it can be compared to an annual covenant service within Methodism.

The New Year's Fiest at *Inhlangakozi* can be a prolonged and lively festival where singing of Shembe's hymns with their characteristic rythm is an integral element[28]. The climax of the fiest is the procession uphill *Inhlangakozi* with the sermon of the prophet and the ritual on the peak of the mountain. At a terrass below the peak, the prophet, at present a grand-son of Isaiah Shembe, gives a sermon, which is based on the Bible and functions as an annual confirmation of the Law[29].

After the sermon, which can last for more than an hour the prophet invites his people to climbe the peak. There new rituals including dances and a Communion Service take place. There each participant also performs a particular rite: takes a stone, spits on it and throws it on a cairn. No prayers are said, the ritual as such is seen to bring blessing[30]. The holy mountain functions as an effective symbol of divine presence[31].

In his Hymnal, Isaiah Shembe expresses the significance of the new year ritual on the holy mountain[32]. In one of these hymns Shembe encourages his people:

> The enemies of Jehova
> rise up against you.
> Rise up, rise up
> Ye Africans.
>
> Those are given kingly authority
> upon the mountain.

---

[25] Cf. Sundkler 1975, 215 ff.

[26] Sundkler 1976, 161 ff., where the Zionist characteristics of the *Nazaretha* Church is emphasised.

[27] Sundkler 1976, 167 ff., 178 ff., where the New Year's Fiest at Inhlangakozi is studied with reference also to the annual July festival at Ekuphakaweni, where the prophet lives. In this ritual, too, the mountain symbolism is involved.

[28] Cf. ib., 183 ff.

[29] Cf. Becken 138 ff.

[30] Cf., ib. 148.

[31] Cf. Sundkler 1976, 197 ff., where worship at Ekuphakaweni is interpreted in terms of realised eschatology.

[32] On the interpretation of Shembe's hymnal, cf. Sundkler 1976, 190 ff.

Rise up, rise up
Ye Africans.

They already want to deprive
the eternal kingly authority.
Rise up, rise up
Ye Africans[33].

Compared with what we have learned, so far, of the ritual function of the holy mountain it is interesting to note that what this symbol communicates is interpreted in terms of *ubukhozi,* kingly authority. This should be understood with reference both to the role of divine kingship among Zulu and the relationship of Shembe's family to Zulu royalty[34].

The holy mountain of the *Nazaretha* church is, thus, related both to the sanctified royal ancestry of the Zulu nation and to the God of the Bible. *Inhlangakozi* is both a Mount Zion and a place where Zulu *ubukhozi* is restored and experienced[35].

In the religious function of *Inhlangakozi* as a symbol, thus, we see another example of the characteristic dialectic of continuity and discontinuity in what the symbol referred to in its traditional context and what it represents and communicates in its new christianized framework. It seems, however, as if the continuity here is more radical compared to the Chagga hymn. This hymn represents a more advanced reorientation of the traditional symbol.

5. *Concluding remarks*

These examples of how the symbol of the holy mountain is used in different religious contexts in Africa are, of course, too limited to provide a basis for far-reaching generalizations on how symbols function religiously in the encounter of Christianity and other religions. I dare to suggest, however, that this kind of analysis can be applied also when studying other encounters of religions inside and outside Africa. I furthermore suggest that what I have said of the possibility of the symbol to function both as a carrier of a new religious message and as an indigenous means to appropriate this message locally and give it adequate form in different milieus is relevant not only for the African contexts which I have tried to illustrate.

In one respect this argument should be qualified, however. The symbols, which most likely have the religious functions which I have discussed are those which are of a general nature; light, way, living water, and which some are tempted to speak of as archetypes. Yet the comparison between the Chagga-hymn to the holy mountain and Shembe's interpretation of the

---

[33] Cf. Oosthuizen 159f.

[34] Cf. Berglund 35f., 198f.; Sundkler 1976, 168.

[35] Cf. Sundkler 1976, 195f. and 313ff.

blessing of the New Year's Fiest on *Inhlangakozi* indicates, that in the encounter of Christianity and other religions it is not only the symbols as such which produce the local appropriation of the new religious message and give it adequate localized form. Not even in the encounter of Christianity and other religions the symbols function religiously without human beings as actors in the historical process.

Bibliography

Axelson, S., 1970, *Culture confrontation in Lower Congo.* Diss. Uppsala. Studia Missionalia Upsaliensia 13. Uppsala.

Becken, H.-J., 1967, On the holy mountain, a visit to the New Year's Festival of the *Nazaretha* Church on Mount Nhlangakozi *Journal of African religion* 1.

Berglund, A., 1975, *Zulu thought-patterns and symbolism.* Diss. Cape Town. Studia Missionalia Upsaliensia 22. Uppsala.

Dundas, C., 1968, *Kilimanjaro and its people.* London.

Kenyatta, J., 1961, *Facing Mount Kenya.* London.

— 1968, *Suffering without bitterness.* Nairobi.

Kibicho, S., 1965, Traditional Kikuyu religion, *Report from Ecumenical workshop in religious research.* (Mimeographed) Nairobi.

— 1978, The Continuity of the African conception of God into and through Christianity: a Kikuyu case-study. *Christianity in independent Africa.* Ed. E. Fasholé-Luke, R. Gray a. o. London.

Kyrkohistorisk Årsskrift 1977, Utg. I. Montgomery, Uppsala.

Leakey, L., 1977, *The Southern Kikuyu before 1903,* 1–3. London.

Macpherson, R., 1970, *The Presbyterian church in Kenya.* Nairobi.

Mbiti, J., 1970, *Concepts of God in Africa.* London.

Oosthuizen, C., 1967, *The Theology of a South African Messiah.* Leiden.

Rosenkrantz, G., 1951, *Das Lied der Kirche in der Welt.* Tübingen.

Shorter, A., 1973, *African culture and the Christian church.* London.

Sundkler, B., 1975, The New in the New Religious Movements among Zulu and Swazi. *Scripta Instituti Donneriani Aboensis* 7.

— 1976, *Zulu Zion and some Swazi Zionists.* Studia Missionalia Upsaliensia 29. Uppsala.

The symbolism of Mesopotamian cult images

By HELMER RINGGREN

Is. 44: 12–20 contains a satirical description of the way the pagans, *i.e.*, the Babylonians, make their "gods", *i.e.*, their idols. "The ironsmith fashions it and works it over the coals; he shapes it with hammers, and forges it with his strong arm ... The carpenter stretches a line, he marks it out with a pencil; he fashions it with planes, and marks it with a compass; he shapes it into the figure of a man, with the beauty of a man, to dwell in a house. He cuts down cedars", he plants holm trees and oaks and lets them grow. Some he uses for fuel to warm himself or to bake bread, of others "he makes a god and worships it". With these and similar words the prophet ridicules those who make cult images.

This might of course be an independent literary creation—and perhaps it is—but interestingly enough there is a Babylonian text that could well have served as the prophet's model. In a ritual for the *akītu* festival in Babylon from Seleucid times we read about the third day as follows: "When it is three hours after sunrise, he shall call a metalworker and give him precious stones and gold from the treasury of the god Marduk to make two images for (the ceremonies of) the sixth day. He shall call a woodworker and give him (some) cedar and tamarisk (pieces). He shall call a goldsmith and give him (some) gold."

Then the work shall be distributed: the tail (?) to the metalworker, the breast to the goldsmith, the thigh to the woodworker, the ribs to the weaver. A detailed description of the images follows: 7 fingers high, one of cedar, one of tamarisk, precious stones shall be mounted, one image shall hold in its left hand a snake (made) of cedar, the second a scorpion. They shall be clothed in red garments, and they shall be placed in the house of the god Madan until the sixth day. Then their heads shall be stricken off and they shall be thrown into a fire that has been kindled[1].

It is obvious that the images in question are not cult images in a real sense, *i.e.*, images to be set up in a temple to receive sacrifices and worship, but images intended to be used in a "magical" ceremony: they represent evil forces that shall be annihilated by means of destroying their images in fire. At the same time, the text shows that it was well known how these images were made, but also that this did not detract from their symbolic, or magical, value.

---

[1] Cf. ANET 331 f.

Unfortunately, we are not told how the Babylonians conceived of the relationship between the images and the evil beings which they symbolized. We have to draw our conclusions from what we can, so to speak, read between the lines.

Let us first consider the linguistic usage! "Image" in Accadian is *ṣalmu,* and there are examples of both *ṣalam ilāni,* "image of god(s)" and e.g. *ṣalam ḫurāṣi,* "golden image"[2]. *Ṣalmu* also means "royal image, royal statue", and it is not without interest that kings often set up their images in conquered cities in order to mark their presence and to show that they were ruling there.

In addition, however, the very word *ilu,* "god", can be used with reference to the image or statue of the god. There are such expressions as "to anoint the gods", to carry away gods and men as booty, to remove the gods from their pedestals, to send back (the queen of Arabia and) the gods to their country, to restore or to renew the gods, and so on. It can be said that "the high priest carries (the image of) Marduk, and the king walks before the god (*i.e.* his image)"[3]. All this suggests that the image in some way *was* the god, or that the god let himself be represented by the image.

Other texts bear witness to the same kind of "identity". We are told that a god may become angry because his temple has been neglected and then leave it. Esarhaddon says that Marduk was angry and allowed Babylon to be destroyed, and then "the gods who dwelt therein flew away like birds and went up to heaven"[4]. Other texts give reason to suspect that in reality it was enemies that carried away the images and so put an end to the gods' presence.

A Sumerian text called "The Curse of Agade" contains the following passage: "She has gone from the city, left it; like a maid who forsakes her chamber, the holy Inanna has forsaken her Agade shrine; like a warrior with raised weapons she attacked the city in fierce battle."[5] It is not entirely clear if this is a circumlocution for the attack of enemies and their carrying away the image of the goddess, but much suggests that this is the case. It is probable at least that the whole poem deals with the fall of the city as a consequence of the attack of the Gutians.

In any case, "the role of the image was central in the cult as well as in private life"[6], as is shown by the great number of small images that have been found. "The deity was considered present in its image if it showed certain specific features and paraphernalia and was cared for in the appropriate manner" established by tradition[7].

Most images were made of precious wood and were either covered with garments or plated with gold. The eyes were made of precious stones. "The

---

[2] AHw 3, 1078 f.
[3] CAD 7, 102 f.
[4] Quoted in CAD 7, 97.
[5] Quoted from Kramer 63; cf. Albrektson 25.
[6] Oppenheim 1964, 184.
[7] Ib.

garments were changed in special ceremonies according to ritual requirements." Generally the images had human shape [8].

Oppenheim says that "the king and the god Assur [were] often represented in identical attire and pose", which suggests that "the image of the national god could reflect that of his priest, the king"[9]. In support of this he refers to an inscription on the bronze reliefs mounted on the gate of the New Year's Chapel in Assur, "the figure of Assur going to battle against Tiamat is that of Sennacherib". But this could also mean that the king played the role of Assur in his battle against Tiamat in the ritual drama of the New Year's Festival.

The image had two main functions: it "served as the focal point for sacrificial activities", and it was carried in the processions of the great cultic festivals[10]. The image stood on its pedestal in the cella and functioned as a king in his palace. The temple was his "house" (E=*bitu*). In general the public was not allowed to enter the cella, but the image was visible from the courtyard through a row of doorways. But it could be seen by the public when it was carried in procession[11].

The sacrifices were regarded as meals and were served in the same way as the meals of the king. Food was placed in front of the image, music was performed, and incense was burned. As Oppenheim observes, the god "was apparently thought to consume [the food] by merely looking at it"[12]. It could also be passed in a swinging motion before the eyes of the image. After the food had thus been presented to the image, it was taken away and sent to the king for counsumption[13]. This privilege of the king is illustrated by Sargon II's remark: "The citizens of Babylon and Borsippa, the temple personnel, the scholars, and the administrators of the country, who formerly looked upon [Merodach-Baladan] as their king, now brought the leftovers of Bel and Sarpanitu, Nabu and Tasmetu to me at Dur-Ladinni and asked me to enter Babylon."[14] In other words, Sargon was offered the privilege that normally belonged to the king of Babylon. It is possible that the high officials of the sanctuary enjoyed the same privilege in some cases.

Jacobsen thinks that there was identity not only between the god and his image but also between the god and his temple. He speaks of "closeness of essence with the power inhabiting it (the temple)", or, in some cases, "making the temple more nearly an embodiment than a habitation"[15]. The argument seems strained; it is built mainly on the fact that temples sometimes have names resembling divine epithets, e.g. E-kur, "house-mountain", cf. Enlil's epithet *Kur-gal,* "great mountain", E-babbar, "house-rising sun".

---

[8] Cf. Ib. 189.
[9] Ib. 185.
[10] Cf. Ib.
[11] Cf. Ib. 186f.
[12] Ib. 192.
[13] Cf. Ib. 189.
[14] Ib.
[15] Jacobsen 16.

We now revert to the making of images. In order to make an image suitable as a symbol of a god it must be consecrated. This was done by means of a ritual that was called *pet pī*, "opening of the mouth". At least two versions of the ritual are preserved, the most complete one was published by Sidney Smith[16] and later by Ebeling[17]. The procedure was the following.

Two pots of holy (pure) water were set up in the workshop, a red cloth was placed in front of "the god" (i.e. the image) and a white cloth beside him (red is the colour of death, white of life), and a preliminary "washing of the mounth" (*mes pī*) was performed on the newly made image. The officiating priest recited incantations, as e.g. "You who are born in heaven", and "From this time forth you shall go before your father Ea". In the night the image was carried in the light of torches to the bank of the river and placed on a reed-mat (symbol of the mother goddess, i.e. of birth) facing east. Sacrifices and libations were performed, incantations recited and the washing of the mouth repeated. The god was turned towards the west, and new sacrifices, incantations and mouth-washing were performed. Each incantation was obviously intended to make a certain part of the statue "perfect". A ram was sacrificed, then followed the incantation "Holy image that is perfected by a great ritual". The priest "opened the god's eyes" by touching them with a twig of tamarisk. Then the god was taken by the hand and led to his temple, accompanied by the incantations "Foot that advances", and "When he goes in the street". At the gate, sacrifices were performed, the god was taken into the temple and seated on his throne. Another washing of the mouth took place, whereupon the god received his divine insignia.

Everything goes to show that the ceremony was the symbol of a birth, the image was given "life". This is further illustrated by a text quoted by Ebeling, "This god of the New Moon ... the work of human beings ... without opening of the mouth he does not smell the incense, does not eat herbs, does not drink water."[18] Ebeling concludes: "Also bewirkt die Mundöffnung, der die Mundwaschung mit heiligem Weihwasser vorangeht, die Belebung der Gottesstatue, die vorher nichts als Materie (*titu*) ohne Leben (*napistu*) oder Geist (*saru*) des Gottes gewesen ist."[19]

The last lines of the ritual suggest that it was the insignia and not the shape of the image that were essential. Oppenheim has also shown that the garments of the divine image, in many cases at least, represented the sky, the adornments being the stars, etc.[20]. As is well known, most of the gods were celestial gods.

The aim of the ritual was obviously to make the image a true and living representative of the god and to enable him to partake of the sacrificial

---

16 Cf. Smith 37 ff.

17 Cf. Ebeling 100 ff., see also Oppenheim 1964, 186.

18 Ebeling 100.

19 Ib.

20 Cf. Oppenheim 1949, 172 ff.

meals presented to him. Unfortunately, the ancient Babylonians have not told us how they conceived of the relationship between the image and the god in heaven. It is obvious, though, that through his image the god was thought to be present in his temple.

Bibliography

AHw	Soden, W. von, Akkadisches Handwörterbuch
ANET	Ancient Near Eastern Texts related to the Old Testament. Ed. by J. Pritchard
CAD	Chicago Assyrian Dictionary
JNES	Journal of Near Eastern Studies
JRAS	Journal of the Royal Asiatic Society

Albrektson, B., 1967, *History and the gods* (Coniectanea Biblica, O.T. series 1). Lund.

Ebeling, E., 1931, *Tod und Leben nach den Vorstellungen der Babylonier* 1. Berlin.

Jacobsen, T., 1976, *The treasures of darkness.* New Haven.

Kramer, S., 1963, *The Sumerians.* Chicago.

Oppenheim, A., 1949, The golden garments of the gods. *JNES* 8.

— 1964, Ancient Mesopotamia. Chicago.

Smith, S., 1925, The Babylonian ritual for the consecration and induction of a divine statue. *JRAS*

Man as Symbol of God

By ANDERS HULTGÅRD

It is a well-known fact that Judaism and Zoroastrianism, being prophetic religions with a monotheistic character, present many affinities (Winston, Hultgård). One point of similarity is a clear tendency towards aniconic representation of the Divine, which, from the beginning, was the mark of Judaism as well as Zoroastrianism, being religions with a nomadic background. As a result of the confrontation with the agricultural and urban civilisations of the ancient Near East, attempts were made to introduce iconic representations of the Divine to be used in the cult. Many groups within Judaism, and most probably also within Zoroastrianism[1], levelled a vigorous resistance to these attempts. As a consequence, there arose in both religions a strong movement to prohibit cult-images, which in Judaism also tended to develop into a prohibition of figurative art in general[2]. This movement became victorious in the end and its aniconic conception of the Divine has ever since remained the normative attitude of both Jews and Zoroastrians. What were the reasons for these attitudes in Judaism and in Zoroastrianism? And were there theological ideas that could function as a substitute to cult-images of the Divine? These are the questions that briefly will be discussed in this paper.

As to Judaism, it is important to point out that from the time of the Second Temple and onwards, the prohibition of making any image of YHWH was beyond all dispute. It is during the Second Temple period also that a resistance to all forms of man-like representations is taking shape and receives some of its clearest expressions. Thus, the Hasmonaeans never put their effigies on the coins they issued and the same is true of Herod the Great[3], although he introduced figurative art and freestanding sculptures in the non-Jewish parts of his kingdom[4]. In the first century A.D., the attitude towards human images became more rigorous and was linked to a growing opposition against the Roman rule[5]. The Jewish historian Josephus reports some incidents which bear witness to a strong reluctance felt by the Jews against

---

[1] It is the merit of Mary Boyce, 98 ff., to have called attention to an iconoclastic movement within Zoroastrianism.

[2] For a discussion of this development, cf. the studies of Gutmann 10 ff.; Roth 505 ff.

[3] Cf. the documentation of ancient Jewish coins found in Reifenberg, 10 ff., and Meshorer, 41 ff.

[4] Cf. for exemple Josephus *Antiquities* XV,364; cf. also Roth, 507.

[5] Cf. Roth, 507.

any form of images[6]. It seems, however, that a distinction was made in this respect between the holy city of Jerusalem and the rest of Palestine[7]. From the middle of the second century and up to the sixth, a more tolerant attitude concerning figurative art appeared. This is demonstrated by some sayings in the Talmud[8] and above all by the lavishly decorated synagogues of Palestine and Syria constructed during this period[9]. Here, we find animal figures and, what is more remarkable, representations of human and angelic beings[10] which probably meant more than pure decorations to the Jews who gathered in these synagogues for prayer and religious instruction[11]. However, from the late sixth century, a more rigorous attitude towards images of human beings can be observed, which also seems to have produced iconoclastic movements[12]. When coming under the rule of Islam, most of the Jewish communities rejected any form of figurative art[13].

The reason put forward by classical Judaism for an objection to images of the Divinity and representations of human figures is that it is forbidden by the torah. This is the answer given already by Josephus in various passages of his works[14]. But it must be borne in mind that the rejection of the making of iconic figures of man was based on an interpretation of the Second Commandment (*Exodus* 20,4, *Deuteronomy* 5,8; see also *Deut.* 4,15). These passages, however, were in need of a precision since they could be interpreted in different ways according to varying contexts and historical situations[15]. The main theological reason for not representing YHWH in any

---

[6] Pilate introduces into Jerusalem Roman standards which had the images of the emperor attached to them. This was felt as a violation of the law against the making of an iconic figure of man and caused an immense excitement among the Jews and Pilate was forced to remove them, see *Antiquities* XVIII,55 ff., and *War* II,169 ff. The whole Jewish world is stirred up by the attempt of Caligula to have his statue set up in the temple of Jerusalem, see *Ant.* XVIII,261 ff. and *War* II,184 ff.

[7] In *Ant.* XVIII,55 the incident mentioned above is explained by Josephus with a reference to the Second Commandment: "our law forbids the making of images". In *War* II,170 he gives a precision by stating that the law permit no image to be set up in Jerusalem. According to *Ant.* XV,277 images of men could not be tolerated in Jerusalem. Cf. also *Talmud Yer. Avodah Zarah* 3,1 which seems to hint at special laws for the holy city when reporting that before the destruction 70 A.D. all likenesses were to be found in Jerusalem except those of man.

[8] Cf. *Talmud Yer. Av. Zar.* 3,3; 4,1; cf. also Roth, 508.

[9] It is noteworthy that the synagogue of Dura Europos, constructed in the middle of the third century, was preceded by an earlier one whose pictures were without figures of man and animals.

[10] Let us mention as examples the synagogue of Dura Europos, of which Goodenough 12,158 ff., gives a detailed description. Further, Beth Alpha (Saller 23 ff.) and Gerasa (Saller 43 f.) with their rich mosaics depicting also human figures. In Chorazin there can still be seen *in locu,* as was by the present author in 1978, a sculptured column representing a human face, probably an angelic being.

[11] For a discussion of Jewish symbols found in the synagogues, cf. Goodenough 12,64 ff.

[12] Some synagogues in Galilee show traces of iconoclastic activity, as for instance those of Barʿam and Capernaum (Loffreda, 60).

[13] Cf. Roth, 521.

[14] Cf. *Antiquities* XVIII,55 and 121, XV,277 *War* II,195 and *Against Apion* II,75 and 191.

[15] The opposition against Rome favoured a rigid interpretation of the Second Commandment. In Babylonia at a later period, however, the rabbis could frequent synagogues

image was no doubt to preserve his transcendental character, but this reason could apparently not be applied to the prohibition of representations of man. However, the idea found in *Genesis* 1,26–27 and 9,6 that man was made in the image of God, would constitute an excellent theological argument against the use of iconic figures of man, because in that case something of the Divinity would also be represented. The idea of man as created in the image of God is, however, as far as I have been able to ascertain, never explicitly connected to the objection of making images of human beings. One ground for this may be that rabbinic Judaism tends to interpret the statement of Genesis 1,26–27 in the sense that man is not an image of God but of the angels or of Adam as primordial man[16]. Neither intertestamental nor rabbinic sources enlarge on the interpretation of the idea of man's godlikeness[17]. But some texts from the Second Temple period offer a more precise meaning, which seems to stress an identity between God and man. Here, we may speak about man as symbol of God. The *Testament of Naphtali* thus states: "There is no inclination and no thought (of man) which the Lord knoweth not, for He created every man after his own image."[18] We read in the *Wisdom of Salomon* 2,23 that: "God created man for immortality and made him the image of His own eternal self."[19] These passages reveal the intimate relation thought to exist between God and man. It seems to me probable that, to many Jews in the time of the Second Temple, man could function as a symbol of God which would tacitly imply an objection to iconic figures of man.

Zoroastrianism, as well as other forms of the ancient Iranian religion, is characterized by an aniconic conception of the Divine. Herodotus records that it is not the custom of the Persians to make and set up statues, temples and altars. Instead, they ascend to the peaks of the mountains and there offer sacrifice to the God of heaven[20]. The negative attitude towards cult-images is reflected in many actions performed by the Achaemenians[21].

---

where, for patriotic reasons, statues of the ruler were erected, see *Talmud Babli Av. Zar.* 43b and *Rosh Hashanah* 24b. The archaeological evidence from the synagogues of the third to the sixth centuries must be explained in the light of a less rigid interpretation of the Second Commandment.

16 Cf. the texts and the discussion given by Jervell, 84 ff., 96 ff.

17 This idea appears mostly as a quotation from *Genesis* without any precise interpretation. Cf. for instance of earlier texts: *Sir.* 17,3; *Jub.* 6,8; *Pirqe Aboth* 3,14. In *Jub.* 16,26 we find the interpretation that Israel is created in the image of God. For all the passages from the Second Temple period which allude to *Gen.* 1,26–27, cf. Jervell, 21 ff. One reason for passing over *Gen.* 1,26 f. without an interpretation seems to have been the rabbinical view not to instruct the common people in the meaning of the first chapter of *Genesis*.

18 *Test. Napht.* 5,2: ὅτι οὐκ ἔστι πᾶν πλάσμα καὶ πᾶσα ἔννοια ἥν οὐκ ἔγνω κύριος' πάντα γὰρ ἄνθρωπον ἔκτισε κατ'εἰκόνα ἑαυτοῦ.

19 The Greek text runs as follows: ὅτι ὁ θεος ἔκτισεν τὸν ἄνθρωπον ἐπ' ἀφθαρσίᾳ καὶ εἰκόνα τῆς ἰδίας ἀϊδιότητος ἐποίησεν αὐτόν.

20 *Hist.* I,131.

21 When Xerxes destroys a temple with pagan idols (*daivadāna*), most probably in Babylon, he proclaims on a rock relief: "the idols (*daivas*) shall not be worshipped." The text is found in Kent, 151. The violent attacks of

But, on the other hand, it is precisely the Achaemenians who introduce a symbol of the highest god, Ahura Mazda, in the form of a winged disc in which the god himself appears as a human being[22]. The iconography is clearly based on Assyro-Babylonian models. It is not easy to decide whether these images, found on reliefs, were worshipped as deities or were made for the glorification of the king of the kings only. Anyhow, we do not find free-standing images or temples at this stage. With the reign of Artaxerxes II (404–359) something new is being introduced: the making of images of the goddess Anahita that were housed in temples erected in the principal cities of the empire[23]. No doubt, the introduction of fire-temples also goes back to the same period[24]. According to Strabo[25], there were in Parthian times two kinds of temples: sanctuaries (ἱερά) for a particular deity, most often Anahita, in which the image of the goddess (or god) was worshipped, and fire-temples (πυραιθεῖα) where only the holy fire was burning. Against the background of primitive Zoroastrianism with its aniconic conception of the Divine, the image-cult established by Artaxerxes must have provoked a fierce opposition from many Zoroastrian groups. Owing to the lack of sources for this period, we do not know anything about an anti-iconic movement within Zoroastrianism in late Achaemenian and Parthian times. When we come to the Sasanian period however, the objection to images for adoration marks the Zoroastrian religion, now being that of the state itself. But the kings continue to represent the principal Zoroastrian deities on the rock reliefs showing their royal enthronement accomplished by the gods[26].

Mary Boyce has recently shed some light on the history of the anti-iconic attitude which has been inherited by modern Zoroastrianism. She maintains that the term *uzdēs,* traditionally interpreted to mean "idol", may instead refer to cult-images of Zoroastrian deities[27]. Even if the etymology proposed by Boyce is correct, only the context in which the term *uzdēs* is found, will help us to decide whether pagan idols or images of Iranian gods are meant. The exhortations found in the Pahlaviliterature to keep away from *uzdēz-paristišnēh* are recorded in a context which strongly suggests an image-

Kambyses on Egyptian and Phoenician temple cults must be seen as an expression of the Iranian aniconic conception of the Divine. These actions of Kambyses are recorded in Herodotus *Hist.* III,13, 16, 27 ff.

22 Sometimes the winged disc is found without a human figure (examples Hinnells, 100, 103), which indicates that the winged disc could function as a symbol of the god even without the human figure. It seems clear to me that the figure in the disc represents Ahura Mazda and not the king or his genius. The rock relief of Behistun 73 makes it very clear that it is the god who is represented by the figure in the disc.

23 The evidence is given by Berossos as quoted in Clemens Alexandrinus *Protrepticus* V,65,3 and in Agathias II,24. Cf. also Wikander, 61 ff.

24 Cf. Wikander, 60; Boyce, Mary, 98.

25 *Geography* XV,3,15.

26 Cf. the documentation in Ghirshman, 119 ff.

27 Boyce, Mary, 96. She proposes an etymology from the Avestic root *d*aes- "show". *Uzdēs* should thus mean a "showing forth, representation".

worship inside the Zoroastrian community and makes it clear that this was looked upon as a danger for the faithful[28]. A comparison between certain Avestan traditions and the Pahlavi-texts dependant on them shows that the problem of image-worship became a matter of great concern during a fixed period and some time after. The beginning of the seventh book of *Dēnkart* describes the transmission of the Divine Word (*vaxš*) from Ahura Mazda to Zoroaster by the intermediary of some mythical figures. With regard to the Avestan Taxma Rupa, the text follows first the statement of *Yašt* 19,28 that this hero conquered demons and wizards mastering even the Evil Spirit himself. It then adds, however, that Taxma Rupa also fought against image-cult and propagated among mankind the cult of fire and the worship of the Creator[29]. The passage clearly alludes to the aniconic conception of Ahura Mazda, who is instead represented by his creation and by fire, and contrasts to this the iconic representation of the Divine. The coming saviours, as described in *Yašt* 19,88–96, are in some later texts also said to be the destroyers of those who within the realm of Iran serve these images[30]. This redaction and reinterpretation of ancient Zoroastrian traditions should probably be dated to the time when the veneration of images was introduced and was fluorishing, that is the late Achaemenian, the Seleucid and the Parthian periods. In the beginning of the Sasanian period temples with images of Zoroastrian deities were still in existence but they were gradually transformed into fire-temples[31]. By the end of the Sasanian period, the use of cult-images was wholly suppressed.

There seem to have been several motives involved in the rejection of cult-images of Zoroastrian deities. The aniconic conception of the Divine, professed by primitive Zoroastrianism as part of its Indo-european heritage, has certainly favoured the resistance to image-worship. However, theological arguments were no doubt more influential in this respect. The distinction made in Zoroastrian theology between the non-material (Avest. *mainyava-*, Pahl. *mēnōk*) and the material (Avest. *gaeθya-*, Pahl. *gētīk*) is fundamental to Zoroastrianism[32]. Ahura Mazda and the *yazatas* (spiritual beings worthy of worship) belong to the non-material, intangible existence. To make and consecrate an image of God or his *yazatas* meant to transfer something from an immaterial sphere into a material, which should not be there. It could also be considered as a violation against the prerogative of

---

[28] In addition to the passages with *uzdēs* and its compounds, given by Mary Boyce, the following are worth quoting: *Mēnoi i xrat* 2,93: *hac uzdēz-paristišnēh i dēv-izakēh dūr pahrēc.* Further the same writing 36,11, which tells us that the one who serves the idols commits one of the heaviest sins. The Pahlavi text of those passages is found in Nyberg 71,82.

[29] *Dēnkart* VII,1,19: *u-š apāc apakand uzdēs-paristakēh ud ravakēnīt andar dāmān niyāyišn ud parastišn i dātār.* The term *niyāyišn* is used particularly to denote the worship of fire.

[30] Cf. *Mēnoi i xrat* 2,93 ff.

[31] Cf. Boyce, Mary, 105.

[32] For this distinction, cf. the analys given by Lommel 93 ff.; Shaked, 59 ff.

God who is the sole creator. Furthermore, because the evil powers do not possess a material form, they would use an image in which to appear and "misappropriate the worship intended for the divinity."[33]

If then Ahura Mazda is not permitted to be represented in a material form as a cult-image, he is nevertheless thought to reveal himself to mankind on the earth. According to Zoroastrian belief, God is made manifest by His creation and in particular by the fire, which is invoked as "the son of Ahura Mazda". But there is in Zoroastrianism an idea which corresponds to the *imago Dei* theology of Judaism. *Bundahišn,* a theological compendium based on Avestan traditions states in 26,10f.: "His (sc. Ohrmazd's) material sign is the righteous man, he who brings joy or affliction to the righteous man, has also brought joy or affliction to Ohrmazd."[34] A kind of identity is here presupposed and we may thus consider the righteous man as the earthly symbol of God. But who is understood to be a righteous man? Man himself is for Zoroastrianism the foremost creation in the material world[35] and man reaches his perfection in the righteous man, embodied in Gayomart, the primordial man, and in Zoroaster the prophet himself[36]. At the same time, the pious Zoroastrian may be regarded as a representative of the righteous man. In the royal ideology the same idea is to be found. The king representing by his position the righteous man can be styled as the image of God. The Iranian king is, according to a passage from Plutarch, "an image of the God who saves the universe".[37]

Thus, in both Judaism and Zoroastrianism, a similar theological idea of man as created in the image of God appears, which may have been felt as a corrective counterpart to image-worship and, for Judaism, also to representations of human figures. Man means in this respect to Judaism either the Israelite as a member of the chosen people or man in general. To Zoroastrianism man is above all the perfect man as represented by the primordial man, the prophet, the king and the faithful of the Zoroastrian community.

---

[33] The wording is that of Boyce, Mary, 97.

[34] The Pahlavi-text runs: *u-š gētīk daxšak mart i ahrāv, kē mart i ahrāv ramēnēt ayāp bēšēt, adak-iš Ohrmazd ramēnīt ayāp bēšt būt.* This passage alludes by its wording to another passage in *Bundahišn* (chapter 4) where Gayomart is the righteous man who is attacked by the whoredemon Jeh: *beš apar mart i ahrāv.* According to *Zātspram* 35,13 Zoroaster was made in the likeness (*handāzakēh*) of Ahura Mazda.

[35] Cf. for instance *Dēnkart* 124,14f.; cf. also Bailey, 87.

[36] For Zoroaster as *mart i ahrāv* cf. especially *Dēnkart* VII, 2,20.

[37] Plutarch, *Themistokles,* 27, reproduces an Iranian conception put in the mouth of an Iranian nobleman: ἡμῖν δὲ πολλῶν νόμων καὶ καλῶν ὄντων κάλλιστος οὗτός ἐστι, τιμᾶν βασιλέα καὶ προσκυνεῖν ὡς εἰκόνα θεοῦ τοῦ τὰ πάντα σώζοντος.

Bibliography

Bailey, H., 1972, *Zoroastrian problems in the ninth century books.* Oxford.
Boyce, Mary, 1975, *Iconoclasm among the Zoroastrians.* Christianity, Judaism and other Greco-Roman cults, 4. Leiden.
Bundahišn, 1908, *The Bundahišn,* being a facsimile of the TD manuscript No. 2., ed. by T. Anklesaria. Bombay.
— 1971, *The Bondahesh,* being a facsimile edition of the manuscript TD 1. ICF, 88.
Codex, 1972, *The Codex DH,* being a facsimile edition of Bondahesh, Zand-e Vohuman Yasht and parts of Denkard. ICF, 89.
Clemens Alexandrinus, 1961, *Protrepticus,* ed. C. Mondesert et A. Plassert. *Sources Chrétiennes,* 2. Paris.
Denkart, 1911, *Denkart:* The complete text of the Pahlavi Dinkart, ed. D. Madan. Bombay.
Flavius Josephus, 1887 s, *Opera* 1 f. Ed. B. Niese. Berlin.
Ghirshman, R., 1975, Les scènes d'investiture royale dans l'art rupestre des Sassanides. *Syria,* 52.
Goodenough, E., 1965, *Jewish Symbols in the Greco-Roman period,* 12. Toronto.
Gutmann, J., 1971, The 'Second Commandment' and the image in Judaism. *No graven images.* Ed. by J. Gutmann. New York.
Herodotus, 1927, *Historiae,* ed. by C. Hude. Oxford.
Hinnells, J., 1973, *Persian mythology.* London.
Hultgård, A., 1978, Das Judentum in der hellenistisch-römischen Zeit und die iranische Religion—ein religionsgeschichtliches Problem. *Aufstieg und Niedergang der römischen Welt,* 2, 16. Berlin.
ICF, Iranian culture foundation. Teheran.
Jervell, J., 1960, *Imāgo Dei.* Göttingen.
Kent, R., 1953, *Old Persian,* grammar, texts, lexicon. New Haven.
Loffreda, S., 1977, *A* visit to *Caphernaum.* Jerusalem.
Lommel, H., 1930, *Die Religion Zarathustras nach dem Awesta dargestellt.* Tübingen.
Meshorer, Y., 1967, *Jewish coins of the Second Temple period.* Tel Aviv.
Nyberg, H., 1964, *A manual of Pahlavi,* 1. Wiesbaden.
Plutarchus, 1972, *Themistocles,* ed. par R. Flacelière. Paris.
Reifenberg, A., 1947, *Ancient Jewish coins.* Jerusalem.
Roth, C., 1971, Art. *Encyclopedia Judaica,* 3. Jerusalem.
Saller, S., 1972, *Second revised catalogue of the ancient synagogues of the Holy Land.* Jerusalem.
Shaked, S., 1971, The notions *mēnōg* and *gētīg* in the Pahlavi texts and their relation to eschatology. *Acta Orientalia,* 33.
Strabo, 1966, Geography Books XV and XVI, ed. by H. L. Jones, London.
Talmud, 1925 f., Der babylonische Talmud, hebräisch und deutsch, ed. L. Goldschmidt.
— 1934 f., Talmud Yerushalmi, ed. H. Dinkels.
Vichitākihā, 1964, *Vichitākihā i Zātspram,* with text and introduction, ed. by B. Anklesaria. Bombay.
Wikander, S., 1946, *Feuerpriester in Kleinasien und Iran.* Acta Reg. Societatis Humaniorum Litterarum Lundensis, 40. Lund.
Winston, D., 1966, The Iranian component in the Bible, Apocrypha and Qumran. *History of Religions,* 5.

Literary Symbols and Religious Belief

By SVEN LINNÉR

Of all the world's religions, I shall here only be dealing with Christianity; this is the religion I know something about. I also impose strict limitations in the matter of literary examples, which are taken predominantly from modern Swedish literature. But I naturally hope that the views presented here will also prove applicable to other religions and literatures.

Characteristic of the modern situation I have in mind is the lack of any distinction between the languages of belief and non-belief. Thus, over a wide area, a believer on the one hand may use symbols which are in no way recognisable as specifically Christian, and may do so even when he wishes to portray experiences of a profoundly religious character; as reader, he can also recognise such experiences in the symbolism of the non-believer. A non-believer, on the other hand, may use Christian symbols without enabling us to attribute to him any conversion to faith.

Let me begin by quoting an example from *The Brothers Karamazov;* the point in question might be called a religious concept rather than a symbol, but it can still serve to illustrate the tendency to which I refer. In the conversation between Alyosha and Ivan (Chap. 3, Book V), Dostoyevsky confronts belief with denial. On one point, however, he lets the brothers agree, that is in the belief that one must "love life more than the meaning of it"[1]. Here the author, himself a devout Christian, has found a formula which was probably intended to be acceptable to the sceptics too among the novel's readers. The concept of "life", as used in the novel, builds a bridge between belief and non-belief.

That the two Karamazov brothers are united on this point is of interest and significance precisely because they disagree fundamentally in other respects. This may serve as an illustration of what is the basis of my subsequent argument, namely the notion, clearly controversial, that there *is* a tangible difference between believing and not believing. At one level, where the brothers talk of "life", the division between the two is admittedly hard to distinguish, even invisible, but at other levels it is clear and all-important. There is a wide gulf between their respective positions. Only when we realise this, do we understand how remarkable it is that they can be united in the same devotion to "life".

The formula on which Ivan and Alyosha are agreed concerns the meaning

---

[1] Dostoevskij 289. The passage is quoted in its context in Linnér 1975, 159. Dostoevsky's concept of "life" is studied in ch. VI, 141 ff., "Life versus the meaning of life".

of life and thus poses an existential question. My account here is limited to questions of this type, that is the meaning of life (or the cosmos, or existence), man's guilt, man's confrontation with death. One could of course claim that religious belief colours our whole range of experience, and that it is therefore misleading to limit the comparison to a few so-called existential themes. Should one not be able to observe equally interesting differences, or equally problematic points of concurrence in other areas too—in the contexts of love, happiness or unhappiness in work, the encounter with nature, social conflicts etc? This is perhaps true, but my account would then require the scope of a book. In an outline of this kind, I consider it permissible to concentrate my argument on a few main points.

And now to my Swedish examples. Almost twenty years ago, Artur Lundkvist was subjected to an unusual and overwhelming experience; he was caught in an earthquake. This is the subject of his collection of poems, *Agadir* (1961). In one of the poems he writes that God "was nowhere to be found"; for those engulfed there was only a vacuum, "only darkness endlessly waiting, unaware of its waiting"[2]. In the following poem the atmosphere has however changed and the poet testifies to God's presence and power, and our duty to surrender ourselves to his will.

—Just as I fell down into darkness I felt that God existed, it seized me like fear and rejoicing: God let his presence be known,
showed his power over the world, showed that against God there is no recourse but God,
no buildings, no walls, no inventions, no machines mean anything to God,
he sets the deep in tremors and all our certainty is crushed like straw,
his will alone sustains all living things, penetrates everything, more immanent than water and air.
What a mistake to seek him, when he is already present in everything, embracing and filling us,
we have only to surrender, to want nothing outside his will,
God has the same inescapable love for everyone,
for me whom he allowed to survive, filled with the knowledge of his presence,
for all those who died in the moment of disaster, happily united with him,
for all those who still move between life and death, imprisoned in the ruins,
those he has given time for insight and transformation[3].

This poem—admittedly cut and revised—has been included in the section, Hymns for Reading, in *Hymns and Songs 76,* published by the Swedish Church[4]. This is not hard to understand. Here is the account of an ex-

---

[2] Lundkvist 81.
[3] Ib. 83 f.
[4] Cf. *Psalmer* 1976, 194.

perience which the believer can recognise, or at least regard as exemplary. But does it follow from this that Lundkvist himself should be called a believer? Notice that it is here a question of how, in religious terms, one should consider the poet, and not the text he has written.

If anyone wishes to interpret the poem as evidence that the poet in a moment of trial and grace has found God, then the commentator must note with disappointment that the production of subsequent years (soon two decades) bears little sign of this encounter. An alternative interpretation emerges instead. When Lundkvist is about to formulate his extraordinary experience—perhaps when he was still in the middle of it—it was the language of religion which offered itself: we know that he had learned this language as a child. With this type of interpretation we avoid calling the poet himself a believer, and thereby avoid the unpleasantness of treating faith as something a person may have at one moment and then lose again.

I have cited Lundkvist's Agadir poem because it provides a case where a literary text can be unconstrainedly characterised in religious terms, but where the poet's own religious position remains difficult to define. For what are the necessary criteria for a person to be called a believer?

The need to maintain the distinction between the religious content of a single statement and the religious position of its author emerges clearly as one studies a notebook in which the young Pär Lagerkvist, during the first World War, recorded aphorisms, drafts of poems etc. Under the heading "On Death. An Essay" we find a number of reflections, including the following: "One day after I have been searching in vain for something in my books, these words suddenly come to me and they seem to me wonderful, and more than this: I a poor sinner—"

Further on in the notebook he has written down the Lutheran General Confession word for word from the beginning "I a poor sinner" upto "Holy and righteous God—". Two theses on the pages opposite to the ones quoted show the state in which Lagerkvist found himself at the time. One says: "As far as God is concerned, I should like to say: [. . .] I do not believe You exist. But I must believe it". The other says: "Those who have never been frightened by life have never been aware of it".

Lagerkvist had heard the General Confession countless times as a child in Växjö Cathedral, where his family regularly attended Sunday Service. But in his last years at school he had abandoned the faith of his home: "one must break away", as he puts it in the autobiographical *Guest of Reality*[5]. When—half a dozen years later—he now requotes the words of the General Confession, what does it mean? A couple of years ago we were still limited to the study of texts he himself had published. We now, however, also have his notes and manuscripts available, and we know more than before about his development. It would not be unreasonable to interpret his note on the

---

[5] Lagerkvist 1925, 136.

General Confession as the expression of a return to his childhood faith, a secret confession which admittedly did not later achieve fulfilment.

But this is not the only possible interpretation. The notes can also be read in such a way as to mean that Lagerkvist has understood the words of faith as relevant to others besides believers; in this case to himself. Much of what he wrote during this stage of his development could be cited in favour of such an interpretation. (I am thinking principally of the artistic manifesto in *Word Art and Pictorial Art* (1913) and its realisation in *Motifs* (1914).)

It is not however my purpose to attempt to solve a problem in Lagerkvist studies, but rather to provide a reminder of two principles of interpretation which we can choose between, and which give different results. In one case we read the individual text according to the linguistic usage prevalent in the writer's environment; in the second case we play closest attention to his own use of language and symbol as we see it in all his work, particularly in the parts which are chronologically close to the problematic text. By the latter method, it is obviously far more difficult to characterise the young Lagerkvist as Christian, although we find in his writings a text taken from the lithurgy. (The corresponding observation is true with regard to Lundkvist's Agadir poem referred to above.)

In another Lagerkvist text, which I shall quote shortly, the symbolism is by contrast unspecific, seen from a religious point of view. This does not prevent the text from being interpreted in a Christian sense. In the poem Who are you, standing turned away? (in *Genius,* 1937) an "I" addresses an unknown figure turned away, a "you". No dialogue is established, perhaps the person turned away is unaware of being addressed, this is not explained. The text of this short poem is as follows:

Who are you, standing turned away?
Standing with your unknown face turned against the evening.

Others I know but not you,
Your countenance is hidden from me like a stranger's.

When shall I see *you*?

No. You I shall never see.
But one day I shall be you,
be your turned away face,
open against the evening[6].

In one respect this text has a biblical ring. The averted/revealed face is one of the Old Testament's great symbols for the relationship between man (or Israel) and God. The concepts which the modern poet uses to indicate the relationship between the "I" and "you" of the poem belong to the sphere of the bible.: face /countenance, turned away, hidden, stranger. The lan-

[6] Lagerkvist 1937, 48 f. For a more detailed analysis of the poem, cf. Linnér 1971, 166 ff.

guage has a biblical tone, especially in the lines "Your countenance is hidden from me like a stranger's./ When shall I see *you*?". Lagerkvist has thus taken over *one* important element from the biblical relationship with God: that this relationship is decisive, the one thing needful. The technique is characteristic of him. His religious dilemma borrows symbols—and thereby force—from the Christian tradition. There is, one might say, something of an Old Testament impatience in the poem's question "Who are you, standing turned away?" But these similarities are limited to the question and the uncertainty. In other respects and taken as a whole, the poem is, as I see it, very remote from the world of the bible.

To interpret the "you" of the poem as God would be to go beyond Lagerkvist's sphere. If, for the present at least, we choose to remain within this sphere, we find that two other interpretations win support. I quote from a book of meditations, *Man Freed* (1939):

> How I must have loved life. When I remember it, it is as one remembers a beloved woman from whom one is separated for ever.
> [. . .] I cannot see her face. Because she is walking away. I see only the actual figure. And she does not turn round.
> Perhaps life no longer has any face for me[7].

From this text, and others which space does not allow me to quote, is derived an interpretation implying that the "you" of the poem is a woman who is life. The content of the poem can be summarised as follows: we may never see the secret of life and we cannot comprehend it rationally, but one day we will be one with it, as a man is united with a woman he loves.

Another interpretation, however, is hardly less justified with reference to Lagerkvist's works. Here too I must be content with a single example. In *The Holy Land,* one of his last books (1964), we are told how Tobias the pilgrim, having passed the three crosses (which are all empty), comes to the bank of a river. He sees a man standing by the bank "turned away, right over the gliding water, as if sunk in contemplation of it".

> He went up and stood at his side. Looked down into the water like him. Saw his own face reflected there, but old, aged, with greying hair, he hardly recognised it. Saw that it was his own face reflected there, and only his. That he was alone, and that there was no-one else but him. That the stranger was himself[8].

The poem from Genius can now be interpreted by analogy with this and other Lagerkvist texts. The answer to the question, Who are you, standing turned away? is: my true self, with which I shall one day be united, and then—perhaps in the presence of death—I shall become whole.

Both of the interpretations I have suggested are well supported. However, it is required that we supplement the text with motifs from other texts, albeit by the same author. If we confine ourselves to this short poem alone,

---

[7] Lagerkvist 1939, 13 f.

[8] Lagerkvist 1964, 82.

without thought of what Lagerkvist has written elsewhere, it is doubtful whether these nine lines can sustain such elaborate interpretations as those suggested, and such interpretations *are not needed either*. The poem about the figure turned away has a meaning, nonetheless. What *matters* in it lies at a level where there are as yet no labels, a psychological level where theoretical concepts have yet to be formulated, or where—in the face of eternity—they have been set aside as unimportant.

If, however, we feel the need to interpret the poem further than this (to fill out its 'Unbestimmtheitsstellen', to borrow Ingarden's term), there is, on the other hand, no obligation to choose precisely Lagerkvist's personal system of symbols as our norm for interpretation. That his poem is meaningful, even when set in another symbolic system likely to be quite foreign to Lagerkvist, was demonstrated by a Swedish critic, Gunnar Edman, a few years ago in a television programme based on "Who are you, standing turned away?". Edman there tried to see the unknown figure as Christ or as a reminder of him. Because of its indeterminacy, Edman might have claimed in support of his interpretation, the text points in this direction too. It is difficult to offer anything against this.

I have tried by my examples to provide a reminder that the believing author (or reader) is not confined to any specific language. Thus Dostoyevsky talks of "life" when he suggests a central religious mystery, and in Lagerkvist's poem about the turned away figure, a Christian critic can glimpse Christ. On the other hand we have seen how authors whom it would not be plausible to call Christian use the language of faith.

Similar cases could be cited in large numbers. Literary symbols seem to have the capacity to cross borders unchecked over the whole religious continent. But this gives us no reason to proclaim that, among writers using symbols, there is no division between believers and non-believers.

Such an opinion would mean that all authors (if they only speak with sufficient seriousness) would appear to be brothers—admittedly not in faith, but brothers in their religious attitude, and beyond this we should have no need for any distinctions. I find such a muddled view unappealing.

But if, then, the division must be attempted, the difficulty of accomplishing it is considerable. When we confine ourselves to the "lexical level" of the symbolic language (Ricœur), that is, only study the individual symbols or very small units of text, the borderline is often invisible; I refer to the examples above. If, however, we leave this plane and direct our attention to *larger* symbolic structures, it may be possible to distinguish who is a Christian believer and who holds some other sort of belief. By "larger" structures, I here mean those which emerge, for example, in a writer's work, or at any rate over a whole period of his development.

The first point about these comprehensive structures is that they offer us rules for interpreting the individual text. To return to the Lagerkvist poem: it is not plausible to read "Who are you, standing turned away?" as referring to Christ. I do not need to repeat that no law exists enforcing the application of this rule for interpretation. There are, on the other hand, good reasons for applying it, although the ultimate choice is the reader's.

In the second place, one can usefully reverse the perspective and look for rules which *govern creation,* and this I find even more interesting. One then begins with a writer's religious belief as given and attempts to show how this governs the creative process. The word "govern" must of course be construed very freely. There is no necessary relationship, either logical or psychological, between belief and art. What I have in mind is a tendency implying—if, for example, we confine ourselves to a poet talking of death—that certain symbols with reference to his belief or lack of belief can seem natural, even expected, and others not. It would be strange if the believer and the non-believer consistently spoke the same langauge on such questions. What to one is the hope giving meaning to existence, is to the other an illusion. The choice and deployment of poetic symbols may be assumed to be dominated by this relationship. The writer's belief could then be said to function as a sort of deep structure, from which the shape of the symbolic language in the surface structure is derived.

But then again, this is an extremely vague metaphor. Artistic creation is a complicated process, and it is by no means certain that a writer's belief (however sincerely it may be held) governs his writing in such a manner as to permit generalisations even within the frame of his own work. I do not therefore wish to launch any model, however hypothetical, for the relationship between belief and literary creation. I am content to emphasise that here is an area worthy of more systematic study than it has hitherto received.

I have so far postponed one question of fundamental importance to my argument, or only touched upon it: what does it mean to have a belief and one which, within the terms of my discussion, can be called Christian? Obviously the fact that an author produces texts which can be understood by others as expressions of Christian faith is not a sufficient criterion where he is concerned. Even less is it a criterion of belief that the reader—albeit with admiration and involvement—utilises such texts.

Let me introduce a new example, Bertil Malmberg's drama *His Excellency* (written in 1938 and published in 1942). It takes place in Austria after the *Anschluss,* and the main character is a great Catholic poet. He is offered the chance to flee from the country, but refuses it and chooses to remain. He dies in a concentration camp, as a martyr. There is a good reason for calling this an unmistakably Christian drama. What conclusions can we draw form it regarding the author's own belief? In his memoirs, *A Writer's Life* (1952), Malmberg claims that *His Excellency* is not only, or even principally a political drama. It also, and above all, portrays a "a writer's path from the chill of perfection, from the melancholy in form and pleasure-seeking, through catastrophe and martyrdom, to experience of

Christ". Malmberg goes on to say that personally he had no such experience "but I made my protagonist undergo it".

So I experienced this miracle in my imagination, as a poet, only as a poet, not as a believer, but it took place with an intensity of illusion (for me). It was my own path as a *true* Christian that I was hypothetically covering, and when it was completed—well, then I found I was still at the point where I started[9].

One should note that these lines were written many years later, when Malmberg had abandoned his Christian commitment. It is conceivable that at this later stage he wished to play down the seriousness of the faith he had professed for a short period of his life. In this case, should we not perhaps regard the drama itself as more reliable testimony than this retroactive denial? Malmberg's example shows us again how much easier it is to determine the religious content of a literary text than it is to determine what the author himself believed.

At this point, under the influence of methodical rigour, it would be tempting to resign. That is to say stop talking altogether about authors' beliefs and instead limit oneself strictly to gauging the religious content of their writing. Artistic texts can of course be incomparably richer and more expressive than other texts, but they provide unreliable "source material". For to the extent that literary creation is characterised by play, acting and the quest for effect, the value of the product as a source correspondingly diminishes when we attempt to reach what may be called the writer's own beliefs.

It is salutary if such a reflection takes the colour from our cheeks. I believe, however, that resignation at this point would be an unreasonable expedient. We must still start from the assumption that the authors we study hold some sort of belief (Christian or non-Christian, the variations here are innumerable). In this they resemble people in general. We assume that the latter believe in something, although these beliefs can change in the course of their lives and often co-exist with doubt or uncertainty. Provided such a general view is legitimate, it would be most remarkable if just authors (perhaps together with other artists) constituted a special group, removed from the rest of humanity. Those who nonetheless believe this to be the case, should give their reasons for this opinion; the burden of proof rests on them.

How then is one to describe the difference between believing and expressing a belief one does not share? I imagine that the essential difference should be seen as resting in the attitude towards the *truth* of the symbol or statement of belief. In addition, at least as far as the Christian faith is concerned, there is also a moral obligation which is a consequence of faith. Furthermore, there is the sense of communion with those who embrace the same faith. But the ultimate criterion for me still seems to be the question of truth.

---

[9] Malmberg 1952, 156 ff.

The title of my talk may be understood as referring to two different areas: firstly, the internal relationship between the belief the work as a whole can be said to express, and the symbolism of the work. This question has not been the main focus of my argument. What I have been most concerned to emphasise is a second relationship, that existing between a writer's belief and his work. I have thereby assumed—to state once again the premise of my argument—that writers, like other people, may be supposed to possess beliefs of some kind. Inasmuch as this assumption is valid, the question arises of what role a writer's belief plays in his choice of symbols and his deployment of them.

A fascinating field of research is opened up here. The literary scholar, however, is not equipped to explore it alone; he must be joined by the scholar of religion. With co-operation between people from these two disciplines, exciting things can happen.

Bibliography

Stockholm
Kungl. Biblioteket
Pär Lagerkvists samling (L 120)

Достоевский, Ф. М., 1958, *Братья Карамазовы*. Собрание сочинений, 9–10. Москва.

Lagerkvist, P., 1913, *Ordkonst och bildkonst. Om modärn skönlitteraturs dekadans. Om den modärna konstens vitalitet* [Word Art and Pictorial Art. On the Decadence of Modern *belles lettres*. On the Vitality of Modern Art]. Stockholm.

— 1914, *Motiv* [Motifs]. Stockholm.

— 1925, *Gäst hos verkligheten* [Guest of Reality]. Stockholm.

— 1937, *Genius*. Stockholm.

— 1939, *Den befriade människan* [Man Freed]. Stockholm.

— 1964, *Det heliga landet* [The Holy Land]. Stockholm.

Linnér, S., 1971, I marginalen till en Lagerkvistdikt. *Lyrik i tid och otid*. Lyrikanalytiska studier tillägnade Gunnar Tideström 7.2.1971. Lund.

— 1975, *Starets Zosima in The Brothers Karamazov*. Acta Universitatis Stockholmensis. Stockholm Studies in Russian Literature, 4. Ekenäs.

Lundkvist, A., 1961, *Agadir. En dikt*. [Agadir. A Poem]. Stockholm.

Malmberg, B., 1942, *Excellensen* [His Excellency]. Stockholm.

— 1952, *Ett författarliv* [A Writer's Life]. Stockholm.

Psalmer, 1976. *Psalmer och visor 76*. Tillägg till den svenska psalmboken, 1. Lund.

On the Semiotic Function of Cucurbits

By RALF NORRMAN

In semiotics signs are classified differently according to which school of semiotic thought the classifier sympathizes with, but most taxonomies recognize at least three categories: icons (real likeness between the sign and what it stands for), indices (a causal relationship) and "signs proper" (whose characteristic feature is their arbitrariness—in the Morse-code, for instance, the "b"-sign could just as well stand for "a" if only everyone agreed on the change).

It is of fundamental importance to anyone trying to understand its nature and function to know whether a sign is arbitrary or not.

The literary symbols that authors use are often arbitrary and vary with the culture and period of the text. Indeed "symbolification" is a term used by some linguists to denote the process whereby an author takes any code element in his syntagm and invests it with a special meaning through manipulation of the context. "Symbol" would thus be associated with lability—that half of the dual nature of language which permits us to use language the way the sculptor uses wet clay, i.e. make of it whatever we wish. In this view "symbol" is the opposite of "code"—which is the other role of language, the role in which it functions as a linguistic supermarket where the user of language can choose from the shelves, among stable linguistic elements, the particular one that will suit his communicative need at the moment.

One of the features distinguishing the former half of the nature of language from the latter is the degree of arbitrariness of the sign. If something is used as a sign because of its intrinsic appropriateness for the task this tends to reinforce stability rather than lability, and in this case the relations of the element to the same, or similar—even if contrasting—elements in other texts (its paradigmatic relations, as it were) will be more important than its relations to other elements in the same text (its syntagmatic relations).

Thus, although literary symbols may be fairly arbitrary, there are some cases when the symbols are very stable. One such case is when man uses something from nature to express in metaphors or figurative language (and maybe some forms of totemism) some idea about himself, or somehow define his own position. Thus one finds that plant and animal symbolism is often very stable. "Goose" as a sign of stupidity is used not only because it is agreed that this should be its role in the code; ultimately it is used because *geese really are stupid* (or, to put it more precisely, because they seem stupid to humans—whether geese, cows and donkeys are stupid from an animal point of view is irrelevant). "Goose" as a sign of stupidity is not arbitrary.

If language had been characterized only by its malleability one could also have expected "intelligent" birds to be used as a sign of stupidity, since in principle it should be possible to invest any linguistic element with any meaning through manipulation of the context. But this does not seem to happen—such meanings, if they occur, do not become established. "Goose" as a sign of stupidity is superior because the sign preserves a link with its origin. Every user of the sign can get at its meaning not only through his knowledge of the code (which could have been arbitrary) but also by deducing on his own the meaning of the sign through observations of that part of nature from which it is taken.

In their symbolic use in literature the various plants and animals are thus often given their semiotic role because of intrinsic suitability for it.

This has many consequences. For the student of literature—and I would imagine for the student of the history of religion—it means that chronology loses much of its importance. Research becomes largely ahistorical. If, for instance, the scholar, in studying one culture, notes that a plant from the family *Cucurbitaceae* occurs in connection with some narrative element depicting abundance, vitality and fertility in a story of the creation, and then finds that the plant occurs in a similar story in a later culture, he need not automatically assume an influence from the earlier culture to the later. In order to understand the semiotic role of the plant it may be much more important to study its physiology (fertility, fast growth, abundant harvest) and its special status in the flora. These signs remain the same provided the nature they refer to remains the same and provided human thought remains essentially the same—which in this context is a reasonable assumption.

In addition to "message" the two central concepts of all semiotic theory are "sender" and "receiver". The process of communication is something collective; sender and receiver share the communicative code. If literature or religion is seen as communication one can concentrate on either the role of the sender (the author, the prophet) or the role of the receiver (the readers, the congregation). Thus one may ponder the question whether literary works are written by the authors or by the readers; whether the author creates something which he forces upon the reader or whether the author is merely "borrowed" to formulate something which is essentially created by the readers. In the same way one may ask whether a prophet forces upon his listeners what he has created or whether the listeners create and the situation then, through some process of selection, filters forth a prophet who formulates individually what was already created collectively.

In plant symbolism, in addition to the role of the sender and the receiver, the message itself plays a very important part. In literary or religious texts these elements very often tend to formulate themselves, as it were, because the perfect, the given form of the element is latently in existence, only waiting for the sifting or filtering processes of human thought to bring it forth into materialization.

In this essay, by looking at some aspects of the semiotic role of the plant family *Cucurbitaceae* (melons, water-melons, cucumbers, pumpkins, gourds, calabashes, squashes, gherkins, marrows etc.). I wish to exemplify four of the ways in which such textual elements "write themselves". The material is taken from a study on the semiotic role of cucurbits in literature which I have undertaken in collaboration with Jon Haarberg. Unfortunately there is no space here to illustrate at length the various connotations of the cucurbits; I shall just have to state them before giving the quote which exemplifies how a literary passage writes itself.

One cluster of cucurbitic connotations is strongly positive. Cucurbits—tropical plants, requiring warmth and moisture—are associated with summer, luxury and abundance. Being fertile plants which grow quickly (and die easily) they are a symbol of life and vitality, usually of cyclical life or the life cycle (in contrast to e.g. evergreens which tend to symbolize eternal or enduring life). Closely connected with their role in symbolizing life and fertility are their sexual connotations which are widespread, numerous and far-branching. In particular the sexual connotations abound in associations with femininity.

The cucurbits are in many respects somewhat extreme—they are a typical "record"-species in garden produce (witness the *Guinness Book of Records*). Thus they acquire in a heightened form the connotations of the place they grow in; they become the epitome of whatever class of concepts they belong to in one or another dimension of their existence. They are the prime produce of a garden; thus they acquire the connotations of gardens in a heightened form, whether this be the scorn of the city-slicker, or the enthusiasm of the back-to-nature romantic. They are usually delicious and thus acquire the symbolic role of the dainty par excellence. They are juicy and thus acquire water connotations.

The cucurbits are even richer in negative connotations than in positive. They are big, immobile (the pumpkin fruit); thus stupid. They are rural, thus anathema to urban people. They grow very quickly and are thus absurd. They are sexy; thus sinful etc.

In our investigation Mr. Haarberg and I found that these connotations are extraordinarily stable. Through the centuries and millennia they remain the same. They also seem to be largely the same in different countries and continents. It is obvious that these signs are very stable. We also noted that although people are usually not consciously aware of it, they unconsciously master the grammar of cucurbits (the semiotic matrix) quite well. Most people realize that a cucurbit often expresses ridicule. An amusing empiric test of people's cucurbitic *competence* (the extent to which the public master a cucurbitic *langue*) is to mention that Shakespeare calls only one of his characters "pumpkin" (pompeon). People familiar with Shakespeare's plays will almost always immediately—and quite correctly—name Falstaff, who is fat (iconic relationship), absurd like a pumpkin, humorous like a pumpkin, a glutton (cucurbits being a glutton's food); who drinks (wateriness connotations), and is at this stage in the *Merry Wives* unsuccessfully trying to seduce a woman (sex connotations).

It is obvious that "pumpkin" is maximally suitable, and the idea of suitability, and the gluttony, conveniently bring me to my first example of the ways in which a literary passage writes itself.

1. *Maximal appropriateness*

The principle could be called simply "maximal appropriateness" and the way the selection works is of course quite obvious; when you choose something from nature to illustrate an idea you choose something suitable. If you want an image of hardness you take steel rather than wax. Before steel was known to man he was likely to take bronze. Today the diamond is the epitome of hardness; before it was known man probably used whatever stone was then the hardest when he needed material for figurative language.

Cucurbits are delicious and gluttons and gourmands are fond of delicious food; therefore a good story of a gourmand or glutton should ideally depict him as eating cucurbits. Investigating this we find that cucurbits are a stock item in stories of gourmands and gluttons. The Roman emperor Clodius Albinus, a glutton on the throne, is said to have eaten "melones Ostienses decem" during one single meal, in addition to a fair amount of peaches, grapes, figs and oysters[1]. Of Carinus it is said that he "inter poma et melones natavit"[2]. This weakness became fatal for a Chinese emperor who was so partial to musk-melons that he actually died of over-eating.

The rule that cucurbits occur in connection with gluttons holds irrespective of genre or stylistic level. It is equally to be expected in a children's book by Richard Scarry (where, true enough, it occurs) as in the *Historia Augusta* (cf. *Scriptores*).

A perfect form of a story of a glutton should thus have cucurbits as an element, and through some process of selection they often seem to get it.

An observer unfamiliar with the thought that literary passages could write themselves (i.e. determine their own form and shape), and wondering about the technicalities involved in such "writing", might object that the *Historia Augusta* states that Clodius ate ten melons from Ostia not because this is semiotically appropriate at this point, but because *the emperor really did so*.

This is the confrontation of a structuralist theory of literature with a

---

[1] Cf. *Scriptores* 1, 482–83.

[2] Ib. 3, 442–43.

mimetic. The structuralist would answer that the emperor eating the melons from Ostia may be a necessary but not a sufficient requirement for it to get into the *Historia Augusta*. Life is immeasurably rich in detail. Therefore literature cannot be indiscriminate imitation but is rather selection, and manipulation and arrangement of the selected material. Literature imitates not life but a refined image of it.

From the numerous things that the emperor can be expected to have done that day the author of the *Historia Augusta* selects one, his eating ten melons from Ostia, which distils the essence of the emperor's gluttonous nature as the author saw it.

The story creates, syntagmatically, a convincing picture of a glutton. Clodius eats, and he eats a lot. In the choice of a dish for his zenith of gluttony (eating ten of something) the author chooses melons, a fruit which is inherently associated with gluttons. Thereby the author displays his mastery of the paradigm as well as the syntagm. The well-wrought context fits perfectly the well-chosen element he puts in it. This is one of the characteristic signs of a good author. An author who knows the paradigm but has no skill in linking elements together into a well-wrought textual chain produces clichés.

To explain how the cucurbit got into the *Historia Augusta* one can imagine three models. The first, the "filter model", assumes some process of selection; of all the things the emperor did the author chose the characteristic one; or else the passage, in order to come into existence, had to "wait" for the emperor to do the characteristic thing. The second model could be called the "lie-model". This assumes that no matter what the emperor did in reality, in the *Historia Augusta* he has to eat ten melons, because this is symbolically so true that it does not matter whether or not it is true literally as well. The third model seeks the explanation in the structure of life itself—being a glutton the emperor did eat ten melons and thus provided the symbol of his gluttony, i.e. lived up to his image.

In our research Mr. Haarberg and I again and again came upon examples where cucurbits were used to epitomize something connected with one of their chief connotations. They were used to symbolize the sexiest, the most absurd, the extremely bathetic, the quickest-growing, the fastest-dying etc., and since they somehow excel in all these areas in reality their being picked for the task to stand as a sign for it in literature was, in retrospect, not surprising.

2. *Antitheses*

Another principle which leads to literary passages determining their own shape is antithetical juxtaposition, which, of course, is closely related to the principle of maximal appropriateness. Dualistic structuring of reality, one of man's simplest intellectual models, also seems to be one of his dearest. Antonymic or antithetic structuring naturally makes the other half of the oppositional pair very predictable once the first is a given. The contrasting element must be different, and as different as possible.

As examples of antithetical structuring I shall take passages where the cucurbit symbolizes life, particularly when this is connected with the wateriness of the fruit. Cucumbers and melons consist chiefly of water, 95–98 %, and wateriness naturally fits in very well with associations with life—water is a life-giving and life-sustaining factor.

The cucurbit as a symbol of life is frequent and widespread through the ages. Explicit testimony of its role can be found in those occurrences where the juxtaposition of opposites is expressly signalled by an adversity-marker such as e.g. "either-or", and the semiotic significance of its partner is known. The lily for the Greeks was the flower of death. The proverb "ἢ κολοκύντην ἢ κρίνον" (i.e. either a pumpkin or a lily) is preserved in fragments by the comic poets Diphilus and Menander[3]. Since the lily stands for death, the antonymic symbol, the pumpkin, must stand for life.

Deserts and cucurbits, as semiotic elements, are perfect natural antitheses. Deserts are sterile, dry, deathly; cucurbits are fertile, watery, life-giving. Therefore when authors think antithetically in extremes, the perfect opposite of desert is cucurbit and the perfect opposite of cucurbit desert. The perfect opposition is so obviously neat that it leads to different literary practice in different modes and genres. In those genres where stereotype is cultivated and desired, such as caricature, allegory, etc. the juxtaposition of deserts and cucurbits predictably occurs, whereas realism tries to avoid such perfectly neat constellations and structures. It is therefore only in artistically very poor realist works that one finds the perfect antithetic structuring deserts—cucurbits.

One such work is Henry Rider Haggard's novel *King Solomon's Mines* (1885). In this work there is hardly any cliché that the reader need wait for in vain. At one stage when the expedition is trekking through an African desert they are in very bad shape: at the limit of thirst and exhaustion. The hot merciless sun beats down on the party, who fear that the end is close at hand. They can see no escape from the hostile desert which is sterile, dry and deathly. Since, in a work of this nature, effect is sought by maximization of the function of the device used (in this case contrast), and the extreme opposite of the desert is the cucurbit—which is fertile, watery and life-giving—the inevitable happens: they discover a patch of melons! "So we sat down under the rocks and groaned, and for one I wished heartily that we had never started on this fool's errand. As we were sitting there I saw Umbopa get up and hobble towards the patch of green, and a few minutes afterwards, to my great astonishment, I perceived that usually very dignified individual dancing and shouting like a maniac, and

[3] Cf. Meineke 4, 420 and 331. For a similar antithetic juxtaposition of lily and cucurbit (death and life) cf. e.g. Tennyson's poem "The Princess", Ll. 80–91. Ricks, 843 f.

waving something green. Off we all scrambled towards him as fast as our wearied limbs would carry us, hoping that he had found water.

"What is it, Umbopa, son of a fool?" I shouted in Zulu.

"It is food and water, Macumazahn", and again he waved the green thing.

Then I saw what he had found. It was a melon. We had hit upon a patch of wild melons, thousands of them, and dead ripe.

"Melons!" I yelled to Good, who was next me; and another minute his false teeth were fixed in one of them."[4]

After this they kill a bird and by and by get out of the desert. Things improve gradually whereas before the melonpassage they had been growing gradually worse. At the point of juxtaposition (the structural node), the two intrinsically antithetical elements, desert and cucurbit, were employed to heighten the dramatic change in fortune.

What I have tried to stress here is the inevitability of the choice of cucurbits. To supersede and be maximally contrasted with the least watery thing imaginable (desert), there is one suitably watery thing: a melon. The only improvement on this passage would have been for the party to discover water itself, but this possibility was discarded by the author, for several reasons. Melons at this stage, which is the climax of the desert episode, appeal more to the imagination. In the escalation of the thirst-theme, which reappears cyclically, "finding water" is an appropriate element at the beginning, but it cannot be repeated (that would blunt the effect; each new episode must be an escalation from the preceding). To find water now would be an anticlimax. Part of the way the picture of the plight of the party has been created until now is the tacit assumption that *they will not find water*. Finding water would damage the maximal appropriateness of desert as the driest thing imaginable (a place could hardly be said to be dry if you find water in it!). As it is they find water; yet do not find water.

The same juxtaposition of wilderness and cucurbit is found in the story of an early Christian hermit, who hung a tempting cucumber in front of him[5]. Primarily one may assume that the monk is castigating his gluttonous desire for a fruit which, with its 98% water content, is a delicacy in the desert. (Although of course it may also be that the monk, living his celibate, sterile life in the sterile wilderness uses a memento which is the symbol of fertility. Thus it is also possible that he is reminding himself of his chastity-vow and the cucumber is a visual instrument to conquer his lust.[6])

Assuming that cucurbits stand for luxury, fertility and abundance, it is possible to predict the type of literary passages in which they are likely to occur. One such place is Num. 11. The Jews have been trekking through

---

[4] Haggard, 83 f.

[5] Cf. *Vitae*, 767.

[6] The idea that cucurbits restrain sexual appetite coexists through the ages with the idea that they induce it. This is the level when the cucurbit has passed into a sign proper. But though interpretations vary arbitrarily (in this case dualistically: does-does not), the kernal, i.e. the connection with sex remains.

the Sinai Desert for ages and discontent flares up regularly. Throughout Numeri this grumbling recurs as a leit-motif at regular intervals. In Num. 11.5–6 the immediate *source of discontent* is the diet.

After 40 years the Jews are tired of manna, and being in the sterile Sinai their thoughts antithetically go to the fertile Goshen, where the menu was more varied: "Will no one give us meat? Think of it! In Egypt we had fish for the asking, cucumbers and water-melons, leeks and onions and garlic. Now our throats are parched; there is nothing wherever we look except this manna." (NEB)

Predictably two cucurbits are introduced in the passage. Eating "the bread of the angels" has become monotonous and the Jews recall, as it were, the taste of the two primary dishes for the main course (meat and fish), nice desserts (cucumbers and melons) and spices (leeks, onions and garlic).

It would be next to irrelevant here to inquire into the plants actually grown in Goshen at the time the Jews were there. What is relevant is the situation of the Jews at the moment: hungry, thirsty and bored; and the semiotic position, in the lexicon, of the things they mention—which in each case is antithetical: hungry (meat & fish), thirsty (cucumbers and water-melons), bored (leeks, onions and garlic). In addition, then, there is the juxtaposition cucurbit–desert (i.e. life–death), expressing the ominousness of their present situation and its difference from their memory of Goshen. The antithesis desert–cucurbit also plays a part in the controversy over the translation, in Jonah IV.6, of the Hebrew word קִיקָיוֹן.

These examples, I hope, sufficiently illustrate the element of predictability, or even inevitability, in the way certain literary passages involving antithesis find their own shape.

3. *Symbols cluster*

Another principle, which like the preceding is also closely related to "maximal appropriateness", is the tendency of symbols to cluster and interrelate, and seek companions which are not only in keeping with the general semiotic drift of the passage in which they occur but paradigmatically congenial.

The principle is one of *amount,* simply that more is better than less, and the simplest cases are those where an author doubles (or trebles etc.) his symbolism for good measure.

The cucurbit grows very quickly. It is therefore often combined with mushrooms when authors wish to double the symbolism of fast growth. The cucurbits also die easily (none can tolerate frost for instance). Dying as quickly as it grows it has accordingly become the image of short-livedness (an aspect significant e.g. in the Jonah translation-controversy).

The life of some insects is also proverbially short in many languages (Sw. "dagslända" or Eng. "ephemeron"), which explains why gourd in the following example should be mentioned with a fly: "... we should have been but as an Ephemeron, Man should have lived the life of a Fly, or a Gourd, the morning should have seen his birth, his life have been the term of a day, and the evening must have provided him of a shroud."[7]

An author wishing to double his symbolism and wanting to use the cucurbit in its role as a symbol of stupidity can for instance couple it with a stupid animal, e.g. the sheep, as in Jerome's *Novel Notes* (1893): "Surely as to a matter of this kind, I, a professed business man, must be able to form a sounder judgment than this poor pumpkin-headed lamb."[8]

In these examples two signs were involved. The principle of "symbols cluster" is related to "maximal appropriateness" in that the symbols in this case too, as in the examples from "maximal appropriateness" (which is maybe hierarchically superior—an inclusive concept), have to suit, as to their paradigmatic nature, the slot in the syntagm that they are chosen for. Their additional, specific feature in "symbols cluster" is that they are paradigmatically related to each other as symbols.

This is fairly simple if the symbols are two and their task is to convey one significance (the same). It becomes much more intricate when you increase the number of items and the number of connotations—then the number of relations increases geometrically.

There is a certain numskull story which according to folklorists is spread over large parts of Asia, Europe and the Southern part of the United States. The numskull thinks that a pumpkin is an Ass's egg. He throws it into a bush. A rabbit which has been hiding in the bush is frightened and jumps out. The numskull thinks the egg has broken and the rabbit is the Ass's colt[9].

In this story practically all the imaginable streams of symbolism converge. The subject is sex; what the numskull is ignorant of are the facts of reproduction. Thus not only is the pumpkin appropriate, with its sex-connotations, but the rabbit is also—rabbits are proverbially fertile. Ignorance of sexual matter is a common theme in this type of humour. But it is not only in the sex aspect that the connection from pumpkin both ways, to the subject and to the animals, is appropriate. The man is stupid; pumpkins are symbols of stupidity and so are asses. The interlacement of relationship in the story is such that every element fits every other.

What I am getting at here is the idea that because of the nature of the case, with two basic ideas involved, sex and stupidity, and three elements of narrative: man, mother-animal and egg/baby-animal, and because of the simple mathematics following from this, there exists latently a perfect form of the story, which tends to force its way, as it were, into existence. Man thinks not in literature, but literature in man.

---

[7] Taylor, 21.

[8] Jerome, 24.

[9] Thompson J1772.1 ff.

An example such as the numskull story is of course interesting to study because the process of the canonization of a text, i.e. its stabilization into a certain form, is slow in orally transmitted literature. There is ample scope for changes towards perfection; for imperfect forms to be discarded; and for a transmitter, who is maybe more clever than the last teller of the story (and masters the semiotic matrix of the elements more fully), to touch into life the element which was waiting for him to take it into the story, where it will remain because it improves the story.

Our findings suggest that even if its importance should not be exaggerated there does seem to exist a tendency for symbols to flock together.

4. *Similar yet different*

If the principle of "maximal appropriateness" was hierarchically superior; and if the first subcategory "antitheses" meant the addition of an abstract relation "difference" plus the introduction of a numbering of the items (two); and if, finally, the second subcategory "symbols cluster" depended on the abstract relation "similarity" (two or more items; one or more connotations) it is to be expected that there should be a category combining the abstract relations of subcategories one and two. Let us call this case simply "Similar yet different".

This, of course, is usually thought of as the basic chart of the metaphor. In "the man is a lion" the man is similar to the lion in his courage, yet different from the lion in that he is not really a lion but a man.

For a passage exemplifying "similar yet different" let me take one where, although cucurbitic symbolism occurs ("punkins" in the passage means important persons—an example of a humorous yet positive meaning of the cucurbit), what I wish to illustrate is expressed in other vegetable symbolism.

"Cabbages" are of extremely low semiotic status. Their low value is sometimes rivalled by that of the cucurbits, but cucurbits are a potentially ambiguous symbol, whereas cabbages are purely negative. The other fruit or vegetable which occurs in the passage, 'pea-nuts', is also very negative. "Mrs. R. had been trying to poke fun at us, behind our backs of course, on the subject of cabbages and pea-nuts. Well, not long after she gave a big ball, and we, being punkins, were of course among the invited. So I went to a clever working jeweller that I knew, and gave him an order to be filled up in all haste from a design of my own, ear-rings imitating pea-nuts in dead gold, and shirt buttons in green enamel, to be the counterfeit presentment of two cabbages; and Clara and I wore our ornaments at the ball (where they were much admired for their originality), and made a point of bringing them under Mrs. Robinson's notice."[10]

In the discussion preceding the story, an Englishman has found it strange

---

[10] Bristed, 216.

that his American friend confesses his regrets at not having become a wine merchant. The American is militantly self-confident and does not want to give up his identity or be above his origin—his ancestors have made their fortune in peanuts and cabbages. So he creates a paradox, a representation of vegetables of the lowest possible value (peanuts and cabbages) in material of the highest possible value (gold and enamel). The nineteenth-century American attempt to reconcile the ideas of democracy and social hierarchy was paradoxical. The paradox involved in uniting the two ideas demanded an equally paradoxical symbol, in this case involving a link through colour: nuts-yellow-gold and cabbages-green-enamel.

But with the aid of the paradoxical symbol the American is also signalling to Mrs. R. a message about his similarity and difference: "I may be rich like you, but I am different, and proud of it." Or maybe: "You may think I am different from you, and so I am, but at least I am as rich as you."

To illustrate the role of the principle "similar yet different" in the autogenesis of literary passages let us return to the role of the cucurbit as a symbol of life.

Since the cucurbit symbolizes life the act of cutting a cucurbit sets the human imagination in motion. Thus a number of related symbolic patterns have come into existence. One finds for instance that an eclectic, slightly hedonistic attitude to life and its pleasures (especially love) can be likened to the arbitrary knife of the melon-vendor, as in Alemán's Gvzman de Alfarache: "No falta en Roma bueno, y mas bueno, a menos peligro, y costa, cõ mas gustos, y me nos embaraços: no sè si lo haze, q̃ nuc̃a yo quiero por querer, sino por salpicar, como los de mi tierra: soy cuchillo de melonero, ando picando cantillos, mudando hitos; oy aqui, mañana en Francia; de cosa no me concoxo, ni en alguna permanezco; a mis horas como, y duerno, no suspiro en ausencia, en presencia bozeço, y con esto las muelo."[11]

Or else, in a case where the tension of the co-present principles similarity–difference is already felt, if the body of a man is cut, the way a cucurbit would be, one feels there should have been a difference, but, alas, there is not. In Stephen Crane's short story "The Blue Hotel", when the Swede is murdered, the author says the knife cuts his body as it would have a melon. "There was a great tumult, and then was seen a long blade in the hand of the gambler. It shot forward, and a human body, this citadel of virtue, wisdom, power was pierced as easily as if it had been a melon. The Swede fell with a cry of supreme astonishment."[12]

A melon, like a man, is a prominent example of life, but a melon is insensitive. What seems similar but should nevertheless be different was similar after all.

[11] Alemán, 250. Cf. Spanish "El melon y el casamiento ha de ser acertamiento" (choose a wife and a melon with care).

[12] Gullason, 505.

The difference between cutting human flesh and cutting a melon, i.e. the material of two varieties of life, one sensitive and the other insensitive, is a cliché which is utilized particularly in connection with ideas of callousness or cruelty. In a thriller by Edgar Wallace there is a female character who is supposed to be the epitome of cruelty. One of her acts is to slash the hand of an admirer to teach him that his attentions are not welcome. The idea of the following quotation is that to normal people there is a difference between cutting a melon and cutting human flesh, but that to this cruel woman it is all the same. "She is wonderful, really, Mrs Meredith, wonderful! I find myself thinking about her at odd moments, and the more I think the more I am amazed. Lucretia Borgia was a child in arms compared with Jean—poor old Lucretia has been malignated, anyway. There was a woman in the sixteenth century rather like her, and another girl in the early days of New England, who used to denounce witches for the pleasure of seeing them burn, but I can't think of an exact parallel, because Jean gets no pleasure out of hurting people any more than you will get out of cutting that cantaloup. It has just got to be cut, and the fact that you are finally destroying the life of the melon doesn't worry you."

"Have cantaloups life?" She paused, knife in hand, eyeing the fruit with a frown. "No, I don't think I want it. So Jean is a murderess at heart?"[13]

Consider, for a moment, this quotation and its implications for the idea that art imitates reality! "The realist myth" with which we sometimes delude ourselves claims that art imitates real life. Now it is just not a fact of real life that one's partner in a conversation happens miraculously to have a cantaloupe in her hand any time you need to make a point about cruelty! Neither is it true in life that people make points about cruelty only when their interlocutresses happen to be cutting cantaloupes—though this is much more likely.

It is well known by students of the history of art that art imitates not so much life as other art. A sonnet imitates not only life but above all other sonnets. But, as the Edgar Wallace example demonstrates, even when art does imitate life it is not life in its raw, unordered state, but life as she should have been lived ideally.

In the dual nature of language, the combination of the two contradictory forces of stability and lability, symbols should by definition belong to the lability half. But in the special case of plant symbolism this does not seem to be so. On the contrary, these signs are very stable, which makes possible research organized along dimensions other than chronological; and shifts the emphasis, in the communicative process, from the sender to the receiver(s) and even to the message itself.

Mr. Haarberg and I did not especially seek out religious texts. But when

---

[13] Wallace, 117f., slashing incident 113.

we did find religious texts it seemed as if the semiotic role of cucurbits was the same in these as in literary texts in general.

This could suggest that it might be of interest to study certain elements in religious texts and religious systems from a predominantly semiotic point of view, and inquire especially into the question of their intrinsic suitability for their task. At least this would seem to be so with certain cases of plant symbolism.

Bibliography

Alemán, M., 1661, Primera y segunda parte de Guzman de Alfarache. Madrid.
Bristed, C., 1852, The upper ten thousand. New-York.
Gullason, T., 1963, The complete short stories and sketches by Stephen Crane. Garden City.
Haggard, H., 1965, King Solomon's Mines. London.
Jerome, J., 1893, Novel notes. London.
Meineke, A., 1841, Fragmenta Poetarum Comodiae Novae, 4. Berlin.
Ricks, C., 1969, The poems of Tennyson. London.
Taylor, J., 1649, The Great Exemplar of Sanctity and Holy Life, 3. London.
Thompson, S., 1957, Motif-Index of Folk-Literature, 4. Copenhagen.
Scriptores, 1921 f *The Scriptores Historiae Augustae,* 1, ed. Capps et al.; 3, ed. T. Page et al. London.
Vitae, 1860, *Vitae Patrum.* Patrologia Latina, rec. J.-P. Migne, 73. Parisiis.
Wallace, E., 1962, The angel of terror. London.

On the Symbol Concept of the Vedic Ritualists

ASKO PARPOLA

In his methodologically remarkable studies of the Ndembu ritual, Victor W. Turner has gained important insights from the native terminology and exegesis of this Zambian people[1]. Naturally, the said materials are most relevant for the analysis of the Ndembu ritual. But, as the wide acknowledgement of Turner's work[2] concretely shows, they are of considerable interest from the crosscultural perspective as well.

Different peoples have in their cultural and linguistic systems created individual conceptual categories which best fit their varying needs and surroundings, thus defining and interpreting the world in different ways[3]. While developing universal theories it is useful to take into account as many as possible independent systems of classification, for they can open up new perspectives and refine prevalent concepts. A striking example is supplied by the ancient Indian grammarians who, in spite of their exclusive preoccupation with Sanskrit, have given a lot of stimulation to modern general linguistics[4].

The aim of the present paper is to contribute to the general study of the "ritual symbol", "the smallest unit of ritual which still retains the specific properties of ritual behavior"[5], by drawing attention to, and sketching in basic outline, some central concepts held in this regard by the Vedic ritualists[6].

The Vedic Brāhmaṇa texts, composed around 1000–600 B.C., expound the esoteric meaning of the sacrifices which at the time were at the very centre of the cultural activity in the heart of North India. They are complemented by the slightly later Śrauta and Gṛhya Sūtras (ca. 700–200 B.C.), in which this extremely complicated ritual is systematically described[7]. The import-

---

[1] Cf. especially Turner 1967, 19 ff., 48 ff.; 1969, 1 ff.

[2] Cf. e.g. Middleton 507.

[3] Cf. e.g. Werner 537 ff.

[4] Cf. Collinder 1 ff.; Staal XI ff.

[5] Turner 1967, 19. Since the religious ritual is a communication system, its minimal unit could be called "sign" in accordance with the general theory of semiotics, "symbol" being just one of the subclasses of "sign", cf. Sebeok 244 ff. In the widely adopted terminology of Pike, 54 ff., the basic unit of any purposeful human behaviour is "eme".

[6] The reader who wants to pursue the theme further is referred above all to the studies of Oldenberg 1919, 1 ff.; Schayer 1925, 259 ff.; and to the works of Gonda cited in the bibliography.

[7] For the Vedic texts cf. Gonda 1975, 1 ff.; 1977, 465 ff. For a synopsis of the Vedic ritual, cf. Gonda 1960, 104 ff., and for a more detailed account, Hillebrandt 1 ff.

ance of the vast, homogenous, spontaneous and direct documentation thereby supplied for the general study of the religious ritual was fully realized by Henri Hubert and Marcel Mauss: they took it as the basic foundation of their classic study of the nature and function of the sacrifice[8].

By about 1000 B.C., when the redaction of the Ṛgveda, the oldest Indian text known to us, was completed, a fundamental change in the religious attitude of the Vedic Aryans had already taken place. This happened most probably as a result of their assimilation with the earlier inhabitants of their new domain in India, the Dāsas[9]. Submission to almighty gods, who are worshipped with reverence and honoured with sacrifices in the old hymns of the Ṛgveda, had given way before a new kind of ritual, mechanistic and magical in its character. The sacrifice now enabled man to control the universe independently of the gods, who were largely reduced to the subordinate position of powers that could be manipulated at his will by an expert ritualist[10].

As told in innumerable myths in the Brāhmaṇa texts, it is the sacrifice that the gods have to thank for their exalted position[11]. The very creation of the world was the primeval sacrifice[12]. Sacrifice in its various forms not only is able to grant man all his wishes but to redeem him from death[13]. It also supports the entire universe, since "this all indeed results from [or: corresponds to, follows: *anu*] the sacrifice" (ŚB 3,6,3,1). Thus, for instance, the Śatapatha-Brāhmaṇa declares (2,3,1,5): "And when he offers in the morning before sun-rise, then he produces that (sun-child) and, having become a light, it rises shining. But, assuredly, it would not rise, were he not to make that offering: this is why he performs that offering."[14]

Although the Vedic ritual in its classical form as represented by the Brāhmaṇa texts is not "magic" in the sociological sense of the word, since it is not directed against the society and its order[15], the principle underlying the Vedic ritual is the basic law of magic: *similia similibus*[16]. Magical equations, which are the most characteristic feature of the Brāhmaṇa texts, are established between the controlling ritual and the earthly, cosmic or mythical phenomena to be controlled[17]. The identifications are exploited by the manipulation of the ritual symbols. The Brāhmaṇa texts consistently

---

[8] Cf. Hubert 7f., 19.

[9] Cf. Parpola 1976, 21ff.

[10] Cf. Gonda 1960, 108ff., 105.

[11] Cf. Lévi 41ff.

[12] Cf. ib. 13ff.

[13] Cf. Gonda 1975, 339f.; Oldenberg 1919, 149ff.

[14] The Vedic texts are generally quoted in standard translations (the ŚB in Eggeling's version, etc., cf. the bibliography), but in a few cases I have taken the liberty of making slight modifications, such as e.g. adding the Sanskrit text in parentheses. Some translations, notably those of the MS and the KS, are my own.

[15] Cf. Gonda 1965, 26; Durkheim 42ff.; Diehl 13ff.

[16] Cf. Gonda 1960, 177; Frazer 14ff.

[17] The equations are often expressly considered at three levels (e.g. in ŚB 10,2,6,16), *adhidevatam* "with regard to the deities", *adhyātmam* "with regard to self", and *adhiyajñam* "with regard to the sacrifice". Cf. Oldenberg 1919, 57f.; Schayer 1925, 286f.

emphasize that knowledge of the secret identity gives the knower power over the entities concerned. These magic identifications are the central object of the "pre-scientific science" (as it has been aptly called by Hermann Oldenberg) of the Vedic ritualists. It is the nature of these equations on which our attention shall be focused in the following[18].

In their earliest accessible form the ritualistic identifications are found in the *yajus* formulae. These are generally muttered by the *adhvaryu,* the chief of the priests responsible for the actual sacrificial operations. Characteristically, they are not, as a rule, addressed to gods but to sacrificial offerings or utensils[19]. Not infrequently the *yajus* is twofold, consisting, first, of the name or epithet of the object, which reveals its secret nature, and, second, of a request activating the inherent power. The sacrificial fire, for instance, is addressed with this formula (cf. ĀpŚS 3,7,6): "Guardian of life art thou, o Agni; guard my life!" (TS 1,1,13 i)[20]. It is apparent from this that a thing which is or represents a certain power is expected to give or diffuse it[21].

In the explanatory prose passages attached to the yajus formulae or to other liturgical elements, that is, in the *brāhmaṇas* in the more restricted sense of the word[22], the identifications are usually stated with an almost mathematical brevity. A nominal sentence may consist of nothing else but the words for the two entities thus equated. But it is also usual to add an emphatic particle, such as *vai, eva* or *vāva,* after the more important part, the predicate noun, which occupies the stressed position at the beginning of the sentence, as it does in the *yajus* formulae. For instance, *brahma kṛṣṇājinam* "the black (antelope's) hide (is) Brahma" (TS 5,1,10,4); *asau* (scil. *dyauḥ*) *kṛṣṇājinam* "the black (antelope's) hide (is) yonder (sky)" (KS 19,4; KapS 30,2); *iyaṃ* (scil. *pṛthivī*) *vai kṛṣṇājinam* "the black (antelope's) hide verily (is) this (earth)" (TS 5,1,4,3; ŚB 6,4,1,9)[23]. Emphasis can also be given by adding a relative and a correlative particle in front of the two parts (*yad . . . tad . . .* "it is the . . . that is . . ."), or by other means[24].

While translating such nominal sentences it is customary to add the copula ("is" or "are")[25]. This is entirely justified by the express use of the verb *as-* 'to be' in parallel equations occurring in *yajus* formulae and in mythical narratives (cf. e.g. *eṣa ha vāva saṃvatsaraḥ prajāpatir āsa* "Verily, Prajāpati was this year" in JB 3,375)[26]. But what is actually implied?

---

[18] For the identifications, cf. especially Oldenberg 1919, 110ff.; Schayer 1925, 267ff.; Mylius 1968, 267ff.; 1976, 145ff.; Gonda 1975, 372ff.

[19] Cf. Gonda 1975, 332ff.

[20] Cf. Oldenberg 1917, 2ff.; Gonda 1975, 332ff.

[21] Cf. Gonda 1957, 32, 58ff.

[22] Cf. ib. 340ff.

[23] The best classified collection of equations in the Brāhmaṇa texts is Vishva Bandhu 1ff. (in Sanskrit only); a representative collection from the Maitrāyaṇī Saṃhitā (in German) is given by Schroeder 128ff. For a content analysis cf. Mylius 1968, 267ff.; 1976, 145ff.

[24] For a linguistic analysis of the nominal sentences cf. Gren-Eklund, Gunilla, 1ff.

[25] Cf. ib. 15ff.

[26] Cf. JB 2,393 *prajāpatir eva saṃvatsaraḥ* "the year (is) Prajāpati".

Should the verb "to be" be taken in the sense of literal identity? Or should one rather replace it by expressions such as "is a kind of", "stands for", "represents", "symbolizes"? I do not think that a single answer is admissible. It is a short step from symbolization to identification, and this makes it often difficult to find out what has been in the mind of the ancient ritualists[27]. It is pertinent to remember that the Christian theologians have not been able to agree whether the bread and wine of the holy communion only symbolize or in actual fact are the body and blood of Jesus[28].

In the Vedic religion the temporal factor has to be taken into consideration in this connection. By the close of the seventh century B.C., approximately, the concept of individuality started being abandoned: one was recognized in all and all in one[29]. The development of this pantheistic world view is intimately connected with the process of "internalization" or "mentalization" of the ritual. In the *prāṇāgnihotra* sacrifice, the concrete ritual acts are replaced by corresponding psychic acts taking place in the mind of the sacrificer[30]. This leads to the change of the *kārmamārga* into the *jñānamārga,* where the mere knowledge of the magical identities is sufficient: ritual technology becomes contemplative mysticism[31].

The exact sense of the magic equations in the Brāhmaṇa texts can be best studied by analysing parallel expressions. Thus it can be noted that instead of identifications, comparisons formed with the particle *yathā* or *iva* "as, like" can occur. The expression *máma iva hí prajā́patiḥ* "for Prajāpati is like the mind" (TS 2,5,11,5) is exactly paralleled by the straight identification *mano hi prajāpatiḥ* "for the Prajāpati is the mind" (SVidhB 1,1,1)[32].

A term used for the other component of the equation is *prati-mā́,* literally "counter-measure" and more freely "copy, image, symbol". Let us take for an example the equation of the creator god Prajāpati with the sacrificial year. This magic identity is usually expressed in the Brāhmaṇa texts with a nominal sentence of the usual kind[26]. But in ŚB 11,1,6,13 the year is said to be the *pratimā* of Prajāpati. The text runs as follows: "Prajāpati bethought himself, 'Verily, I have created here a counterpart of myself, to wit, the year'; whence they say, 'Prajāpati is the year'; for he created it to be a counterpart of himself: inasmuch as *saṃvatsara* 'year' as well as *Prajāpati* consist of four syllables, thereby it [i.e. the year] is a counterpart of him."[33]

One of the best clues to the meaning that the Vedic ritualists themselves attached to the identifications is supplied by the term *rupa*[34]. This term

[27] Cf. Schroeder 127 ff.; Oldenberg 1919, 120 ff.; also O'Flaherty, Wendy, 34.
[28] Cf. Oldenberg 1915, 18.
[29] Cf. Schroeder 130; Oldenberg 1915, 35 ff.
[30] Cf. Bodewitz 211 ff.
[31] Cf. Schayer 1925 a, 61.
[32] Cf. Oldenberg 1919, 115; Schayer 1925, 299 (: *upamā*).
[33] Cf. Oldenberg 1919, 114 f.; Schayer 1925, 275; Silburn, Lilian, 50.
[34] For the term *rūpa* cf. especially Oldenberg 1919, 102 ff., 114; Schayer 1925, 276; Gonda 1957, 97 ff.; Silburn, Lilian, 58 f., 84 f.

forms an exact counterpart to the identifications in sentences like the following. On the one hand the texts say *brahma kṛṣṇājinam* "the black (antelope's) hide (is) the brahma" (TS 5,1,10,4), on the other *etad vai brahmaṇo rūpaṃ yat kṛṣṇājinam* (KS 19,4) or *brahmaṇa* [°*ṇo vā* TB] *etad rūpaṃ yat kṛṣṇājinam* (TS 5,4,4,4; TB 2,7,1,4) "the black (antelope's) hide (is) a *rūpa* of the brahma". There seems to be no real difference in meaning between these two kinds of expression[35].

In contexts like the above one, the word *rūpa* is translated as "Erscheinungsform" or "Gestalt" by Oldenberg[34], as "form" or "type" by Eggeling[36], as "characteristic mark" or "feature" or "nature" by Caland[37], as "manifestation" or "representation" by Gonda[34], and as "symbol" by Keith[38], Renou[39] and Silburn[34]. Monier-Williams's dictionary[40] records among others the following meanings of this word as being valid for the Vedic language: "any outward appearance or phenomenon or colour, form, shape, figure; nature, character, peculiarity, feature, mark, sign, symptom". Macdonell's dictionary[41] gives in addition the meanings "likeness, image, reflexion; indication, token, symbol, manifestation". The central meaning is "form, shape". In the classical Sanskrit, the derivative *rūpa-ka* has, as an adjective, the signification "designating figuratively", and as a technical term of the poetics, "metaphor" as well as "drama". The corresponding denominative verb *rūpayati* of the post-Vedic language means "to give form to, represent, act on the stage, represent in pantomime, notify by a gesture"[40–41].

It will be clear from the following passages that the word *rūpa* is used in the Brāhmaṇa texts in a meaning fairly close to our "symbol". In the Aitareya-Brāhmaṇa (2,1,6) we read:

"He who desires nutritious food and he who desires prosperity should make his sacrificial post of bilva wood. Year by year, the bilva tree is fruitful; therefore it is a *rūpa* of nutritious food. Up to the root, it is beset all along with branches; therefore it is (a *rūpa*) of prosperity. He prospers in offspring and cattle who knowing thus makes the sacrificial post of bilva wood. Now as to (his using) bilva wood, they say about bilva that '(it is) light'; a light he becomes among his own people, the chief of his own people he becomes, who knows thus."[42]

The archaic *mahāvrata* rite is connected with a turning point of the sun's course and marks the end of the old year and the beginning of the new. It is celebrated with many characteristic ritual acts. One is described in the Kaṭha-Saṃhitā (34,5: 39,3–6), one of our oldest sources here, as follows: "An Āryan and a Śūdra [i.e. a member of the darkhued servile class] fight

---

35 Cf. Oldenberg 1919, 108 n. 4.

36 Cf. Eggeling 3, 360 (on ŚB 7,3,2,16); 5,125 (on ŚB 11,7,4,4).

37 Cf. Caland 1931, 83 (on PB 5,5,21), 127 (on PB 6,9,25).

38 Cf. Keith 135 (on AB 2,1,6).

39 Cf. Renou 1954, 73.

40 Cf. Monier-Williams 885 f.

41 Cf. Macdonell 257.

42 Cf. Keith 134; Gonda 1957, 97.

for a hide by pulling it in different directions. The gods and demons, forsooth, fought for the sun by pulling it in different directions. The gods won it. He makes the Aryan class [literally, the Aryan colour] to win; it is himself that he makes to win. The Aryan should be inside the sacred space, the Śūdra outside the sacred space. The hide should be white (and) circular, (as) a *rūpa* of the sun [*śvetaṃ carma parimaṇḍalaṃ syād, ādityasya rūpam*]." In the corresponding passage of the Pañcaviṃśa-Brāhmaṇa (5,5,14–17) based on the KS[43] the last sentence reads: "The hide is circular; it is the sun whose *rūpa* is thereby made [in this hide (comm.)] [*parimaṇḍalaṃ carma bhavaty, ādityasya tad rūpaṃ kriyate,* scil. *asmin carmaṇi*]". The mediaeval commentator, Sāyaṇa, explains: "It was namely for the sun that the fight of the gods was made in ancient times; this has been told [scil. above in the text]. For that very reason this hide is a counterfeit of the sun." The gloss here is *prati-rūpaka,* literally, "having counterform".

Some other passages are very instructive with regard to the instrumental function of the *rūpa*. This function is, of course, one of the basic characteristics of ritual symbols in general[44]. When the sacred fires are established a second time (which may happen, for instance, if the year following the first establishment has been unlucky, if one has lost a son, etc., cf. ĀpŚS 5,26,3), the gifts to the priests include, according to MS 1,7,2: 110,12 ff., a cloth that has been mended by sewing it up again, an ox that has been let loose a second time, and a chariot that has been repaired again. This is explained in the text as follows: "Verily, these (gifts) are *rūpa*s of the renewed foundation (of the sacred fires) [*etāni vai punarādheyasya rūpāni*]. He obtains it after having reached its *rūpa*s [*rūpāṇy evāsyāptvāvarunddhe*]." The parallel passage in KS 8,15: 98,19 ff. has for the last sentence this: "It is by means of the rūpas that he perfects that (renewed foundation of the fires) [*rūpair evainat samardhayati*]."

The here used verb *sam-ṛdh-* which in the causative has the meaning "to perfect, make complete", occurs even elsewhere in connection with the word *rūpa*. Commenting upon the relation between the ritual formula and the corresponding sacrificial act which is somehow illustrated by the formula, the Aitareya-Brāhmaṇa (1,4,9) says: "That, indeed, is perfect in the sacrifice which is perfect in *rūpa* [or: abundantly furnished with *rūpa*] [*etad vai yajñasya samṛddhaṃ yad rūpasamṛddham*]."[45] Similarly it is said a little later in the same text (1,19,6): "what in the sacrifice is con-formable (to it) that is perfect [*yad yajñe 'bhirūpaṃ tat samṛddham*]".

The term *sam-ṛddha* "completed, perfect" is nearly synonymous with *sarva* "whole, complete, entire". In ŚB 5,1,4,5 the verb *samardhayati* "makes to attain or succeed fully, completes, perfects" is followed by the

---

[43] Cf. Parpola 1968, 81, 85 ff., 93 f.

[44] Cf. e.g. Turner 1967, 32, 37; Diehl 22 ff.

[45] Cf. Oldenberg 1919, 245.

synonymous expression *kṛtsnaṃ karoti* "makes (the object) whole"[46]. The word *samṛddha* qualifies the term *rūpa* in ŚB 6,4,4,17, where the plants are said to have their "perfect form" when they are blossoming and full-berried. Similarly in ŚB 6,5,1,10 the woman has her "perfect form" when she is fair-knotted, fair-braided, fair-locked; by pronouncing the formula where the goddess Sinīvalī is addressed as such a woman with beautiful hair, he thus makes her perfect (*smardhayaty evaināṃ etat*)[47]. The Jaiminīya-Brāhmaṇa (3,115) explains that water is placed close by while the chanter priests sing the mahānāmnī stanzas in order to make the sacrificial song complete (*sāmnas sarvatvāya*), "for verily, water is the complete manifestation [*sarvaṃ rūpam*] of the mahānāmnī stanzas"[48].

The importance placed on the abundance of symbolic manifestation apparent from the above quotations is connected with the central position occupied by the idea of integrity and wholeness in the Vedic thought. It is the state of not being defective or ill: Sanskrit *sarva* is etymologically the same word as Latin *salvus*[49]. The Chāndogya-Upaniṣad (7,26,2) states that "he who (truly) sees does not see death, nor illness nor any distress; he who (truly) sees sees the All [i.e., wholeness, completeness, integrity], he reaches [or: obtains] the All in all respects [or: entirely]."[50] *Idaṃ sarvam* "all this" means "the complete universe", which is very frequently identified with Prajāpati or Brahma[50]. In ŚB 10,4,3,3–8 the gods are trying to attain immortality by performing sacrificial rites. They do not, however, succeed until Prajāpati intervenes and says to them: "Ye do not lay down [or: put on me] all my forms [*na vai me sarvāṇi rūpāṇy upadhattha*]; ye either make (me) too large or leave (me) defective: therefore ye do not become immortal." The sacrifice is the counterpart of Prajāpati; it is the counterpart of the universe or "this all", which means "integrity", "being whole" and thus "being safe from illness and death", i.e. "immortality"; and this sacrifice-Prajāpati-immortality cannot be reached except by making it complete, by perfecting it[51].

Further insight into the nature of the *rūpa* concept and Prajāpati's completeness is provided by two passages of the Śatapatha-Brāhmaṇa. In 6,5,3,6–7 we read: "He makes these (bricks) from (clay) prepared with prayer, the other from (clay) prepared without prayer; for these are defined, the others undefined; these are limited (in number), the others unlimited. 7. That Agni [i.e., the fire altar built of these bricks] is Prajāpati; but Prajāpati is both of this, defined [*nirukta*] and undefined [*anirukta*], limited [*parimita*] and unlimited [*aparimita*]: thus when he makes (bricks) from (clay) prepared with prayer, he thereby makes up that form [*rūpa*] of his [i.e. Prajāpati's] which is defined and limited; and when he makes up

---

46 Cf. Gonda 1955, 55.
47 Cf. Oldenberg 1919, 106 n. 2.
48 Cf. Gonda 1957, 99.
49 Cf. id. 1955, 67 f.
50 Cf. ib. 62 f.
51 Cf. Silburn, Lilian, 58 f.

them from (clay) prepared without prayer, he thereby makes up that form of his which is undefined and unlimited. Verily, then, whosoever knowing this does it in this way, makes up the whole and complete Prajāpati." The passage 7,2,4,29–30 is otherwise identical, but the actions done with and without a prayer differ: instead of making bricks, one yokes oxen, ploughs furrows, etc. Moreover, there is an important addition at the end: "The outer forms [*bāhyāni rūpāṇi*] are defined, and the inner ones [*antarāṇi*] are undefined; and Agni is the same as an animal: hence the outer forms of the animal are defined, the inner ones undefined."

The term *nir-ukta,* which in the above quoted translation by J. Eggeling has been rendered "defined", literally means "expressly stated", "clearly or distinctly uttered". In the Vedic ritual it refers to hymns and formulae recited in a loud voice (*uccaiḥ*); or to sacrificial songs sung according to the original, intelligible syllables; or to formulae which contain (to use a term of the slightly later Śrautasūtra period) a *liṅga,* that is, a "characteristic element" such as the name of a specific deity. *Nir-ukta,* in other words, explicitly states the meaning. It thus corresponds to another important term often used in the Brāhmaṇas, namely, *praty-akṣa* "that which is before the eyes, visible, perceptible, manifest, open, plain".

The opposite term *a-nir-ukta,* literally "that which is not expressly stated or distinctly uttered", refers in the ritual to "inaudibly, silently" (*upāṃśu, tūṣṇīm*) or "mentally" (*manasā*) uttered stanzas and formulae; or to songs based on unintelligible syllables substituted for the original, meaningful text; or to formulae without a *liṅga. Anirukta* corresponds to the term *paro-'kṣa* "that which is beyond the sight, invisible, inperceivable, cryptic, mystical".

Nirukta is thus everything that has a definite outline or shape or structure, while *anirukta* goes beyond all such defined things and is needed to complete and perfect them. For the whole (*sarva*) transcends all (*viśva*), its elements. According to AB 2,31,5, there must be, at the end of the audible recitations or the explicit lauds, a silent praise (*tūṣṇīṃ-śaṃsa*), which perfects (*saṃ-sthā-*) the sacrifice[52].

The terms *praty-akṣa* and *paro-'kṣa* occur also in the magical equations. A noteworthy passage is PB 22,10,3–4: "What presents itself in a visible way to men (presents itself) in a cryptical way to the gods, and what (presents itself) in a cryptical way to men (presents itself) in a visible way to the gods. 4. The *viśvajit* (rite) is, in a cryptical way, the (*mahā*)*vrata* (rite); in a visible way he, by means of this (rite) obtains food [*vrata*]."[53] The here stated opposition is resorted to when secret connections are established through etymologies which do not entirely fit the observable facts. Thus the Bṛhad-Āraṇyaka-Upaniṣad (4,2,2) says: "*Indha* 'kindler' by name is

---

[52] For this discussion of the terms *nirukta, anirukta,* etc., cf. Renou 1954, 68 ff.

[53] Cf. Caland 579.

this person here in the right eye. Him, verily, who is that *Indha* people call *Indra,* cryptically, for the gods are fond of the cryptic, as it were, and dislike the evident." It can be seen from this that the secret, speculative knowledge was highly appreciated, and the value of the empirical knowledge correspondingly underestimated[54].

The terms *pratyakṣa* and *paro-'kṣa* refer to the eye (*akṣa*) and the sight. In the philosophy of the Upaniṣads (cf. e.g. BĀU 3,2,5; 3,9,20), the *rūpa* or "form, shape" is the object of the sight, just as the sound is the object of hearing. Already the Ṛgveda-Saṃhitā (6,47,18) says of Indra that "this is his *rūpa* for looking at [*tád asya rūpám praticákṣaṇāya*]". In ṚS 1,164,44 it is said of the wind that only its swiftness is seen, not its *rūpa* (*dhrā́jir ékasya dadṛśe ná rūpám*). The Śatapatha-Brāhmaṇa (11,8,3,8) states that "he [i.e., the sun] took to himself the wind's form [*rūpa*]; whence people hear it, as it were, shaking, but do not see it; and verily, he who knows this, takes away the form of his spiteful enemy."[55] The wind and the bodily breaths are among the principal things called *anirukta* in the Brāhmaṇa texts along with mind, yonder world (of heaven), the whole, *brahman* (m. & n.), and Prajāpati. The wind is according to KB 19,2 a perceptible (*pratyakṣaṃ*) *rūpa* of Prajāpati[56].

That the Vedic term *par excellence* for "symbol" should be specifically connected with the sense of sight is not surprising. Turner, for example, reports that "in discussing their symbols with Ndembu, one finds them constantly using the term *ku-solola* 'to make visible' or 'to reveal'"[57]. Such modern terms as "hierophany", "kratophany" and "theophany" applied to religious symbols i.a. by Mircea Eliade[58] are derived from the Greek verb *phaínō* "to bring to light, cause to appear", hence "manifest, reveal, make known, disclose"[59], which also primarily refers to visible manifestations[60].

A particularly interesting distinction made by the Vedic ritualists is that between the "outer" (*bāhya*) and "inner" (*antara*) forms. Modern semiotics defines "symbols" as signs which have no denotata in the phenomenal world but in the mind only[61]. The distinction between extensional and intensional is, however, in semiotics limited to the denotatum[61], while the Vedic ritualists have extended it even to the "form" of the sign. (We may note here in passing also the exact coincidence of the Vedic term *rūpa* as "form" with the terminology of modern linguistics and semiotics.) Not only the object symbolized by the symbol but even the form of the symbol itself is unextensional, at least in such cases as that exemplified by the prescription of the Āśvalāyana-Śrautasūtra (2,3,19): "He should always m e n t a l l y think upon Prajāpati whenever a s i l e n t oblation is performed." Cf.

[54] Cf. Oldenberg 1919, 221 ff.
[55] Cf. ib. 104.
[56] Cf. Renou 1954, 74 f.
[57] Turner 1967, 48.
[58] Cf. Eliade 437.
[59] Cf. Liddell 1912 f.
[60] Cf. Walde 1, 454 f.
[61] Cf. Sebeok 246 f.

also ŚB 1,6,3,27: "What is (uttered) inaudibly that is the *rūpa* of Prajāpati."

The basic model of thought underlying the use of the term *rūpa* is, as has been pointed out by Hermann Oldenberg, the distinction between a Platonic sort of idea and its physical manifestations[62]. The latter may be quite numerous, and we have seen above the importance placed on representing a manyformed being symbolically as completely as possible. One method often resorted to in order to do this in the Vedic ritual is to enumerate all the names of the multisided being concerned. Thus we meet with long lists of "wind names", "horse names", "snake names", not to mention the *śata-rudriya* (cf. TS 2,4,9,1; ĀpŚS 20,5,9; 20,11,1; ŚB 7,4,1,25 ff.; VS 16, etc.)[63].

Already in the ṚS (3,38,7; 7,103,6; 10,169,2) the term *rūpa* occurs in connection with the term *nāma* "name"[64]. In Buddhism, *nāma-rūpau* "name and form" stands for the concept of "individuality" or for "individual being", since these immaterial and material principles make up the individual and distinguish it from other individuals[65]. That similar views were prevalent in the Brāhmaṇa period can be seen from the myth explaining the structuring of the chaotic universe, told thus in the Taittirīya-Brāhmaṇa (2,2,7,1): "Prajāpati created the beings. Once created, they were joined closely together [*sam-ā-śliṣṭa-,* apparently as an undifferentiated mass, chaos being inherent in the creative act]. He entered them with the form [*rūpa*]. Therefore they say, 'Prajāpati, verily, is the form' [*rūpaṃ vai prajāpatir iti*]. He entered them with the name [*nāman*]. Therefore they say: 'Prajāpati, verily, is the name.' "[66]

The close relation between the concepts of name and form in the Vedic thought is also illustrated by a well known myth related in ŚB 6,1,3,7 ff. Agni or Fire was born as a boy [*kumāra*] to the creator god Prajāpati. He cried, because he had no name as yet and was therefore not freed from evil. The text continues: "10. He (Prajāpati) said to him, 'Thou art Rudra'. And because he gave him that name [*tan nāma*], Agni became such-like [or: that form, *tad-rūpam*], for Rudra is Agni: because he cried [*rud-*], therefore he is Rudra." The text goes on to describe how Prajāpati on Agni's request gives him seven other names, and each time the relation of the name to his corresponding form is explained[67].

The very next chapter in the same text is interesting here for several reasons. It shows how a godly power is able to adopt new *rūpas* at will, and particularly *rūpas* or forms that at the first sight are perplexing and obscure. It also gives a concrete example of the logic and criteria applied by the Vedic ritualists for the discovery or identification of such a secret *rūpa*. (The Vedic exegete is here represented by the mythical archetype of the

---

[62] Cf. Oldenberg 1919, 106 f.
[63] Cf. ib. 104.
[64] Cf. ib. 102 f.
[65] Cf. Rhys-Davids 350 a.
[66] Cf. Silburn, Lilian, 58.
[67] Cf. Oldenberg 1919, 103 f.

brahmanical offer priest, the creator god Prajāpati.) In ŚB 6,2,1 we read: "1. Prajāpati set his mind upon Agni's forms. He searched for that boy who had entered into the (aforesaid different) forms. Agni became aware of it—'Surely, Father Prajāpati is searching for me: well, then, let me be suchlike [*tad-rūpam*] that he knows me not.' 2. He saw those five animals, —the man, the horse, the bull, the ram, and the he-goat. Inasmuch as he saw [*paś-*] them, they are (called sacrificial) animals [*paśu*]. 3. He entered into those five animals; he became those five animals. But Prajāpati still searched for him. 4. He saw those five animals ... 5. He considered, 'They are Agni: I will fit them unto mine own self [or: I will make them part of mine own self, *imān evātmānam abhisaṃskaravai*]. Even as Agni, when kindled, glares, so their eye glares; even as Agni's smoke rises upwards, so vapour rises from them; even as Agni consumes what is put in him, so they devour; even as Agni's ashes fall down, so do their faeces: they are indeed Agni ... 6. ... He slaughtered them."[68]

As noted above, the *rūpa* or form is the object of the sight. The perception of a secret *rūpa* is however conceived as a mental activity. ŚB 11,2,3,6 states that "it is by mind that one knows 'This is form'". Yet, as the above quoted myth shows, this perception is thought of as a sort of vision, for the Brāhmaṇa texts use the verb *paś-* "to see" of the discovery of secret forms and connections. Vision was considered as the most reliable source of knowledge, as can be seen from ŚB 1,3,1,27: "for the eye is indeed the truth. If, therefore, two persons were to come disputing with each other and saying, 'I have seen it!' 'I have heard it!' we should believe him who said, 'I have seen it!' and not the other." It is understandable that the Chāndogya-Upaniṣad (8,12,5) calls the mind (*manas*) the "divine eye" (*daivaṃ cakṣus*). Asceticism and sacrifice can give the gods and the sages the superhuman ability to see the secret and powerful realities such as holy texts, rituals and identities, which, though existing, are closed from the eyes of the mere mortals (cf. e.g. TS 5,3,5,4)[69].

In the famous creation hymn of the Ṛgveda (10,129,4) the "heart" (*hṛd*) is spoken of as the place where the sages discovered the secret connection[70]. "Heart" takes the place of "mind" as the instrument of conceiving the forms also in the following discussion between Śākalya and Yājnavalkya recorded in BĀU 3,9,19–20: "'Since you know the quarters of heaven together with their gods and their bases, what divinity have you in this eastern quarter?' 'The sun.' 'That sun—on what is it based?' 'On the eye.' 'And on what is the eye based? [*kasmin nu cakṣuḥ pratiṣṭhitam iti*]' 'On appearances, for with eye one sees appearances [*rūpeṣv iti cakṣuṣā hi rūpāṇi paśyati*].' 'And on what are appearances based?' 'On the heart', he said, 'for with the heart one knows appearances [*hṛdayena hi rūpāṇi jānāti*], for

---

[68] Cf. ib. 108.

[69] Cf. ib. 222 ff.; Gonda 1963, 27 ff. For the eye as truth cf. also KS 8,3; MS 1,8,1; 3,6,3; Śb 4,2,1,26; AB 1,6.

[70] Cf. also Gonda 1963, 63.

on the heart alone appearances are based.' 'Quite so, Yājnavalkya.' "[71] This passage introduces us to a term important for the understanding of the magic identifications, namely *pratiṣṭhā* "firm foundation, ground, basis, support", and the corresponding verb which consists of the preverb *prati* "towards, against, upon" and the root *sthā-* "to stand, stay"; the latter is often used in the causative, with the meaning "to make stand firmly, establish"[72]. The word *pratiṣṭhā* is among other things used for the home or native country of a person in the sense of a reliable place where he gets support, where he is free from danger, and to which he always naturally resorts as his own[73].

The Vedic man appreciated *pratiṣṭhā* "foundation" as a benefit and a source of welfare. It was a possession that he sought to acquire for himself by ritual means. He also resorted to the sacrifice when he wished to deprive his enemy of food and foundation, for this meant destruction[74]. Ritual was likewise the instrument to provide the powerful potencies of the universe with strong resting places: it was necessary to prevent them from wandering about arbitrarily (which would mean infringement of the cosmic norms and cause of dangerous disorder), and this could be done by "establishing" them "on their proper places" where they naturally belong. The sacrificial acts, which were supposed to be connected with the cosmic processes, could be used to produce any desired "establishment" of a given person or object[75].

The knowledge of its foundation thus provides the means for the attainment of the desired object[76]. It is for this reason that Naciketas asks in the Kaṭha-Upaniṣad (1,14): "How can the infinite world be attained and what is its foundation (*pratiṣṭhā*)?"[77] An answer to a somewhat similar problem is attempted in AS 17,1,19, where the sage says: "In the non-existent (*asat*) is the existent (*sat*) established (*pratiṣṭhitam*); in the existent is being (*bhūtá*) established; being is set in what is to be; what is to be is established in being." Here being and what is to be are said to be established in one another, as indissolubly co-existent[78]. In the creation hymn ṚS 1,129 this relation is expressed in a different way (verse 4): "the sages have found in their heart the *bandhu* of the existent in the non-existent."[79]

The word *bandhu* literally means "bond" and is etymologically of the same origin as this English word. In the Brāhmaṇa texts it denotes above all the mysterious connection or relation between the entities of this world and the transcendental "ideal" entities of the divine world, which are the foundation and origin of the perceptible things[80]. As Oldenberg has put it,

---

[71] Cf. Hume 123; Gonda 1954, 24. According to TB 3,10,8,5, "the eye is based on the heart" (*cakṣur hṛdaye pratiṣṭhitam*).
[72] Cf. Gonda 1954, 1f.
[73] Cf. ib. 6f. For the related concepts of *āyatana* and *yoni* ("womb"), which cannot be discussed here, cf. ib. 7,10; id. 1969, 1ff.; Schayer 1925, 279f.
[74] Cf. Gonda 1954, 13ff.
[75] Cf. ib. 4,7,11f., 18,20.
[76] Cf. ib. 17,30.
[77] Cf. ib. 25.
[78] Cf. ib. 27f., 24; Whitney 810.
[79] Cf. Gonda 1965, 29; id. 1966, 689.
[80] Cf. ib. 689; id. 1965, 1ff.

the knowledge of the Brāhmaṇas is above all knowledge about the *bandhus*[81]. We cannot fully understand the nature of the Vedic identifications if we do not take into consideration this term and its connotations[82]. The most important of the latter are its non-technical meanings "kinship tie, connection in blood or through marriage" and hence "relation, relative". In the archaic societies with blood-revenge, levirate marriage etc., "relationship" is much more than the state of having genealogical or other relations to another person; it is "a form of existence in its own right, from which one cannot release oneself", communion in the truest sense of the term, including an intense consciousness of unity. Gonda, from whom I have quoted the preceding sentence, is certainly right in seeing this meaning in the word *bandhu* used of a mystical identity in ŚB 2,1,4,17 *eṣa hy evānaḍuho bandhuḥ* "for that (fire) is a relation of the ox"[83].

This passage and interpretation makes it perfectly clear what is meant in ŚB 13,8,4,6, where the ox is said to be *āgneya* "of Agni's nature or descent". That the derivative adjective, normally used in patronyms, is here really used to express a magical equation, is secured by the parallel—also to the preceding quotation with *bandhu*—in ŚB 7,3,2,1, where the mystic identification has the normal form of a nominal sentence with a predicate noun: *agnir eṣa yad anaḍvān* "the ox (is) Agni"[84].

Bibliography

ALB The Adyar library bulletin
AUU Acta Universitatis Upsaliensis. Uppsala
BI Bibliotheca Indica. Calcutta
DRT Disputationes Rheno-Traiectinae. The Hague
HIL A history of Indian literature
HM A handbook of method in cultural anthropology. Ed. R. Naroll, R. Cohen. New York
HOS Harvard Oriental series. Cambridge
IS Indische Studien. Berlin
VIS Vishweshwarananda Indological series. Hoshiarpur

A. *Vedic texts*

For translations see B under the name mentioned here in parentheses

AB *Aitareya-Brāhmaṇa*. Ed. T. Aufrecht. Bonn 1879. (See Keith.)
ĀpŚS *Āpastamba-Śrauta-Sūtra*. Ed. R. Garbe 1–3. BI 92, 1882 ff.
AS *Atharvaveda-Saṃhitā*. Ed. D. Sātvalekar. Pardi 1957. (See Whitney.)
ĀśvŚS *Āśvalāyana-Śrauta-Sūtra*. Ed. R. Vidyāratna. BI 49, 1874.

---

[81] Cf. Oldenberg 1919, 4; Gonda 1965, 3.

[82] For *bandhu* and the closely related term *ni-dāna*, which cannot be discussed here, cf. especially Gonda 1965, 1 ff.; Gonda 1969, 63 ff.; Renou 1946, 55 ff. Cf. also Oldenberg 1919, 117; Schayer 1925, 276 f.

[83] Cf. Gonda 1965, 22 f.

[84] Cf. ib. 22; Oldenberg 1919, 115 f.; Schayer 1925, 298 f.—For the evidence presented as grounds for the identifications by the Vedic ritualists cf. Oldenberg 1919, 118 ff.; Schayer 1925, 288 ff.

BĀU *Bṛhad-Āraṇyaka-Upaniṣad*. Ed. J. Śāstrī, *Upaniṣatsaṅgrahah*. Delhi 1970. (See Hume.)
ChU *Chāndogya-Upaniṣad*. (As BĀU.)
JB *Jaiminīya-Brāhmaṇa*. Ed. Raghu Vira, Lokesh Chandra. Sarasvati Vihara Series 31. Nagpur 1954.
KapS *Kapiṣṭhala-Kaṭha-Saṃhitā*. Ed. Raghu Vira. Delhi 1968.
KB *Kauṣītaki-Brāhmaṇa*. Ed. S. Sarma. Verzeichnis der orientalischen Handschriften in Deutschland. Supplementband 9,1. Wiesbaden 1968. (See Keith.)
KS *Kaṭha-Saṃhitā* (*Kāṭhaka*). Ed. L. v. Schroeder 1–3. Wiesbaden 1970 ff.
KU *Kaṭha-Upaniṣad*. (As BĀU.)
MS *Maitrāyaṇī Saṃhitā*. (As KS.)
PB *Pañcaviṃśa-Brāhmaṇa* (*Tāṇḍya-Mahā-Brāhmaṇa*). Ed. with Sāyaṇa's commentary C. Śastri 1–2. The Kashi Sanskrit series 105. Benares 1935 f. (See Caland.)
ṚS *Ṛgveda-Saṃhitā*. Ed. T. Aufrecht 1–2. IS 6–7, 1861 ff.
ŚB *Śatapatha-Brāhmaṇa* (in the Mādhyandina recension). Ed. A. Weber. London 1855. (See Eggeling.)
SVidhB *Sāma-Vidhāna-Brāhmaṇa*. Ed. R. Sharma. Kendriya Sanskrit Vidyapeetha Series 1. Tirupati 1964.
TB *Taittirīya-Brāhmaṇa*. Ed. N. Goḍbole 1–3. Ānandāśrama-saṃskṛtagranthāvali 37. Poona 1898.
TS *Taittirīya-Saṃhitā*. Ed. A. Weber 1–2. IS 11–12. Berlin 1871 f.
VS *Vājasaneyi-Saṃhitā* (in the Mādhyandina recension). Ed. A. Weber. London 1852.

B. *Modern authors*

Bodewitz, H., 1973, *Jaiminīya-Brāhmaṇa I, 1–65*. Orientalia Rheno-Traiectina 17. Leiden.
Caland, W., 1931, *Pañcaviṃśa-Brāhmaṇa*. BI 255.
Collinder, B., 1962, *Les origines du structuralisme*. AUU. Acta Societatis Linguisticae Upsaliensis. N. S. 1,1.
Diehl, C., 1956, Instrument and purpose. Diss. Lund.
Durkheim, É., 1976, *The elementary forms of the religious life*. London.
Eggeling, J., 1882 ff., *The Śatapatha-Brāhmaṇa according to the text of the Mādhyandina school translated* 1–5. Sacred Books of the East 12, 26, 41, 43, 44. Oxford.
Eliade, M., 1958, *Patterns in comparative religion*. London.
Frazer, J., 1957, *The golden bough*. London.
Gonda, J., 1954, Pratiṣṭhā. *Saṃjñāvyākaraṇam. Studia Indologica Internationalia* 1. Poona.
— 1955, Reflections on *sarva-* in Vedic texts. *Indian Linguistics* 16.
— 1957, *Some observations on the relations between "gods" and powers in the Veda, a propos of the phrase* sūnuḥ sahasaḥ. DRT 1.
— 1960, *Die Religionen Indiens* 1. Die Religionen der Menschheit 11. Stuttgart.
— 1963, *The vision of the Vedic poets*. DRT 8.
— 1965, *Bandhu-* in the Brāhmaṇa-s. *Brahmavidyā: ALB* 29.
— 1966, De kosmogonie van Ṛgveda 10, 129. *Tijdschrift voor Philosophie* 28.
— 1969, Āyatana-. *Brahmavidyā: ALB* 33.
— 1975, *Vedic literature* (*Saṃhitās and Brāhmaṇas*). HIL 1,1. Wiesbaden.
— 1977, *Ritual Sūtras*. HIL 1,2. Wiesbaden.
Gren-Eklund, Gunilla, 1978, *A study of nominal sentences in the oldest Upaniṣads*. Diss. AUU. Studia Indoeuropaea Upsaliensia 3. Uppsala.

Hillebrandt, A., 1897, *Ritual-Litteratur, vedische Opfer und Zauber*. Grundriss der Indo-Arischen Philologie und Altertumskunde 3,2. Strassburg.
Hubert, H., Mauss, M., 1964, *Sacrifice: its nature and function*. London.
Hume, R., 1931, *The thirteen principal Upanishads translated*. Oxford.
Keith, B., 1920, *Rigveda Brahmanas translated*. HOS. 25.
Lévi, S., 1898, *La doctrine du sacrifice dans les Brāhmaṇas*. Bibliothèque de l'École des Hautes Études. Sciences religieuses 11. Paris.
Liddell, H., Scott, R., 1940, *A Greek-English Lexicon*. Oxford.
Macdonell, A., 1929, *A practical Sanskrit dictionary*. Oxford.
Middleton, J., 1970, The religious system. *HM*.
Monier-Williams, M., 1899, *A Sanskrit-English dictionary*. Oxford.
Mylius, K., 1968, Die Identifikationen der Metren in der Literatur des Ṛgveda. *Wissenschaftliche Zeitschrift der Karl-Marx-Universität Leipzig. Gesellschafts- und Sprachwissenschaftliche Reihe* 17.
— 1976, Die vedischen Identifikationen am Beispiel des *Kauṣītaki-Brāhmaṇa*. *Klio* 58.
O'Flaherty, Wendy, 1973, *Asceticism and eroticism in the mythology of Śiva*. London.
Oldenberg, H., 1915, *Die Lehre der Upanishaden und die Anfänge des Buddhismus*. Göttingen.
— 1917, *Zur Geschichte der altindischen Prosa*. Abhandlungen der Kgl. Gesellschaft der Wissenschaften zu Göttingen. Phil.-hist. Kl. N. F. 16,6. Berlin.
— 1919, *Vorwissenschaftliche Wissenschaft*. Göttingen.
Parpola, A., 1968, *The Śrautasūtras of Lāṭyāyana and Drāhyāyaṇa and their commentaries* 1,1. Societas Scientiarum Fennica. Commentationes Humanarum Litterarum 42,2. Helsinki.
— 1976, The encounter of religions in India, 2000–1000 B.C. *Temenos* 12.
Pike, K., 1964, Towards a theory of the structure of human behavior. *Language in culture and society*. Ed. D. Hymes. New York.
Renou, L., 1946, 'Connexion' en védique, 'cause' en bouddhique. *A volume of Indological studies presented to Dr. C. Kunhan Raja*. Madras.
Renou, L., Silburn, Lilian, 1954, Nírukta and Ánirukta in Vedic. *Sarūpa-Bhāratī: The homage of indology, Dr. Lakshman Sarup memorial volume*. Ed. J. Agrawal, B. Shastri. VIS 6.
Rhys-Davids, T., Stede, W., 1925, *The Pali Text Society's Pali–English dictionary*. London.
Schayer, S., 1925, Die Struktur der magischen Weltanschauung nach dem Atharva-Veda und den Brāhmaṇa-Texten. *Zeitschrift für Buddhismus* 6.
— 1925 a, Über die Bedeutung des Wortes upaniṣad. *Rocznik Orjentalistyczny* 3.
Schroeder, L. v., 1887, *Indiens Literatur und Cultur in historischer Entwicklung*. Leipzig.
Sebeok, T., 1974, Semiotics. *Current trends in linguistics* 12. The Hague.
Silburn, Lilian, 1955, *Instant et cause*. Diss. Paris.
Staal, F., 1972, *A reader on the Sanskrit grammarians*. Studies in linguistics 1. Cambridge.
Turner, V., 1967, *The forest of symbols*. Ithaca.
— 1969, *The ritual process*. London.
Vishva Bandhu, 1966, *Brāhmaṇic Citations*. VIS 38.
Walde, A., Hofmann, J., 1938, *Lateinisches etymologisches Wörterbuch* 1–2. Indogermanische Bibliothek 1,2. Heidelberg.
Werner, O., Fenton, Joann, 1970, Method and theory in ethnoscience and ethnoepistemology. *HM*.
Whitney, W., 1905, *Atharva-Veda-Saṁhitā translated* 1–2. HOS 7–8.

The Symbolism of Liminality

BY JUHA PENTIKÄINEN

1. The rites of the threshold: van Gennep's prestructuralism

Arnold van Gennep belongs to such a group of scholars as were not particularly appreciated by his own generation. His work *Les rites de passage* was published as early as in 1909, but his theory had no greater influence on anthropological studies of religion before than at mid-century. The English edition was published as late as in 1960. Durkheim had more readers and followers than van Gennep at his time. Later on, van Gennep's ideas seem to have been forgotten under the influence of functional theories of the 1920's. The British social anthropology criticizes him for generalizing too much and for neglecting a thorough analysis of any particular society. It is typical what M. Gluckman writes when introducing van Gennep's theory in the book *Essays on the ritual of social relations*[1]. Referring to Junod's classic monograph on the Tsonga, Gluckman makes the following statement: "Nevertheless I would myself still advise a student, wishing to study *rites de passage*, to go to the persisting excitement of Junod rather than to van Gennep himself. Van Gennep is dull to me in the same way as Sir James Frazer's *The Golden Bough* is dull. [– – –] Van Gennep for me illustrates strikingly how a man can make an important discovery, and sense that he is on the way to further problems, yet be prevented from going on to exploit his discovery because he tries to prove his initial point beyond doubt in a form which his contemporaries and probably he himself, thought convincing."[2]

It is, of course, clear that many of van Gennep's thoughts do not hold in the light of current research. Consequently, his concepts have got redefinitions and his classifications reformulations[3]. It can be mentioned, for example, that he did not make any difference between the three main categories[4] of rites, i.e. rites of passage, calendar rites and rites of crisis. He did not pay particular attention to the analysis of social structure and social relations in any society either[5]. He was also too eager to show that his model

---

[1] Cf. Gluckman 1962, particularly 1 ff.

[2] Ib. 9ff.

[3] E.g. Chapple 484 ff.; Beals 55; Gluckman 1962, particularly 1 ff.; Honko 1964, 129 ff.; Glaser 1971, 1 ff., 157 ff.

[4] Cf. Honko 1976, 71 ff. Honko summarizes his distinction in the following way (ib. 84):

	Definition criteria		
Rite category	Social orientation	Repeatable	Predictable
Rite of passage	Individual	–	+
Calendar rite	Group	+	+
Crisis rite	Individual/ Group	–	–

[5] Cf. Gluckman 13 ff.

was universal and concerned every ritual context and every society. But is this not true what comes to scientific and theoretical development in general? Some people prefer to generalize, some others to analyze. The progress of science needs both analysts and universalists.

One dilemma in the criticism concerning van Gennep's ideas might have been in putting his theory violently into too functional categories. Van Gennep has in general been regarded as a prefunctionalist[6] whose categories would have been better understood when using the concepts of social structure and functional relationships à la Malinowski or Radcliffe-Brown. I would prefer to consider him as a *prestructuralist*. He clearly strived after a structural pattern which should be universal and concern every ritual complex as well as every society. Because the contemporary formalistic schools[7] had not yet come far enough in their definitions, his concepts could not be very precise as far as structural analysis is concerned.

Van Gennep's basic idea is structural. According to his definition, *rites de passage* are rites which accompany every change of place, state, social position and age. In primitive communities these changes are generally made public and their importance is hallowed by rites which follow a pattern. First comes the *séparation* in which the individual is removed from his previous social position. This is followed by an interim period, *marge,* during which the individual is poised on the borderline between the two positions. The third and last phase is the full entry into the position (*agrégation*). Hence, *rites de passage* are divided into three groups: 1. rites of separation, 2. rites of transition, 3. rites of incorporation[8].

The structural emphasis becomes very clear in the last chapters of the introduction where van Gennep describes the phenomenon of crossing frontiers and other territorial passages. This part of the book has particularly been criticized by functionalists because it seems to confuse the universal borderline between "this world" and "the other-worldly". Van Gennep describes regional moves as follows: "Precisely: the door is the boundary between the foreign and domestic worlds in the case of an ordinary dwelling, between the profane and sacred worlds in the case of a temple. Therefore to cross the threshold is to unite oneself with a new world. It is thus an important act in marriage, adoption, ordination and funeral ceremonies. [– – –] Consequently, I propose to call the rites of separation from a previous world, *preliminal rites,* those executed during the transitional stage *liminal* (or threshold) *rites,* and the ceremonies of incorporation into the new world *postliminal rites*."[9]

He closes the chapter on "The Territorial Passage" with the following

---

[6] Cf. Gluckman 1962, particularly 1 ff.; Honko 1964, 129 ff.

[7] E.g. Propp 20 f., 60 ff., 95; Dundes 1964, 58 ff.; Greimas 203 ff.; Pentikäinen 1978 a, 23 ff.

[8] Cf. Van Gennep 8 f.

[9] Ib. 20 f. The term *limen* is Latin meaning 'threshold' and for van Gennep 'transition between'.

statement: "In order to understand rites pertaining to the threshold, one should always remember that the threshold is only a part of the door and that most of these rites should be understood as direct and physical rites of entrance, of waiting, and of departure—that is, as rites of passage."[10]

2. *The liminal stage in the ritual performance*

In his several writings[11], Victor W. Turner has further developed van Gennep's idea on liminal rites. Turner's way of analysis is mainly symbolic and process oriented. He also speaks about the structural analysis of rites and symbols. In his terminology, the concept of "structure" coincides with that of "social structure", according to the usage of British social anthropology. The concept of "anti-structure" and "communitas" are used in the description of the liminal stage: "In liminality, *communitas* tends to characterize relationships between those jointly undergoing ritual tradition. The bonds of *communitas* are anti-structural in the sense that they are undifferentiated, equalitarian, direct, extant, nonrational, existential, I–Thou relationships. *Communitas* is spontaneous, immediate, concrete—it is not shaped by norms, it is not institutionalized, it is not abstract."[12]

Under the liminal stage, people, for example the *initiands,* are beyond the boundaries of the normal social structure, its values, norms and obligations. The marginal state which starts from the rites of separation is an abnormal condition, outside society and time. For that reason it is possible for people to behave according to the habits and norms which do not coincide with those of the "normal" social structure and its conditions. For example, sexual freedom is a common characteristic of the marginal period in the initiation rites of many peoples. The marginal abnormal condition is ended by rites of aggregation which make new status relationships public to the community. The general three-phase scheme of rites of passage can be illustrated by the following figure[13]:

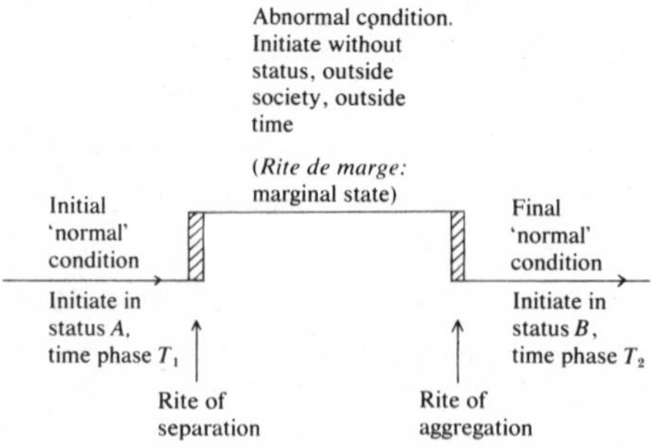

[10] Ib. 25.

[11] E.g. Turner 1969, 94 ff.; 1974, 1 ff.; 1974 a, 13 ff., 231 ff.; 1975, 145 ff.; 1975 a, 207 ff.; Ms 1 ff.

[12] Turner 1974 a, 272 ff.

[13] Cf. Leach 78.

Van Gennep characterized the condition of the initiates in the following way: "The novices are outside society, and society has no power over them, especially since they are actually sacred and holy, and therefore untouchable and dangerous, just as gods would be."[14] Turner expresses the same as follows: "They are dead to the social world, but alive to the asocial world. [– – –] In liminality, profane-social relations may be discontinued, former rights and obligations are suspended, the social order may seem to have been turned upside down, but by way of compensation, cosmological systems (as objects of serious study) may become of central importance for the novices, who are confronted by the elders, in rite, myth, song, instruction in a secret language, and various non-verbal symbolic genres, such as dancing, painting, clay-moulding, wood-carving, masking, etc., with symbolic patterns and structures which amount to teaching about the structure of the cosmos and their culture as a part and product of it, in so far as these are defined and comprehended, whether implicitly or explicitly. Liminality is a complex series of episodes in sacred space–time, and may also include subversive and ludic events."[15]

3. *The ritual movements of the Karelian wedding drama*

From the structural point of view, the liminal stage could also be regarded as a crucial phase in the sequence of the ritual drama. When rites of passage are investigated as structured symbolic behaviour, it is also possible to find and isolate smaller units of analysis. In my study on the White Sea Karelian wedding ceremonies I used the ritual movement[16] from one status to another as the basic unit of structural analysis.

Concerning the transformations of statuses, we can differentiate six basic positions[17]. In the case of the girl, she is moved from her 1. previous statuses as daughter (of her parents) and member of family (group and family line), youth etc., to that of 2. a wooed girl, 3. *antilas* ("the girl to be given away" referring to liminality) and 4. bride in the course of the wedding ceremony. After these steps there are still two positions which are made public later on, namely that of 5. wife after having become officially registered by an Orthodox priest, and that of 6. spouse and mother after having borne her first child. In the case of the boy, we can differentiate the statuses of 1. son, member of family groups, youth, etc., 2. suitor, 3. *seniehhä,* 4. bridegroom during the wedding ceremony itself; and after that 5. husband, and in the last phase 6. spouse and father.

The wedding itself took only a few days from the first step to the last, sometimes everything took place during one day. The whole process concerning transformations of statuses, however, could take several years. So

---

14 Van Gennep 114.

15 Turner Ms 10f.

16 Cf. Lawson Ms 18ff.; Pentikäinen 1978, 182ff.

17 More thoroughly in Pentikäinen 1978, 199ff.

prolonged a period was significant from the functional point of view: it gave enough time for the young couple, particularly the new wife, to become emotionally separated from her previous groups and to become united into a new solidary group in their own nuclear family.

The structural sequence of the ritual movements and status transformations in the wedding ceremony

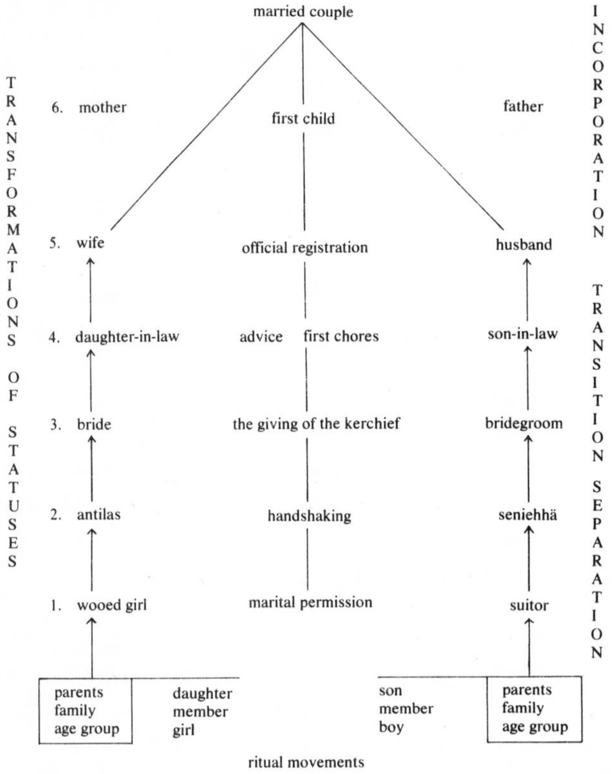

4. *Ritual as transmission of symbols*

Ritual behaviour is always the communication of the symbols which transmit some religious or other messages to the participants aware of their meanings. According to Firth, "symbols are instruments of expression, of communication, of knowledge and of control"[18]. He strongly emphasizes the importance of political symbols as instruments of power and control. Turner seems to share this idea when writing in his book *The forest of symbols* as follows: "I could not analyse [these] ritual symbols without studying them in a time series in relation to other 'events', for symbols are essentially involved in social processes. [– – –] From this standpoint

[18] Firth 77. Cf. Turner 1975, 145 ff.

the ritual symbol becomes a factor in social action, a positive force in any activity field."[19]

According to Firth, symbols are "storage units", which consist of a maximum capacity of information. Hence, he continues, the total significance of a symbol is only understood once it has been viewed from each ritual context in which it is found. Turner sees three levels of interpretation: 1. an *exegetical,* given by the participants themselves, 2. an *operational* which is drawn from the context in which the symbol is found, and 3. the *positional* meaning, which is obtained by way of comparisons[20].

Symbols are communicated in the interactional situations between individuals in certain social groups. From this point of view, symbolic behaviour and its learning is a process meaning "becoming human through culture". Geertz writes: "When seen as a set of symbolic devices for controlling behaviour, extrasomatic sources of information, culture provides the link between what men are intrinsically capable of becoming and what they actually, one by one, in fact become. Becoming human is becoming individual, and we become individual under the guidance of cultural patterns, historically created systems of meaning in terms of which we give form, order, point, and direction to our lives. And the cultural patterns involved are not general but specific—not just 'marriage' but a particular set of notions about what men and women are like, how spouses should treat one another, or who should properly marry whom; not just 'religion' but belief in the wheel of karma, the observance of a month of fasting, or the practice of cattle sacrifice. Man is to be defined neither by his innate capacities alone, [...] nor by his actual behaviour alone, [...] but rather by the link between them, by the way in which the first is transformed into the second, his generic potentialities focused into his specific performances."[21]

5. *Emics of the ritual: the world view of the rites*

Marett at his time summed up his ideas about the nature of "primitive religion": "Primitive religion is danced out, not thought out." It is only natural that ritual is the most decorative and observable side of the religion. Marett's sentence is onesided, however, because it emphasizes too much the behavioural aspects of the so-called "primitive religions". There are dogmas, myths, folk beliefs and other cognitive elements in every religion, although they cannot be observed as easily as ritual behaviour but, rather, are expressed by informants in conversation. There is a world view[22] behind every ritual performance. It were as great failure to study rites only on the basis of textual observations concerning the ritual acts. Malinowski re-

---

[19] Turner 1974, 20.
[20] Cf. Turner 1965, 82f.
[21] Geertz 52.
[22] On the concept, cf. e.g. Pentikäinen 1978, 34ff. Cf. Dundes 1971, 93ff.; Jones 79ff.; Smith 68ff.; Kearney 247ff.; Manninen 3ff.

marked as early as in 1926: "The text, of course, is extremely important, but without the context it remains lifeless."[23] The context analysis of the ritual performances means a careful study of the uses, meanings as well as functions, both latent and manifest, of any ritual act[24].

In the *emic*[25] study of the ritual we put a great emphasis on ideas, interpretations, attitudes, feelings, and meanings expressed by the informants themselves, either spontaneously or in an interview between a scholar and an informant. This material brings afore the "native's point of view", as some cultural anthropologists have expressed the matter. Meanings concerning the same ritual act can vary even in a small community. The cognitive and conative knowledge of the active leader of the rite is usually wider than that of the passive participants. For that reason, we can speak about the specialized knowledge of the rite performer, i.e. the ritual repertoire[26] of a specialist. He is usually more aware of the old symbolic links of the ritual units than the other participants. Their opinions are important because they usually are a testimony of the collective tradition, i.e. the knowledge shared by most people in the community.

This is why, the emic study of the ritual is holistic and process oriented. It concerns rites both as social and individual acts. Abrahams characterizes "the oral performance" as follows: "A performance is a coming together occasion on which performer and audience bring mutual patterns of expectation to the situation of performance. The performer then, gives his ability to actively produce a narrative will be relying heavily upon the audience's understanding of the lineaments of both the type and its individual manifestation. Of importance in such an approach is not the items itself but the total event in which the item provides the primary focus. The performer serves to heighten awareness of this possibility of participation. His role as presented is to activate the sense of meaningful encounter, meaningful transaction. He differs from the members of his audience only in that he has a productive competence within that type of performance, while their's is, at least at the moment, a receptive competence."[27]

In his micro studies when dealing, e.g., with Ndembu ritual processes, Turner often describes ritual acts and symbols using local and regional terms. It is clear that this kind of culture bound terminology often gives a more trustful picture than the alternative analysis using only internationally accepted concepts. Turner describes Isoma ritual in the following way: "My main aim [in this chapter] is to explore the semantics of ritual symbols in Isoma, a ritual of the Ndembu, and to construct from the observational and exegetical data a model of the semantic structure of this symbolism. The first step in such a task is to pay close attention to the way the

---

[23] Malinowski 17f., 24.

[24] Cf. e.g. Berglund 19ff.; Pentikäinen 1978, 51ff.

[25] Cf. Pike 8ff.; Pelto 67ff.; Harris 1968, 568ff. 1976, 465. Pentikäinen 1978, 28ff.

[26] Cf. Pentikäinen 1978, 324f.

[27] Abrahams 15f.

Ndembu explain their own symbols. [– – –] We are here trying to discover 'the Ndembu inside view', how the Ndembu themselves felt and thought about their own ritual."[28]

In his later papers, Turner makes an attempt for an *etic* study of symbols. According to him, symbology is not only "the study or interpretation of symbols" but also "representation or expression by means of symbols". He continues: "The term 'comparative' merely means that this branch of study involves comparison as method, as does, for example comparative linguistics. Comparative symbology is narrower than 'semiotics' or 'semiology', and wider than 'symbolic anthropology' in range and scope of data and problems."[29] He also makes a distinction "liminal" vs. "liminoid" and emphasizes the need of a terminology for the description of the ritual life even in modern society. According to him, "liminoid" belongs to the analysis of the industrialized high cultures. Turner writes: "In the so-called 'high cultures' of complex societies, the liminoid is not only removed from a *rite de passage* context, it is also 'individualized'. The solitary artist *creates* the liminoid phenomena, the collectivity *experiences* collective liminal symbols. This does not mean that the maker of liminoid symbols, ideas, images, etc. does so *ex nihilo;* it only means that he is privileged to make free with his social heritage in a way impossible to members of cultures in which the *liminal* is to a large extent the sacrosanct."[30]

6. *Liminality and the supernatural*

Most examples above have concerned rites of passages. Liminality is then a marginal phase between old and new statuses, a period lasting some limited time and in most cases leading to a normal condition and a new social membership and status. The liminal stage is abnormal and anti-structural, deviates from the usual one even so far that—depending on the religion in question—people at that phase are considered to be more apt to the influence of the supernatural than usually. For example, the frequency of the supranormal experiences is quite high during or around the liminal periods among people going through rites of passages and their intimate groups as well. The presence of the supernatural thus somehow belongs to the normal picture of the liminal phase. Supernatural experiences are even expected for, and the manifestations of the supranormal beings have a positive function for the community. It is important from the point of the community in question that the liminal stage can safely be passed by and the normal life started after that.

Liminality can also become a continuous problem which will disturb the life of the community and have supernatural manifestations. This concerns,

---

[28] Turner 1969, 10f.

[29] Turner Ms 1.

[30] Ib. 47.

for example, religious beliefs dealing with the so-called "dead without status".

My religio-phenomenological study[31] shows that the exceptional character of these dead appears in many cultures in at least three different ways: 1. Burial ceremonies differ from normal usage. Those who died a "bad death" are buried with special rites—without a coffin, without ceremony, apart from others or they are left unburied. 2. There is no group which feels obliged to equip the dead or to concern itself about what will happen to the dead in the after-life. He who has died a bad death is from this point of view similar to a stranger who is unprovided for. 3. An individual who has undergone a bad death is not believed to succeed in reaching the community of the dead. It is feared that he will only get half way and remain in an eternal transition phase and haunt the living in one form or another.

Dead-child beings are a typical example of the departed without status. From the religio-scientific point of view the problem with abandoned, murdered, unbaptized, aborted or stillborn children is that they have died before the necessary status-giving rites have been carried out. Their position is problematical in that they have never belonged to the group of the living and for this reason cannot belong to the group of the dead either. Burial ceremonies are either performed in a special way or left unperformed. From all this it is evident that the child is considered an "outsider"; he has at no point been a member of the family, nor has he been accepted in the group of the dead, which is the object of a cult.

The problem of the dead without status seems to be in their "eternal" liminality. It is an exceptional, unsatisfactory condition which is mostly suffered and experienced by those who are regarded as responsible for the supranormal manifestations. For that reason, it is quite natural that it is the mother of the murdered child which is attacked by the dead-child being. According to the ancient Nordic tradition, *utbörding* or *aepparâš* sucks or kills its mother after it has been given permission or an order to do so. This order can be given in a stereotyped formula incantation, as for example: "Suck your mother!" "Kill your mother!" or "Go and do your mother what she has done to you."[32] The family's response in the matter becomes clear in the following proverb, very common in Central Scandinavia and Finland: "Utbördingen är värst på släkten sin". (*Utbörding,* a dead-child being is worst for its family)[33]. Another rite which was considered to be very effective for the final elimination of the supranormal disturber was baptism. When the child got the name it was lacking for it was supposed to get peace and cease haunting. The double liminality was dependent both on the neglect of baptismal rites after childbirth and ordinary burial rites after death.

[31] Cf. Haavio 129; Pentikäinen 1968 a, 92 ff.
[32] Pentikäinen 1968, 212 ff., 310 ff.
[33] Cf. ib. 217 ff.

"OK (=Olavi Korhonen): People have perhaps heard something like weeping in the forest?

SV (=Susanna Valkeapää): I do not know. Then perhaps it was *aepparâš*. I think you mean that. It is said that people have hidden a child where it was born and not told about it to others. Then it becomes a ghost. It also cries sometimes. And some hear it and also see it. But they see it in the form of a bird.

OK What sort of a bird?

SV Any bird. A white grouse, for example. Once at Palojaw're a white grouse was seen in the autumn, in the thicket and it screamed like a baby. And it was that sort of a child. There was a child to which they gave a name. You know, when it has got a name it did not haunt any longer.

OK In what manner was the name given to it?

SV Well, I don't know. I remember that I have heard that one should read the Lord's prayer backwards. Then it disappears easily. Just backwards it should be read when it is baptized. And a human name should be given to it. [– – –] Two names were given. A boy's name and a girl's name were given, when it was not of either group."[34]

7. *Marginality—A way of life*

A study of the threshold experiences and the liminal stage might also open some perspectives for a better understanding of creativity. It is a well-known phenomenon from the world of the arts that many authors, painters, and musicians seem to live a kind of continuous marginality. They also seem to enjoy their way of life and put a great emphasis on their marginal exceptional experiences which seem to be a necessary catalysator for their creativity. There are several examples about shaping under the influence of hallucinogenics and narcotics. Being a member of an oppressed minority has often meant an exceptionally great productive power. This concerns for example many famous Jewish scientists and artists. An immigration or a flight to an alien environment has also sometimes meant a new orientation into life. Feelings and experiences on marginality as a continuum have often meant remarkable impulses for creativity. This concerns both more developed and traditional societies. My Karelian informant Marina Takalo could be considered an example of a creative personality in a traditional rural community[35].

She was born in White Sea Karelia in 1890 but lived most part of her life as a refugee in Finland (i.e. from the year 1922 until her death in 1970). She was a representative of four different minorities. Her nationality was that of the U.S.S.R. until her death, she was a representative of a *staroviero* (the

---

[34] Ib. 332.

[35] More thoroughly in Pentikäinen 1978, 58 ff., 326 ff.

Old Belief) minority group within the Russian Orthodox Church. Her ethnic identity was White Sea Karelian and, last but not least, she was illiterate in an almost totally literate society. All these minority identities which she emphatically wanted to preserve all her life through meant strong feelings on marginality and deprivations to her. Her family had great difficulties in finding any stable or satisfactory place in Finnish society. This can be seen from the fact that they were obliged to shift their place of accomodation in Finland over 30 times. Marina Takalo often felt to be an outsider in Finnish society. Her statuses in many social circles seemed to be very temporary. She would hardly have become a creative personality and at the same time an aware bearer of her Karelian culture without her marginal experiences.

In the following two examples on Marina Takalo's repertoire are quoted. The first part of her life history deals with her begging expeditions in her childhood. The second tells about the same period according to the generic grammar of an autobiographical lament.

"When mother came to be married into Vanhatalo, it was among the richest houses in Karelia. When accidents started to follow one another, then I—they had 12 children, I was the 11th one—had to run with a basket in my arms, walk about the village, collect bread, not for myself but for home. Forty kilometres from home sister was a maid in a house, I was there as a lodger. Every day I ran round the village, went to houses. When I went to the steps, I listened from behind the door to see whether there were any visitors. If there were, I didn't dare go, I went to other houses. When I returned, if there were still men from the village, again I didn't dare go. I used such cunning: I split a piece of bread into two, so as if I had gone to every house; because sister ordered me to visit every house. Then they gave me something to eat in that house where sister was a maid and I a lodger. When sister made soup, then in her meanness she put the film of the soup in my bowl. When I ate it, yes every time I put it in my mouth—first I always ate that—, I felt that I should vomit it, but it didn't help. Woe!, woe! It was the winter there, the next summer at home; in autumn I was sent travelling again. I certainly have not had such an onerous job in this world. I have worked hard all my life, but that was the hardest job of all. In autumn I had to go to live on the other side of the river of the village. I travelled by boat. The owner of that house came one time and asked if I would go to the river as his "fishnet-rower" (i.e. to row while he dragged the fish net). Never have I had any news more joyful than that, that I would be able to support myself from my own work. I was there till Christmas. Then mother came to fetch me home. For wages I was given two sacks of potatoes, one sack of grain, also clothes to wear. After that I was at home for my entire girlhood. Winters I had to go to drive logs, but what harm could that work do!"[36]

---

[36] Ib. 67 f.

Autobiographical Lament 340 (A.D. 1962)
"Ever since a doll-child I've grown up with a wretched lot and as a doll-child I've wandered (as a beggar) with a basket, asking from behind dorr-sills of the more flourishing for pieces of bread for a meal
and as a little duckling-child I've asked below the windows of the more generously fated for alms pieces for the first meal.
So, ever since a small duckling-child I've grown up with a lowly lot, and all my dear lifetime I've lived with a lowly lot at the jobs of those more generously fated,
ever since I wound up from there, the higher parts [i.e. Viena] of the dear world to wander here in the very foreign parts [i.e. Finland] of the world."[37]

The religious genres known by Marina Takalo offered her a large scale of ways for engaging in sacral intercourse. The messages transmitted through these genres were not always traditional ones. For example, autobiographical laments were for her the way of sacral intercourse with which she particularly wanted to address her God. Marina Takalo's ritual practices and world view underwent greater changes in course of her life history. Many norms, rites and customs crucial in Orthodox Karelian upbringing (such as prayers, the making of the sign of the cross, fasting) dropped off in the course of the emigrant phase. Despite that, her personal devotion did not weaken. The peculiar character of her religious views and interpretations which has respectedly been pointed out in this study clearly indicated that Marina Takalo, as an Orthodox, was an uncontrolled outsider.

Bibliography

1. *Manuscripts*

Helsinki
The author's archiv

Lawson, T. Ritual language. A problem of method in the study of religion.
Turner, V., Liminality, play and ritual. An essay in comparative symbology.

ARA Annual review of anthropology
FFC Folklore fellows communications

Abrahams R., 1976, Genre theory and folkloristics. *Folk narrative research.* Ed. by Tuula Juurikka, J. Pentikäinen. Pieksämäki.
Beals, R., Hoijer, H., 1961, *An introduction to anthropology.* New York.
Berglund, A.-I., 1976, *Zulu thought-patterns and symbolism.* Uppsala.
Chapple, E., Coon, C., 1947, *Principles of anthropology.* London.
Dundes, A., 1964, *The morphology of North American Indian folktales.* FFC 195. Helsinki.

[37] Ib. 252.

— 1971, Folk ideas as units of world view. *Journal of American Folklore* 84.
Firth, R., 1973, *Symbols, public and private*. Ithaca.
Geertz, G., 1973, *The interpretation of cultures*. New York.
Glaser, B., Strauss, A., 1971, *Status passage,* a formal theory. Chicago.
Gluckman, M., 1962, Kinship and marriage among the Lozi of Northern Rhodesia and the Zulu of Natal. *African systems of kinship and marriage*. Ed. by A. Radcliffe-Brown, D. Forde, s. 1.
Greimas, A. 1966, *Sémantique structurale*. Paris.
Haavio, M., 1959, *Essais folkloriques*. Studia Fennica 8. Porvoo.
Harris, M., 1968, *The rise of anthropological theory*. New York.
— 1976, History and significance of the emic/etic distinction. *ARA* 5.
Honko, L., 1964, Siirtymäriitit. *Sananjalka* 6.
— 1976, Riter: en klassifikation. *Nordisk Folktro*. Ed. Klintberg o. a., Lund.
Jones, W., 1972, World view, their nature and their function. *Current anthropology* 13.
Kearney, H., 1975, World view theory and study. *ARA* 4.
Leach, E., 1976, *Culture and communication*. Cambridge.
Malinowski, B., 1926, *Myth in primitive psychology*. London.
Manninen, J., 1976, *Maailmankuvan käsitteestä monitieteisen tutkimuksen työvälineenä*. Helsingin Yliopiston filosofian laitoksen julkaisuja 3. Helsinki.
Pelto, P., 1970, *Anthropological research, the structure of inquiry*. New York.
Pentikäinen, J., 1968, The Nordic dead-child tradition. *FFC* 202. Helsinki.
— 1968 a: Grenzprobleme zwischen Memorat und Sage. *Temenos* 3.
— 1978, *Oral repertoire and world view*. Helsinki.
Pentikäinen, J., Apo, Satu, 1978 a, The structural schemes of the fairy-tale repertoire, a structural analysis of Marina Takalo's Fairy-Tales.—*Varia Folklorica*. Ed. by A. Dundes. The Hague.
Pike, K., 1957, *Language in relation to a unified theory of the structure of human behaviour*. The Hague.
Propp, V., 1958, *Morphology of the folktale*. Austin.
Smith, R., 1972, The structure of esthetic response. *Toward new perspectives in folklore*. Ed. by A. Paredes, R. Bauman. Austin.
Turner, V., 1965, Ritual symbolism among the Ndembú. *African Systems of Thought*. Ed. by M. Fortes, G. Dieterlen. London.
— 1969, *The ritual process*. Chicago.
— 1974, The forest of symbols. Ithaca.
— 1974 a, Dramas, fields and metaphors. Ithaca.
— 1975, Symbolic studies. Chicago.
— 1975 a, Revelation and divination in Ndembu ritual. Ithaca.
Van Gennep, A., 1960, *The rites of passage*. London.

Symbolism and Magical Acts

By SVEIN BJERKE

1. However the field of magic in non-literate cultures is delimited and defined, probably most students of comparative religion and anthropology today conceive magic as falling either wholly or partly within the broad field of religion. While many writers on the subject endorse the Frazerian two principles of magic—the imitative and the contagious—few agree with his conception of magic as the primitive equivalent of our science. Now if people do not look upon their magic as technology pure and simple and consequently do not view the relationship between the rite and its effect in a mechanistic-causal manner, how in fact is the relationship thought of? Why do people believe in the efficacy of magical acts? And how can we explain this belief? Various answers have been given to these questions, but in this brief paper I have chosen to concentrate on the presentation and criticism of one particular analytic framework closely associated with the discipline of social anthropology. The British philosopher Skorupski has given the name "symbolist" to this approach because its adherents consider magical and religious actions and beliefs to be systems of messages cast in symbolic codes, about the social (and in some cases also the natural) order[1]. This approach has also been called neo-Durkheimian[2]. The study of magic does not occupy any privileged position in this analytical framework, but I have focused on it here because I am of the opinion that precisely the study of magical acts and ideas provides us with a touchstone for probing the validity of the symbolist approach in general. There exists several varieties of the symbolist approach but in this paper I have chosen to concentrate on Beattie's theory. This because his anthropology can be characterized as "orthodox"[3], and because in several publications he has succeeded in formulating his variety most forcefully and explicitly—also with reference to magic[4]. But before I give a brief account of his theory I shall try to outline a few features which I think are central to symbolist theories of magic and religion.

a. In the old debate concerning differences and similarities between the modes of thought of traditional and modern societies—a debate that is still going on[5]—the symbolists, like Durkheim, maintain that there is no fundamental difference in this respect between traditional and modern societies. The symbolist approach tends to understand traditional religions on the

---

[1] Cf. Skorupski 18 ff.

[2] Cf. Runciman 153.

[3] Cf. Peel 73.

[4] Cf. Beattie 1964, 65 ff., 202 ff.; 1966, 60 ff.; 1970, 240 ff.

[5] Cf. *Modes* 1 ff.

model of 20th century western Christianity for which science, not God, serves to explain events in this world of space and time. Religious convictions and dogmas are not really concerned with the empirical world but with metaphysics, and are thus not subjected to any criteria of verification or falsification[6]. A sharp contrast is seen between magic and religion on the one hand, and science on the other, a contrast that is neo-Durkheimian rather than Durkheimian[7]. The intellectualist, neo-Tylorian thesis that religion in traditional societies has an essentially explanatory function is most emphatically denied.

b. Emphasis is placed on magic and religion as forms of action. The term "ritual" is basic, denoting magico-religious actions as well as beliefs, values and attitudes. Action is prior to belief and myth which are often conceived as rationalizations of ritual activities. Belief, therefore, cannot explain ritual activity, on the contrary it is part of forms of activity. It is this totality that should be explained.

c. Ritual is symbolic. In so far as beliefs are not mere rationalizations, these are symbolic as well. This means that in general a distinction must be drawn between the conscious and explicit level of the actor, the literal meaning, and the level on which such acts and beliefs must really be understood. Magical and religious acts cannot be understood adequately in the actor's frame of reference—that is, on the literal level—the real meaning must be sought on a symbolic level which is most often hidden from the consciousness of the actor. Thus when an African villager kills a goat, the meaning on the literal level may be that he is making a sacrifice to his ancestors. But the symbolists maintain that what the man is really doing is to make a statement on lineage structure and values. "Ritual" in any given society constitutes a symbolic system which describes, demonstrates, or expresses social relations, groups, categories and values. Or, to quote Leach's well known dictum to the effect that "ritual action and belief are alike to be understood as forms of symbolic statement about the social order"[8].

Ritual acts are thus not primarily ways of "doing" something, they are ways of "saying" something. This also applies to magical acts. On the literal level they are admittedly ways of doing something, often something very definite and practical, but symbolist theory demands that they are basically ways of saying something. The contrast between Frazer's conception of magic as the primitive equivalent of our science, and that of the symbolists as a kind of language, could hardly be greater.

2. When we now turn to Beattie and his theory of magic, it is first of all necessary to point out the distinction he makes between two kinds of human

---

[6] Cf. Leach 1969, 107 f.
[7] Cf. Horton 258 ff.
[8] Cf. Leach 1954, 14.

behaviour which he calls expressive and instrumental. This distinction is crucial to his theory of ritual—it is the foundation on which it is built. "Instrumental behaviour must be understood in terms of the consequences it aims at and achieves; expressive behaviour in terms of the meanings, the ideas, it expresses."[9] As examples of instrumental behaviour he mentions various agricultural techniques with associated empirical knowledge[10], the wearing of clothes and wielding authority[11]. Religious and magical behaviour belongs to the expressive category. Although it is analytically of the utmost importance to distinguish between these two kinds of behaviour, in real life instrumental activities often have expressive aspects, and expressive activities instrumental aspects.

At this point it should be emphasized that Beattie considers the category expressive behaviour to include also kinds of activities other than magic and religion. His category "ritual" is delimited by being related to beliefs in non-empirical powers, whether personalized or not[12], a definition agreed upon by most anthropologists. He thus does not share the position of Leach whose category "ritual" comprises all expressive acts (and expressive aspects of "technical" acts), such as custom, etiquette, and ceremonial. According to Leach, the difference between social communicative behaviour in general and magical and religious behaviour, is either illusory or trivial[13]. Beattie emphasizes that ritual is more than expressive, it is also symbolic. Ritual is consequently characterized by a symbolism that is not necessarily characteristic of non-ritual expressive or communicative behaviour. A decisive importance is thus given to the concept of symbol which is a particular type of signs, that is "things that have meanings and which stand for something other than themselves"[14]. Thus, "when we speak of symbols we refer to comprehensible (i.e. 'graspable') entities, whether objects, ideas, or patterns of behaviour, which represent, by means of an underlying rationale, some more or less abstract notion (power, social or group unity, 'maleness' and 'femaleness', life, the dangerous and unfamiliar, are examples), to which social or cultural value, either positive or negative, is attached"[15].

Within the category of ritual, objects, ideas as well as acts, have a symbolic nature. Supernatural, or non-empirical, powers like spirits and gods are thus also symbols[16]. Unless I have totally misunderstood him, Beattie's thought on magic and religion requires a distinction to be made between the literal level on which people believe themselves to be interacting with supernatural beings whose reality they do not doubt, and a deeper, symbolic level on which people's religious activities as well as the supernatural

---

[9] Beattie 1964, 72.
[10] Cf. ib. 202.
[11] Cf. ib. 72.
[12] Cf. Beattie 1970, 241.
[13] Cf. Leach 1966, 404; 1968, 523.
[14] Beattie 1964, 69.
[15] Beattie 1970, 242.
[16] Cf. Beattie 1964, 224.

beings are correctly understood as "symbolizing certain important aspects of the physical and socio-cultural environment"[17]. When applied to magical acts in particular this means that belief in the efficaciousness of magic belongs to the literal level. On the symbolic level the actor is not doing anything at all, he is saying something.

3. When turning now to Beattie's account of magic, one feels the need for a detailed analysis of at least one particular magical rite where his theoretical framework could be demonstrated and applied, if not verified. Such an analysis might have enabled him to show, first, that the magical act is basically a means for saying something, not doing something; second, as the rite is symbolic, how it relates to its significatum by means of an underlying rationale; third, that the significatum is an abstract idea which has a social value; and fourth, why an essentially expressive and symbolic act should be believed to be effective by the actors. Unfortunately, however, I have been unable to find an analysis of this kind in Beattie's writings. His account of magic moves on a much more general and abstract level. Thus he uses the generalized and almost unavoidable magical rite where a man sticks a pin in a wax model of his enemy while uttering the appropriate spell[18]. I hasten to add, however, that the kind of ritual micro-analysis that I am missing is of a kind that probably would be out of place in the writings of Beattie referred to in this paper. His main concern is undoubtedly to argue for the very general thesis that magical acts belong to the category of expressive action. The man who attempts to kill his enemy by means of magic is engaged in an enterprise different in kind from that of the person who waylays and murders him. The first man says what he wants, the other does what he wants[19]. This position is quite the opposite of that of Frazer who thought of magical rites as acts performed in order to achieve particular ends, the acts being causes that in a mechanical way lead to the desired goal. Beattie considers Frazer's theory to represent "a travesty of magical thinking, which is essentially symbolic thinking"[20]. Magical acts cannot be understood on the basis of what the actors want to accomplish by performing them: "Serious mistakes have arisen from attempts to interpret types of behaviour which are primarily symbolic in intention as though they were misguided attempts to be practical and scientific."[21]

Magical acts should therefore not be understood as inadquate means for attaining empirical aims, but as dramatic assertions which may be ends in themselves. When writers like Malinowski and Evans-Pritchard list a number of reasons why people do not disclose the futility of their magic, they do not mention this reason which is the most important of them all[22].

---

[17] Beattie 1970, 263.
[18] Cf. Beattie 1966, 63.
[19] Cf. ib.
[20] Beattie 1964, 66
[21] Ib. 72.
[22] Cf. Beattie 1966, 68.

The examples of magical acts given by Beattie in order to illustrate his general thesis, belong to the Frazerian category of imitative magic. In such cases of magic, based on "the law of similarity", it is not difficult to demonstrate that the magical act is related to its significatum by means of an underlying rationale. The act of sticking a pin in a wax model of your enemy comes into this category, and so does the pouring of water or the producing of heavy smoke in order to make rain. As I shall argue later, we clearly have to do with symbolism in cases like these, but Beattie generalizes from these cases and argues that *all* kinds of magic are symbolic.

According to Beattie's definition of symbol, magical acts as symbols should refer to more or less abstract notions with social value and preferably to the social or natural order. Thus when people perform a rain-making ceremony by means of the pouring of water or the producing of heavy smoke, they symbolically assert the importance that they attach to rain and their earnest desire that it should fall[23]. And when a man sticks a pin in a wax model of his enemy he is expressing his desire for the enemy's death by making a little picture of what he wants[24]. Although it is hardly an abstract notion, rain clearly qualifies as a social value. Also the death of an enemy may imply a social value, but not necessarily so, and again no abstract notion would seem to be involved.

While it is obvious that rituals are symbolic for Beattie, he is well aware that they need not be symbolic for the actor: "The total procedures which we label 'magical' need not be, and often are not, viewed by their practitioners as purely symbolic (or even as symbolic at all). They are ways of getting what they want, what is done in such and such a situation in a given culture."[25]

Now it is quite obvious that a person who performs a magical rite has no difficulties in verbalizing and making explicit that he is acting in order to achieve a particular end, magical acts are clearly instrumental on the literal level. Beattie therefore raises the crucial question "in what sense, if any, can we say that people's institutionalized behaviour is symbolic if, as may well be the case, they themselves do not seem to know what it is?"[26]

The most important argument for his thesis seems to be that the symbolic level of consciousness is implicit or unconscious, but that the anthropologist can show that it really does exist by placing the rites and symbols which he observes in a total social and cultural setting[27]. The conclusion must be that people who perform magical rites act explicitly and consciously on the instrumental and literate level, but not on the expressive level which is the level on which an adequate understanding of such acts must be obtained.

---

[23] Cf. Beattie 1964, 203.
[24] Cf. Beattie 1966, 66.
[25] Beattie 1970, 251.
[26] Beattie 1966, 66.
[27] Cf. ib. 67.

To the last question, why should people who perform magical acts which are really expressive and symbolic be convinced of their efficaciousness, Beattie's answer is that the conviction of efficaciousness is grounded in their symbolic quality. "What I am asserting, then, is that fundamentally ritual's efficacy is thought to lie in its very expressiveness."[28]

In my opinion this assertion can best be illustrated by means of magical acts in which the relation between the signans and the significatum has a metaphorical nature, that is, rites which are based on the Frazerian "law of similarity". Although I shall later modify somewhat Beattie's argument, in these particular cases we can understand that the dramatized expression of a wished-for state of affairs may convince the actors that this dramatization is an adequate means for attaining it. But Beattie argues that *all* rites which are regarded by the actors as efficacious, should be understood on the background of the expressive nature of these acts.

Beattie's arguments for this assertion are very brief. He quotes with approval Malinowski's assertion to the effect that the expression of emotions in verbal utterances and gestures have a certain power. And the explanation for this is to be found in the psychology of children. To the child words are not merely means of expression but efficient modes of action[29]. He thus seems to endorse, at least in part, Malinowski's emotionalist theory of magic.

As Beattie explicitly states, the general thesis that magical acts are believed to be efficacious because they are expressive and symbolic, cannot be validated by reference to what informants say. If the Azande state that their magic is effective because of the power present in the magical substances used in the rites, "by what conceivable right do we assert that these informants are mistaken, that we know better than they do what they 'really' think, and that even though they do not know it, what underlies their behaviour is a belief in the power of symbolic expression itself?"[30]

In attempting to anser this question he refers to his previous arguments for the ascription of symbolism in cases where it is unknown to the actors, and then advances the assertion that no other explanation of the thought that underlies ritual institutions can make sense of people's behaviour[31].

4. During the last twenty years or so, symbolist theories of magic and religion have been discussed and criticised by anthropologists (Horton, Goody, Spiro), sociologists (Peel, Turner, Runciman), philosophers (Jarvie, Agassi, Skorupski)., and students of comparative religion (Ray). I cannot refer or take a stand on these discussions here. My own approach is most probably to be labeled "literalist", a term which in the discussions

---

[28] Ib. 69.
[29] Cf. ib.
[30] Ib.
[31] Cf. ib.

has been used to characterize those students of traditional religions who are opposed to the symbolist thesis as well as in some degree to the more extreme intellectualist approach of the neo-Tylorians whose most energetic spokesman is Horton. In my perspective it becomes necessary to question the fruitfulness of Beattie's classification of human behaviour in expressive and instrumental, and consequently his thesis that magic and religion are essentially symbolic. Instead of a distinction formulated from the observer's point of view, I prefer a distinction made from the point of view of the actor in accordance with the Weberian principle of *Verstehen*.

Beattie defines instrumental activity as activity which must be understood "in terms of the consequences it aims at and achieves"[32]. Instrumental activities are thus not only goaldirected, but they are also means that really (that is, as judged by our own reality definitions) lead to the desired goal. On the basis of an observer oriented definition of instrumentality it is obvious that magical acts cannot be instrumental because *we* know that magic does not work. But when Beattie states that magical acts, which "in reality" are expressive, also have an instrumental aspect, he defines instrumentality from the actor's point of view. The concept instrumental is thus ambiguous, and our dilemma consists in whose definition we should choose, that of the observer or that of the actor. As we have seen, Beattie attempts to solve this dilemma by postulating that the actors on some level of consciousness somehow are aware that magical acts are really symbolic and expressive. He thus approaches the position of Marett who saw magic "as a more or less clearly-recognized pretending, which at the same time is believed to project itself into an ulterior effect"[33]. But Beattie is conscious of the fact that one is confronted by very serious problems in verifying the thesis that magical acts are symbolic when the actors do not intend them as such. Beattie finds no reason to doubt that the actors are of the serious opinion that their magical acts are adequate means for obtaining certain ends. Marett's magician somehow knows that he is pretending, that his act is symbolic in the sense of not real, in other words, he suppresses his unbelief in the magical act. But Beattie knows that the actors are convinced that their magical acts are effective, that they are not pretending. At the same time Beattie knows that magical acts cannot have the effects imputed to them by the actors. I find it hard to see that Beattie has succeeded in verifying the thesis that magical acts for the actor on any level of consciousness, are not instrumental, but expressive and symbolic. The concepts of expressive and instrumental I find very useful, but in my opinion they should be used within the frame of reference of the actor. From this perspective magical acts are necessarily instrumental.

5. In the foregoing I have been critical of the central symbolist thesis which maintains that religion and magic *as such* have a symbolic nature

[32] Beattie 1964, 72.

[33] Marett 48.

whose referents are the social, or alternatively, the natural order. I will not deny that we often find symbols in magic and religion, of course we do. Our first task must therefore be the construction of a fruitful concept of symbol and the emphasis that I place on the actor's point of view demands that we for our understanding of the nature of symbols must start with what are *intended* as symbols by the actors. This does not mean that it is always obvious when an object is symbolic, or a statement a metaphor, there will always be a number of border line cases. What I should like to do here is to suggest a concept of symbol which harmonizes with a "literalist" conception of magic and religion, and more particularly, one that is fruitful for the understanding of magical acts. By the term "ritual symbol", then, I shall understand a physical object (or the objectivation of linguistic elements) which stands in a culturally defined relationship of representation or participation to an entity in a given socially constructed world. I find no particular reason to emphasize that the signification should have a logical rationale, or have a metaphoric character[34]. Nor do I want to stipulate that the significatum should be an abstract notion with social value. What I should like to emphasize is that the symbol object, the signans, is quite concretely a stand-in for its significatum. In ritual situations it consequently tends to be treated *as if* it is the entity which it represents. I fulle agree with Beattie and others[35] when they underline the tendency of the entity symbolized to participate in or float over into the symbol object.

If we apply this perhaps somewhat restrictive definition of symbol, the property "symbolic" can also be ascribed to magical acts provided that the rite includes a symbol on which the magical act is an operation. In such cases the action with reference to the symbol will as a whole represent an action with reference to the entity symbolized. The symbolic-ritual act must be defined on the basis of the use of a symbolic object in the ritual[36]. Proceeding from this understanding of ritual symbols I shall—following Skorupski—suggest that a particular type of magical acts are based on a cognitive pattern that implies control by means of symbols. The characteristic features of this form of magic is probably best seen when it is compared with some other elementary forms of magic. I want to emphasize, however, that these different forms of magic are not to be understood as an exhaustive classification within a field with well defined limits. In any given magical act, moreover, two or more of these elementary forms can be combined.

6. The elementary form of magic that is of central concern in the present context can briefly be called *symbolic magic*. The magical act is typically

---

[34] Cf. Leach 1976, 12 ff.
[35] Cf. Firth 1973, 15 f.
[36] Cf. Skorupski 119, 123.

an operation on objects that serve as symbols, or alternatively, on objectivated linguistic elements, most often the names of persons and things. In those cases where the rite includes a spell, this serves typically to identify the ritual symbol with the entity which it represents. The cognitive pattern on which this kind of magic is based, Skorupski calls *symbolic or mimetic identification:* "Some form of change is produced in an object, *s*, which is taken as standing for, or 're-presenting', the goal object, *g*. So, *s* 'is' *g*. Therefore the same change is produced in *g*."[37]

As an example of this form of magic we can use the by now very familiar operation on the wax figure. When a magician sticks a pin in a wax model that represents his enemy, this enemy undergoes the same change as the wax model which is a stand-in for him in the rite. His breast is pierced and he dies. In cases belonging to this kind of magic I shall presuppose that the actor *knows* that the ritual object is a symbol. If he is asked I expect that he can give an explicit answer to the effect that the ritual object is a stand-in for the entity he wants to affect. For the actor the act is instrumental because he is convinced that he can exercise real control by means of the manipulation of symbols. The symbol is here to be seen as being connected with the instrumental aspect of the magical act as seen from the point of view of the actor. This position is rather different from that of Beattie who connects the symbol with the expressive aspect of the magical act and the belief in its efficacy with the literal level, as seen from the point of view of the observer. The conviction of control by means of symbols should not be interpreted by us as "make-believe" or symbolic in the sense of not real as Marett maintained[38]. Neither is it the case that the actor fails to disclose the falsity of his own magic because overpowering emotions shut off his cognitive reality definitions[39].

The kind of magic I am here concerned with comprises the Frazerian imitative magic, but I think that it is not necessary to emphasize—as Frazer does—that there should be an element of similarity between symbol and entity symbolized. Thus in rites of vengeance magic that I observed among the Zinza of Tanzania, pepperfruits were used to represent the persons who were the targets of the magical act. Also Frazer's category of contagious magic belongs to the present kind of magic. Nail parings, excrements, hair, shreds of clothing, etc., are in magical acts used as symbols of the person (or other entity) to whom they used to belong.

In this connection there is another point of considerable theoretical importance that must be mentioned. As we know Frazer viewed the magical act and its effect as two quite distinct events between which there was a causal relationship. But in the case of symbolic magic we are well advised

---

[37] Ib. 135.
[38] Cf. Marett 41 ff.
[39] Cf. Widengren 6f.

to consider whether the operation on the symbol is seen as merging with the effect on the entity symbolized so that there is only one event[40].

In the other elementary forms of magical acts the ritual use of symbols is not a necessary feature. In the cognitive pattern which can be called *the magical power of words,* it is ritual language itself—called "the formula spell" by Evans-Pritchard[41]—in which the efficient power is believed to inhere. Quite a few of the examples given by Malinowski for the Trobrianders[42], and by Firth for the Tikopia[43] are good examples of magical acts based on this cognitive pattern.

Skorupski suggests that the two forms of magic mentioned above may be considered by us as being magic in the strict sense of the term. His argument is that in both these cases we have to do with cognitive patterns that are based on a lack of differentiation between natural and culturally defined connections[44]. However this may be, I shall briefly mention two other kinds of rites often characterized by anthropologists and others as magical. The first one comprises acts based on the cognitive pattern that Skorupski calls *contagious transfer*[45]. In this kind of magic a property which according to the actors is present in a certain substance is by means of some physical contact transferred to a person or some other entity. (It should be emphasized that this kind of magic is not identical with Frazer's contagious magic.) The second kind can be called *interactive magic*. Rites belonging to this category are based on the belief that the efficaciousness of the act is due to some mediating supernatural agency like the power in magical substances or some personal supernatural being. The spells used in these rites typically take the form of orders given to the agency which brings about the desired effect.

Bibliography

Beattie, J., 1964, *Other cultures*. London.
— 1966, Ritual and social change. *Man* 1.
— 1970, On understanding ritual. *Rationality*. Ed. B. Wilson. London.
Evans-Pritchard, E., 1929, The morphology and function of magic. *American anthropologist* 31.
Firth, R., 1967, *Tikopia ritual and belief.* London.
— 1973, *Symbols public and private*. London.
Horton, R., 1973, Levy-Bruhl, Durkheim and the scientific revolution. *Modes.*
Modes, 1973, *Modes of thought*. Ed. R. Horton, Ruth Finnegan. London.
Leach, E., 1954, *Political systems of highland Burma*. London.
— 1966, Ritualization in man in relation to conceptual and social development. *Royal Society of London, Philosophical transactions*. *Series* B 251.
— 1968, Ritual. *International encyclopaedia of the social sciences* 13.
— 1969, *Genesis as myth and other essays*. London.

---

[40] Cf. Skorupski 141 ff.
[41] Cf. Evans-Pritchard 625.
[42] Cf. Malinowski 136 ff.
[43] Cf. Firth 1967, 195 ff.
[44] Cf. Skorupski 156 f.
[45] Cf. ib. 134 f.

— 1976, *Culture and communication*. Cambridge.
Malinowski, B., 1966, *Coral gardens and their magic* 1. London.
Marett, R., 1914, *The threshold of religion*. London.
Peel, J., 1969, Understanding alien belief-systems. *British Journal of sociology* 20.
Runciman, W., 1969, The sociological explanation of "religious" beliefs. *Archives européennes de sociologie* 10.
Skorupski, J., 1976, *Symbol and theory*. Cambridge.
Widengren, G., 1969, *Religionsphänomenologie*, Berlin.

12†–782459 H. Biezais